Instructor's Resource Manual

for

Adler, Proctor, and Towne's

Looking Out/Looking In

Eleventh Edition

Mary O. Wiemann
Santa Barbara City College

Marion Boyer
Kalamazoo Valley Community College

THOMSON

WADSWORTH

Australia • Canada • Mexico • Singapore • Spain • United Kingdom • United States

Printed in the United States of America
1 2 3 4 5 6 7 07 06 05 04

Printer: Darby Printing

0-534-63633-0

For more information about our products, contact us at:
Thomson Learning Academic Resource Center
1-800-423-0563

For permission to use material from this text or product, submit a request online at
http://www.thomsonrights.com
Any additional requests about permissions can be submitted by email to
thomsonrights@thomson.com

Thomson Wadsworth
10 Davis Drive
Belmont, CA 94002-3098
USA

Asia
Thomson Learning
5 Shenton Way #01-01
UIC Building
Singapore 068808

Australia/New Zealand
Thomson Learning
102 Dodds Street
Southbank, Victoria 3006
Australia

Canada
Nelson
1120 Birchmount Road
Toronto, Ontario M1K 5G4
Canada

Europe/Middle East/South Africa
Thomson Learning
High Holborn House
50/51 Bedford Row
London WC1R 4LR
United Kingdom

Latin America
Thomson Learning
Seneca, 53
Colonia Polanco
11560 Mexico D.F.
Mexico

Spain/Portugal
Paraninfo
Calle/Magallanes, 25
28015 Madrid, Spain

CONTENTS

CONTENTS

PART FOUR **TEST BANK**   137

CONTENTS

INTRODUCTION

Any successful course is a special mixture of the instructor's teaching style and competencies, the students' interests and abilities, course requirements, time strictures, and choice of text. This Instructor's Resource Manual for Looking Out/Looking In is a compilation of various materials we have found useful in teaching our basic interpersonal communication courses. We offer these suggestions with the hope that they will help you develop your own successful blend of ingredients.

You might use the teaching strategies given here in the way a good chef uses recipes. Although they're a starting point, your own special talents and the needs of the specific classroom may call for an adaptation of the basic formula--or even the creation of a new approach. You'll find that the format of *Looking Out/Looking In* will allow this kind of flexibility. The text is organized into ten chapters, each covering material available for one unit in a course. Chapters 2 through 7 are written so that they may be arranged in any sequence that suits your needs.

This *Instructor's Resource Manual*, the separate *Student Activities Manual*, and the text itself provide more exercises and activities than you can probably use in a one-semester course. Once again, we have offered this abundance so that you may pick and choose from among the exercises the ones that will work best for you. We're sure you have many of your own favorite exercises to add to the blend as well.

The *Instructor's Resource Manual* is organized into three parts as follows:

Part I The <u>Resource Integration Guide</u> is a useful grid that provides chapter-by-chapter instructional ideas and corresponding supplemental resources. At a glance, you'll know which activities, website materials, quizzes, and videos are appropriate for each chapter. Meticulously organized, the Resource Integration Guide helps you prepare more effectively, in less time, and with less effort.

Part II provides general suggestions concerning course format and grading options. A detailed course syllabus is included to illustrate how to organize a course using the text, the *Student Activities Manual*, and the *Instructor's Resource Manual*. New to this edition of the *Instructor's Resource Manual* are lists of internet sites that relate to chapter material. Instructors can easily find links to journals, publications, collections, bibliographies, teaching strategies, and other course-related materials such as audiotapes and videotapes.

Part III contains chapter objectives. Notes for class and student activities in each chapter are found here. Exercises found in the text are listed in boldface type by title in the index of *Looking Out/Looking In*. Activities from the *Student Activities Manual* are listed by number (e.g., 1.4 for the fourth activity in Chapter 1).

Part IV is a test bank of over 1000 questions and answers keyed to each chapter. They are organized by chapter and then by question type (T = true/false, M = multiple choice, Matching = matching, and E = essay). In addition, you will find that each question is referenced to the text page(s) on which it can be found and by cognitive type. Thus, each question looks like this:

How many parts are there in this *Instructor's Resource Manual*?

      a.   four
      b.   three
      c.   two
      d.   one
      e.   This *Instructor's Resource Manual* is not divided into parts.

Answer: a   **Type: M**   **Page 123**   **Knowledge**

Please note that the cognitive type identifiers will help you construct quizzes or exams that are easier or more difficult, depending on your purpose. The cognitive types are:

KN = knowledge (remembering terms, facts, or theories)

CO = comprehension (understanding, summarizing material)

AP = application (use of learned material in new and concrete situations)

AN = analysis (understanding content and structural form by differentiating, inferring, or outlining)

SY = synthesis (categorizing, combining, or organizing parts to form a new whole)

EV = evaluation (judging, comparing, or contrasting the value of material for a given purpose)

Starting with the 9th edition of the test bank, we added one more category of test item:

RE = recall (simple recall of reading--no course content)

We include this category for instructors who like to give simple quizzes on the chapters to check that their students are keeping up with the reading. Other instructors prefer not to use these types of questions because they do not test course concepts. By separating out this category, and grouping the questions together at the beginning of the true/false and the multiple choice sections, instructors who want these questions can find them easily and those who don't want to use them can skip over them quickly.

The test bank is available on computer disk for adopters of *Looking Out/Looking In*.

Ideas for Instruction	Student Workbook	Media Resources for Instructors	Media Resources for Students

Instructor's Resource Manual (IRM):
Objectives
Notes on class and student activities

Class Activities
1. Name Calling
2. Introductions
3. Autograph Party

Test Bank
For chapter 1, features over 140 questions in multiple-choice, true/false, matching, and essay formats. Also available in **ExamView®** electronic format, which can be customized to fit your needs.

Film in Communication Database
A list of feature films tied to chapter concepts that can stimulate concept processing. Detailed descriptions of the following films are found at the end of Chapter 1:
- About Schmidt
- Erin Brockovich
More films can be found on the database.

Chapter Outline

Activities
1. Communication Skills Inventory
2. Expanding Your Communication Effectiveness
3. Recognizing Relational Messages

Mediated Messages
Applies communication principles to mediated contexts.

Your Call
Paragraph-length case study to prompt analysis and ethical choices.

Dear Professor
Applies instructor responses to chapter relevant interpersonal problems revealed by students.

Study Guide
Approximately 50 questions in matching, true/false, completion, and multiple-choice format with answers for self-testing practice.

Book Companion Web site
Visit the Looking Out/Looking In Web site, accessible only through the Looking Out/Looking In CD-ROM, for online access to the Instructor's Resource Manual and InfoTrac® College Edition resources.

Relevant Web Sites (URLs located in IRM)
- What Employers Want vs. What They See in Job Candidates
- Applications of an Interpersonal Model to Educational Environments
- Establishing and Maintaining Interpersonal Relationships
- Making Friends in Cyberspace
- What Makes a Good Communicator?
- Interpersonal Competence Resources

And more . . . .

WebTutor™ Toolbox on WebCT and Blackboard
Online course management tool available in WebCT or Blackboard pre-loaded with text-specific content and resources. This tool is useful for all chapters of the text.

Multimedia Presentation Manager: Microsoft® PowerPoint® Presentation Tool for Interpersonal Communication
Using this Microsoft® PowerPoint® tool, choose from a variety of text images, graphs, and tables from the text to customize your own media lecture. This tool is useful for all chapters of the text.

CNN® Today Video: Interpersonal Communication
Vol. 1: Latch-Key Kids (2:23)
Vol. 1: Gulf War Forces Use of Email (2:02)
Vol. 4: Internet Spam (1:37)
Vol. 4: Wireless Widgets (2:03)
Vol. 4: Technology and Communication (2:30)

CNN® Today Video: Human Communication
Vol. 3: Email Geography (2:30)
Vol. 4: Multi-racial Communication (3:45)
Vol 4: E-Mail Dependence (1:43)

Book Companion Web site
Visit the Looking Out/Looking In Web site, accessible only through the Looking Out/Looking In CD-ROM, for online access to
- InfoTrac® College Edition
  - Why We Communicate
  - Practical Goals
  - Technology and Interpersonal Communication
- Web links
  - Setting Communication Goals
  - Making Models Meaningful
  - Assessing Your Communication Skills
- Interactive activities
- Review quizzes
- Feature film database

Looking Out/Looking In CD-ROM

CNN Clips
Watch CNN news clips to analyze the application of interpersonal concepts in every day situations.
- Social Contact Cures Colds

WebTutor™ Toolbox on WebCT and Blackboard
Expanded online study tools flash cards, practice quizzes, chapter outlines and learning objectives, Web links, and discussion questions. This tool is useful for all chapters of the text.

InfoTrac® College Edition
Keywords: communication; morality in interaction; impact on others; intrapersonal communication; communication types; communication systems; observing communication; communication models; interpersonal communication; interpretation; feedback; conversation; technology, communication; communication criticism; communication objectives; human communication; communication assessment, cognitive complexity.

Ideas for Instruction	Student Workbook	Media Resources for Instructors	Media Resources for Students

Instructor's Resource Manual (IRM):
Objectives
Notes on class and student activities

Class Activitiess
1. Your Personal Coat of Arms
2. Interpersonal Interviews

Test Bank
For chapter 2, features over 140 questions in multiple-choice, true/false, matching, and essay formats. Also available in **ExamView®** electronic format, which can be customized to fit your needs.

Films In Communication Database
A list of feature films tied to chapter concepts that can stimulate concept processing. Detailed descriptions of the following films are found at the end of Chapter 2:
- ◆ Boyz in the Hood
- ◆ Stand and Deliver
- ◆ Catch Me if You Can

More films can be found on the database.

Chapter Outline

Activities
1. Who Do You Think You Are?
2. Self-Concept Inventory
3. Ego Boosters and Busters
4. Your Self-Fulfilling Prophecies
5. Success in Managing Impressions

Mediated Messages
Applies communication principles to mediated contexts.

Your Call
Paragraph-length case study to prompt analysis and ethical choices.

Dear Professor
Applies instructor responses to chapter relevant interpersonal problems revealed by students.

Study Guide
Approximately 50 questions in matching, true/false, completion, and multiple-choice format with answers for self-testing practice.

Book Companion Web site
Visit the Looking Out/Looking In Web site, accessible only through the Looking Out/Looking In CD-ROM, for online access to the Instructor's Resource Manual and InfoTrac® College Edition resources.

Relevant Web Sites (URLs located in IRM)
- ◆ Self-Monitoring: Do You Censor What You Say?
- ◆ Identity Management in Cyberspace
- ◆ Self-Esteem Self-Evaluation Survey
- ◆ Evaluate Your Self-Esteem by Responding
- ◆ How Can We Strengthen Our Children's Self-Esteem?
- ◆ Symptoms of Low Self-Esteem
- ◆ Shaping Body Image
- ◆ US/Chinese Memories Show Impact of Culture on Self-Concept
- ◆ Face: It Just Depends on Your Perspective

And more . . . .

CNN® Today Video: Interpersonal Communication
Vol. 1: Bilingual Storyteller (3:41)
Vol. 2: Weight Hate (5:13)
Vol. 3: The "Ugly Bill" (2:11)

CNN® Today Video: Human Communication
Vol. 3: Who Is an African? (2:43)
Vol. 3: Only Child (4:15)
Vol. 4: Teen Culture (2:20)

Book Companion Web site
Visit the Looking Out/Looking In Web site, accessible only through the Looking Out/Looking In CD-ROM, for online access to
- ◆ InfoTrac® College Edition
  - • How the Self-Concept Develops
  - • Sex and Gender
  - • Identity Management
- ◆ Web links
  - • Your Self-Esteem
  - • Your Personality Profile
- ◆ Interactive activities
- ◆ Review quizzes
- ◆ Feature film database

Looking Out/Looking In CD-ROM

CNN Clips
Watch CNN clips to analyze the application of interpersonal concepts in every day situations.
- ◆ Accent Reduction

InfoTrac® College Edition
Keywords: identity; self-esteem; personality; endorsement; self-evaluation; recognition; race; self-disclosure; self-evaluation; self-serving bias, stereotypes; culture; person-centeredness; personal constructs; perceptions; social perceptions; perspectives; social perspectives; identity; personal opinion; social comparisons; self-concept; self-confidence; inner dialogues; evolution of self; identity, in cyberspace; self-sabotage; self-fulfilling prophecy.

Chapter 3: Perception: What You See is What You Get

Ideas for Instruction	Student Workbook	Media Resources for Instructors	Media Resources for Students

Ideas for Instruction

Instructor's Resource Manual (IRM):
Objectives
Notes on class and student activities

Class Activities
1. Perception-Checking Stimuli
2. Empathy skills

Test Bank
For chapter 3, features over 140 questions in multiple-choice, true/false, matching, and essay formats. Also available in **ExamView®** electronic format, which can be customized to fit your needs.

Films in Communication Database
A list of feature films tied to chapter concepts that can stimulate concept processing. Detailed descriptions of the following films are found at the end of Chapter 3:
◆ White Man's Burden
◆ The First Wives Club
◆ The Doctor
More films can be found on the database.

Student Workbook

Chapter Outline

Activities
1. Guarding Against Perceptual Errors
2. Examining Your Interpretations
3. Shifting Perspectives
4. Observation and Perception
5. Perception Checking Practice
6. Perception Checking

Mediated Messages
Applies communication principles to mediated contexts.

Your Call
Paragraph-length case study to prompt analysis and ethical choices.

Dear Professor
Applies instructor responses to chapter relevant interpersonal problems revealed by students.

Study Guide
Approximately 50 questions in matching, true/false, completion, and multiple-choice format with answers for self-testing practice.

Media Resources for Instructors

Book Companion Web site
Visit the Looking Out/Looking In Web site, accessible only through the Looking Out/Looking In CD-ROM, for online access to the Instructor's Resource Manual and InfoTrac® College Edition resources.

Relevant Web Sites (URLs located in IRM)
◆ The Accuracy and Power of Sex, Social Class and Ethnic Stereotypes
◆ Basic Self-Controls to Interact Effectively With People
◆ Empathy and Listening Skills
◆ Different Drummers
◆ Typical Stereotypes and Misconceptions
◆ Test Your Hidden Racial Biases
◆ Discover Your Emotional Empathy Profile
◆ Experiencing Empathy Online
And more . . . .

CNN® Today Video: Interpersonal Communication
Vol. 1: Teen Roundtable (4:32)
Vol. 1: Tale of Two Kids (5:20)
Vol. 2: Inner-city Teens Talk (2:06)
Vol. 2: Synagogue Fires (2:03)
Vol. 2: The New South Africa (2:17)
Vol. 4: Shattering Stereotypes (1:58)
Vol. 4: Arab Hip Hop (2:55)
Vol. 4: Stereotypes (1:17

CNN® Today Video: Human Communication
Vol. 4: Breaking Cliques (2:03)
Vol. 4: Museum Art Controversy (2:22)
Vol. 4: Race Relations and Attitudes (3:03)

Media Resources for Students

Book Companion Web site
Visit the Looking Out/Looking In Web site, accessible only through the Looking Out/Looking In CD-ROM, for online access to
◆ InfoTrac® College Edition
  • The Perception Process
  • Influences on Perception
  • Empathy and Communication
◆ Web links
  • Exploring Your Biases
  • Understanding Your Personality Type
◆ Interactive activities
◆ Review quizzes
◆ Feature film database

Looking Out/Looking In CD-ROM

Video Scenarios
Watch, listen to, and critique the conversation by completing the Conversation Analysis.
◆ Pillow Method in Action (Planning a Wedding)
◆ Pillow Method in Action (Exotic Dancing)

CNN Clips
Watch CNN clips to analyze the application of interpersonal concepts in every day situations
◆ Culture Clash

InfoTrac® College Edition
Keywords: perception; empathy; stereotyping, schemata, social scripts, prototypes, inference, categorizing, assumptions, ethnocentrism, interpersonal relations; culture; personal constructs; interpretation.

Ideas for Instruction	Student Workbook	Media Resources for Instructors	Media Resources for Students

Instructor's Resource Manual (IRM):

Objectives
Notes on class and student activities

Class Activities
1. How Would You Feel?
2. Would You Share?

Test Bank
For chapter 4, features over 140 questions in multiple-choice, true/false, matching, and essay formats. Also available in **ExamView®** electronic format, which can be customized to fit your needs.

Films in Communication Database
A list of feature films tied to chapter concepts that can stimulate concept processing. Detailed descriptions of the following films are found at the end of Chapter 4:
- ◆ Monster's Ball
- ◆ Riding in Cars with Boys

More films can be found on the database.

Chapter Outline

Activities
1. The Components of Emotion
2. Find the Feelings
3. Stating Emotions Effectively
4. Self-Talk
5. Disputing Irrational Thoughts

Mediated Messages
Applies communication principles to mediated contexts.

Your Call
Paragraph-length case study to prompt analysis and ethical choices.

Dear Professor
Applies instructor responses to chapter relevant interpersonal problems revealed by students.

Study Guide
Approximately 50 questions in matching, true/false, completion, and multiple-choice format with answers for self-testing practice.

Book Companion Web site
Visit the Looking Out/Looking In Web site, accessible only through the Looking Out/Looking In CD-ROM, for online access to the Instructor's Resource Manual and InfoTrac® College Edition resources.

Relevant Web Sites (URLs located in IRM)
- ◆ EQ International Site
- ◆ Advice for Couples: How to Control Anger
- ◆ How Do You Feel Today?
- ◆ Thinking Quiz
- ◆ Who is the Only Person in the World Who Can Make You Angry?
- ◆ Using Rational-Emotive Therapy to Control Anger
- ◆ Rational-Emotive Behavior Therapy
- ◆ An Introduction to Rational Emotive Therapy
- ◆ Understanding Yourself

And more . . . .

CNN® Today Video: Interpersonal Communication
Vol. 1: US Reaction to Princess Diana's Funeral (1:55)
Vol. 2: Synagogue Fires (2:03)
Vol. 1: Teen Roundtable (4:32)

CNN® Today Video: Human Communication
Vol. 3: Emotional IQ (2:59)

Book Companion Web site
Visit the Looking Out/Looking In Web site, accessible only through the Looking Out/Looking In CD-ROM, for online access to
- ◆ InfoTrac® College Edition
  - • Gender & Social Conventions
  - • Guidelines for Expressing Emotions
  - • Managing Difficult Emotions
- ◆ Web links
  - • Measuring Your EQ
  - • Expanding Your Emotional Vocabulary
- ◆ Interactive activities
- ◆ Review quizzes
- ◆ Feature film database

Looking Out/Looking In CD-ROM

Video Scenarios
Watch, listen to, and critique the conversation by completing the Conversation Analysis.
- ◆ Rational Thinking in Action (Annoying Customers)
- ◆ Rational Thinking in Action (Meeting my Girlfriend's Family)

CNN Clips
Watch CNN clips to analyze the application of interpersonal concepts in every day situations.
- ◆ Emotional IQ
- ◆ CNN.com Netiquette

InfoTrac® College Edition
Keywords: criticism; social emotions; emotions; self-disclosure; emoticons; emotions, nonverbal; rationalizing emotions; perceptions; self-talk.

Chapter 5: Language: Barrier and Bridge

Ideas for Instruction	Student Workbook	Media Resources for Instructors	Media Resources for Students

Ideas for Instruction

Instructor's Resource Manual (IRM): Objectives
Notes on class and student activities

Class Activities
1. The World of Abstraction
2. Words That Hurt and Heal

Test Bank
For chapter 5, features over 140 questions in multiple-choice, true/false, matching, and essay formats. Also available in **ExamView®** electronic format, which can be customized to fit your needs.

Films In Communication Database
A list of feature films tied to chapter concepts that can stimulate concept processing. Detailed descriptions of the following films are found at the end of Chapter 5:
◆ Nell
◆ When Harry Met Sally…

More films can be found on the database.

Student Workbook

Chapter Outline

Activities
1. Misunderstood Language
2. Behavioral Language
3. Responsible Language
4. "I" Language Oral Skill Check
5. Effective Language

Mediated Messages
Applies communication principles to mediated contexts.

Your Call
Paragraph-length case study to prompt analysis and ethical choices.

Dear Professor
Applies instructor responses to chapter relevant interpersonal problems revealed by students.

Study Guide
Approximately 50 questions in matching, true/false, completion, and multiple-choice format with answers for self-testing practice.

Media Resources for Instructors

Book Companion Web site
Visit the Looking Out/Looking In Web site, accessible only through the Looking Out/Looking In CD-ROM, for online access to the Instructor's Resource Manual and InfoTrac® College Edition resources.

Relevant Web Sites (URLs located in IRM)
◆ Gender Differences in E-mail Communication
◆ Basic Differences Between Men and Women
◆ Gender Differences in Communication
◆ Styles of Communication: Direct and Indirect
◆ Why Men and Women Don't Always Understand Each Other
◆ More About High- and Low-Context Communication Styles
◆ Language: Say What You Mean
And more . . . .

CNN® Today Video: Interpersonal Communication
Vol. 1: Black English (2:32)
Vol. 1: The Lost Language (2:11)
Vol. 2: Punjab Pop (2:58)
Vol. 2: Future Translators of America (2:29)
Vol. 2: Baby's First Words (2:35)
Vol. 2: The Language of Peace (2:40)
Vol. 4: Language Use in Television Shows (2:13)
Vol. 4: African American Dialect (2:02)
Vol. 4: Language and The Internet (2:48)
Vol. 4: Census Ethnicity (2:59)
Vol. 4: Healthcare and Language Barrier (1:58)

CNN® Today Video: Human Communication
Vol. 3: Managing Jargon (1:52)
Vol. 3: Reaction to Rocker (2:01)
Vol. 4: Baby Talk (3:19)
Vol. 4: Seinfeld: Language and Meaning (2:28)
Vol. 4: Culture Clash (2:12)

Media Resources for Students

Book Companion Web site
Visit the Looking Out/Looking In Web site, accessible only through the Looking Out/Looking In CD-ROM, for online access to
◆ InfoTrac® College Edition
  • The Impact of Language
  • Gender and Language
  • Language and Culture
◆ Web links
  • Avoiding Troublesome Language
  • Expand Your Emotional Vocabulary
◆ Interactive activities
◆ Review quizzes
◆ Feature film database

Looking Out/Looking In CD-ROM

Video Scenario
Watch, listen to, and critique the conversation by completing the Conversation Analysis.
◆ "I" and "You" Language on the Job

CNN Clips
Watch CNN clips to analyze the application of interpersonal concepts in every day situations.
◆ Black English

InfoTrac® College Edition
Keywords: hate speech; perspective of minority groups; sexism, non-sexist language; gender communication; androgyny.

Ideas for Instruction	Student Workbook	Media Resources for Instructors	Media Resources for Students

Instructor's Resource Manual (IRM):
Objectives
Notes on class and student activities

Class Activities
1. Hello and Goodbye
2. Nonverbal Travels

Test Bank
For chapter 6, features over 140 questions in multiple-choice, true/false, matching, and essay formats. Also available in **ExamView®** electronic format, which can be customized to fit your needs.

Films In Communication Database
A list of feature films tied to chapter concepts that can stimulate concept processing. Detailed descriptions of the following films are found at the end of Chapter 6:
- The Birdcage
- Mrs. Doubtfire
- Tootsie
- Life as a House
More films can be found on the database.

Chapter Outline

Activities
1. Nonverbal Description
2. Nonverbal "How-Tos"
3. Evaluating Ambiguity

Mediated Messages
Applies communication principles to mediated contexts.

Your Call
Paragraph-length case study to prompt analysis and ethical choices.

Dear Professor
Applies instructor responses to chapter relevant interpersonal problems revealed by students.

Study Guide
Approximately 50 questions in matching, true/false, completion, and multiple-choice format with answers for self-testing practice.

Book Companion Web site
Visit the Looking Out/Looking In Web site, accessible only through the Looking Out/Looking In CD-ROM, for online access to the Instructor's Resource Manual and InfoTrac® College Edition resources.

Relevant Web Sites (URLs located in IRM)
- Nonverbal Communication in Japan
- Nonverbal Communication in Text-Based Virtual Realities
- An Overview of Nonverbal Communication in Impersonal Relationships
- Dress for Success
- Nonverbal Communication in Asian Cultures
- Nonverbal Communication Abstracts

And more . . . .

CNN® Today Video: Interpersonal Communication
Vol. 1: Eating Disorders (2:09)
Vol. 4: Poise School (2:33)
Vol. 4: Body Language (2:10)
Vol. 4: Baby Sign Language (1:38)

CNN® Today Video: Human Communication
Vol. 3: Demonstrators Gesture Defiance (1:45)
Vol. 4: Nonverbal Communication (2:29)
Vol. 4: Accent Reduction (3:42)
Vol. 4: Feng Shui (2:18)

Book Companion Web site
Visit the Looking Out/Looking In Web site, accessible only through the Looking Out/Looking In CD-ROM, for online access to
- InfoTrac® College Edition
  - Nonverbal Communication Scholarship
  - Male and Female Nonverbal Communication Differs
  - Gestures
- Web links
  - Gestures around the World
  - Exploring Nonverbal Communication
- Interactive activities
- Review quizzes
- Feature film database

Looking Out/Looking In CD-ROM

CNN Clips
Watch CNN clips to analyze the application of interpersonal concepts in every day situations.
- The Story of Uh

InfoTrac® College Edition
Keywords: nonverbal; nonverbal communication; emoticons; gestures; distance; environment; time.

Chapter 7: Listening: More than Meets the Ear

Ideas for Instruction	Student Workbook	Media Resources for Instructors	Media Resources for Students

Instructor's Resource Manual (IRM):

Objectives
Notes on class and student activities

Class Activities
1. Listen to the Little Children
2. Lecture Listening
3. One-Way and Two-Way Listening

Test Bank
For chapter 7, features over 140 questions in multiple-choice, true/false, matching, and essay formats. Also available in **ExamView®** electronic format, which can be customized to fit your needs.

Films In Communication Database
A list of feature films tied to chapter concepts that can stimulate concept processing. Detailed descriptions of the following films are found at the end of Chapter 7:
- Jerry Maguire
- Dead Man Walking

More films can be found on the database.

Chapter Outline

Activities
1. Listening Diary
2. Effective Questioning
3. Paraphrasing
4. Listening Choices
5. Informational Listening
6. Listening and Responding Styles

Mediated Messages
Applies communication principles to mediated contexts.

Your Call
Paragraph-length case study to prompt analysis and ethical choices.

Dear Professor
Applies instructor responses to chapter relevant interpersonal problems revealed by students.

Study Guide
Approximately 50 questions in matching, true/false, completion, and multiple-choice format with answers for self-testing practice.

Book Companion Web site

Visit the Looking Out/Looking In Web site, accessible only through the Looking Out/Looking In CD-ROM, for online access to the Instructor's Resource Manual and InfoTrac® College Edition resources.

Relevant Web Sites (URLs located in IRM)

- Be All Ears
- Active Listening Skills
- Quiz: The Listening Quiz For Couples
- Quiz: What is the Speaker Feeling?
- Improving Listening Skills
- Improving Responding Communication Skills
- Quiz: Are You a Really Good Listener

And more . . . .

CNN® Today Video: Human Communication
Vol. 3: Sleep Hearing (1:34)

Book Companion Web site
Visit the Looking Out/Looking In Web site, accessible only through the Looking Out/Looking In CD-ROM, for online access to
- InfoTrac® College Edition
  - Gender and Listening
  - Faulty Assumptions
  - Ask Questions
- Web links
  - How Well Do You Listen?
- Interactive activities
- Review quizzes
- Feature film database

Looking Out/Looking In CD-ROM
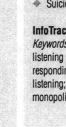

Video Scenario
Watch, listen to, and critique the conversation by completing the Conversation Analysis.
- Paraphrasing on the Job

CNN Clips
Watch CNN clips to analyze the application of interpersonal concepts in every day situations.
- Suicide Prevention

InfoTrac® College Edition

Keywords: noise; listening; listening skills; courtesy; paraphrasing; responding; remembering; selective listening; mindfulness; hearing; monopolizing; literal listening.

Chapter 8: Communication and Relational Dynamics

Ideas for Instruction	Student Workbook	Media Resources for Instructors	Media Resources for Students

Instructor's Resource Manual (IRM):

Objectives
Notes on class and student activities

Class Activities
1. How Fast Should We Go?
2. Self-Disclosure Tales

Test Bank
For chapter 8, features over 140 questions in multiple-choice, true/false, matching, and essay formats. Also available in **ExamView®** electronic format, which can be customized to fit your needs.

Films In Communication Database
A list of feature films tied to chapter concepts that can stimulate concept processing. Detailed descriptions of the following films are found at the end of Chapter 8:
- ◆ About A Boy
- ◆ Bend It Like Beckham
- ◆ Liar, Liar
More films can be found on the database.

Chapter Outline

Activities
1. Discovering Dialectics
2. Relational Stages
3. Breadth and Depth of Relationships
4. Reasons for Nondisclosure
5. Degrees of Self-Disclosure
6. Disclosure and Alternatives

Mediated Messages
Applies communication principles to mediated contexts.

Your Call
Paragraph-length case study to prompt analysis and ethical choices.

Dear Professor
Applies instructor responses to chapter relevant interpersonal problems revealed by students.

Study Guide
Approximately 50 questions in matching, true/false, completion, and multiple-choice format with answers for self-testing practice.

Book Companion Web site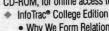
Visit the Looking Out/Looking In Web site, accessible only through the Looking Out/Looking In CD-ROM, for online access to the Instructor's Resource Manual and InfoTrac® College Edition resources.

Relevant Web Sites (URLs located in IRM)
- ◆ Honesty and Intimacy
- ◆ Battle of the Genders
- ◆ Intimacy: Recommended Reading for Men
- ◆ Interpersonal Perspectives and Theories
- ◆ Equivocal Communication
- ◆ Quiz: Self-Disclosure
- ◆ The Johari Window Model: Brief Explanation
- ◆ The Johari Window Model: Lengthy Explanation
And more . . . .

CNN® Today Video: Interpersonal Communication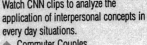
Vol. 1: Love at First Site (:58)
Vol. 2: Valentine's Day On-Line (1:15)
Vol. 2: Love on the Job (1:55)
Vol. 2: Recognizing Domestic Partners (1:41)
Vol. 2: Love at Any Age (1:44)

Book Companion Web site
Visit the Looking Out/Looking In Web site, accessible only through the Looking Out/Looking In CD-ROM, for online access to
- ◆ InfoTrac® College Edition
  - • Why We Form Relationships
  - • Intimacy
  - • Guidelines for Self-Disclosure
- ◆ Web links
  - • Online Attraction Quiz
  - • Relational Satisfaction: An Online Quiz
- ◆ Interactive activities
- ◆ Review quizzes
- ◆ Feature film database

Looking Out/Looking In CD-ROM

Video Scenario
Watch, listen to, and critique the conversation by completing the Conversation Analysis.
- ◆ Self-Disclosure

CNN Clips
Watch CNN clips to analyze the application of interpersonal concepts in every day situations.
- ◆ Commuter Couples

InfoTrac® College Edition
Keywords: commitment; intimacy; relationships; maintaining relationships; starting relationships; liking; love; deception; self-disclosure; equivocation.

Ideas for Instruction	Student Workbook	Media Resources for Instructors	Media Resources for Students

Instructor's Resource Manual (IRM):
Objectives
Notes on class and student activities

Class Activities
1. Pushing My Buttons
2. "Yes, BUT . . . ."

Test Bank
For chapter 9, features over 140 questions in multiple-choice, true/false, matching, and essay formats. Also available in **ExamView®** electronic format, which can be customized to fit your needs.

Films in Communication Database
A list of feature films tied to chapter concepts that can stimulate concept processing. Detailed descriptions of the following films are found at the end of Chapter 9:
◆ Changing Lanes
◆ Antwone Fisher
◆ Stolen Summer
More films can be found on the database.

Chapter Outline

Activities
1. Understanding Defensive Responses
2. Defensive and Supportive Language
3. Clear Messages
4. Nondefensive Responses to Criticism
5. Coping with Criticism

Mediated Messages
Applies communication principles to mediated contexts.

Your Call
Paragraph-length case study to prompt analysis and ethical choices.

Dear Professor
Applies instructor responses to chapter relevant interpersonal problems revealed by students.

Study Guide
Approximately 50 questions in matching, true/false, completion, and multiple-choice format with answers for self-testing practice.

Book Companion Web site
Visit the Looking Out/Looking In Web site, accessible only through the Looking Out/Looking In CD-ROM, for online access to the Instructor's Resource Manual and InfoTrac® College Edition resources.

Relevant Web Sites (URLs located in IRM)
◆ Life Skills: Being Nice
◆ Quiz: Evaluate Your Relationship
◆ Criticism Doesn't Have to Hu
◆ Handling Criticism With Honesty and Grace
◆ Know Yourself and the Communication Clima
◆ Open Communication Climate
◆ Assertiveness Training: Responding to Criticism
◆ Expressing More Appreciation, Gratitude, Encouragement and Delight
And more . . . .

CNN® Today Video: Interpersonal Communication
Vol. 2: The Consequences of Divorce (4:44)
Vol. 4: Love Lab (2:00)
Vol. 4: Old Age and Love (2:04)

CNN® Today Video: Human Communication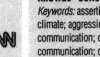
Vol. 3: Cancer Patient Returns to School (2:43)
Vol. 4: Dating (2:20)

Book Companion Web site
Visit the Looking Out/Looking In Web site, accessible only through the Looking Out/Looking In CD-ROM, for online access to
◆ InfoTrac® College Edition
  • Defensiveness
  • Responding Nondefensively to Criticism
◆ Web links
◆ Interactive activities
◆ Review quizzes
◆ Feature film database

Looking Out/Looking In CD-ROM

Video Scenario
Watch, listen to, and critique the conversation by completing the Conversation Analysis.
◆ Responding to Criticism

CNN Clips
Watch CNN clips to analyze the application of interpersonal concepts in every day situations.
◆ Verbal Judo

InfoTrac® College Edition
Keywords: assertion; workplace climate; aggression; supportive communication; defensive communication; communication climates; ethnocentrism.

| Ideas for Instruction | Student Workbook | Media Resources for Instructors | Media Resources for Students |

Ideas for Instruction

Instructor's Resource Manual (IRM):

Objectives
Notes on class and student activities

Class Activities
1. My Favorite Fights
2. Play to Win

Test Bank
For chapter 10, features over 140 questions in multiple-choice, true/false, matching, and essay formats. Also available in **ExamView®** electronic format, which can be customized to fit your needs.

Films In Communication Database
A list of feature films tied to chapter concepts that can stimulate concept processing. Detailed descriptions of the following films are found at the end of Chapter 10:
- American Beauty
- The Joy Luck Club
More films can be found on the database.

Student Workbook

Chapter Outline

Activities
1. Understanding Conflict Styles
2. Your Conflict Styles
3. The End versus the Means
4. Win-Win Problem Solving
5. Conflict Resolution Dyads

Mediated Messages
Applies communication principles to mediated contexts.

Your Call
Paragraph-length case study to prompt analysis and ethical choices.

Dear Professor
Applies instructor responses to chapter relevant interpersonal problems revealed by students.

Study Guide
Approximately 50 questions in matching, true/false, completion, and multiple-choice format with answers for self-testing practice.

Media Resources for Instructors

Book Companion Web site
Visit the Looking Out/Looking In Web site, accessible only through the Looking Out/Looking In CD-ROM, for online access to the Instructor's Resource Manual and InfoTrac® College Edition resources.

Relevant Web Sites (URLs located in IRM)
- Family Life Skills
- Conflict: An Essential Ingredient for Growth
- Managing Conflict Successfully
- Resolving Everyday Conflicts Sooner
- Interpersonal Relationships and Conflict Resolution
- Gender, Conflict and Conflict Resolution
- There Is No Such Thing As a Relationship Without Conflict
- Getting to Yes: Negotiating Agreement Without Giving In
And more . . . .

CNN® Today Video:
Interpersonal Communication
Vol. 1: Sibling Rivalry (7:24)
Vol. 1: Domestic Violence (4:30)

Media Resources for Students

Book Companion Web site
Visit the Looking Out/Looking In Web site, accessible only through the Looking Out/Looking In CD-ROM, for online access to
- InfoTrac® College Edition
  - The Nature of Conflict
  - Direct Aggression
  - Variables in Conflict Styles
- Web links
  - Your Conflict Style
- Interactive activities
- Review quizzes
- Feature film database

Looking Out/Looking In CD-ROM

Video Scenario
Watch, listen to, and critique the conversation by completing the Conversation Analysis.
- Win-Win Problem Solving

CNN Clips
Watch CNN clips to analyze the application of interpersonal concepts in every day situations.
- Sibling Rivalry

InfoTrac® College Edition
Keywords: conflict; covert conflict; overt conflict; conflict scripts; interpersonal conflict; conflict responses; conflict management; workplace conflict.

PART
TWO

GENERAL
SUGGESTIONS

THE INSTRUCTOR IS THE MAIN INGREDIENT

It is our belief that instructors of interpersonal communication have a particularly rewarding but difficult job. In addition to dealing with the problems faced by all instructors in the classroom, the interpersonal communication teacher faces the challenge of being the model interpersonal communicator in the classroom. In recognition of this role, we strongly suggest that as instructor you actively participate in class exercises. Although there will be many times when you must play a specialized role to facilitate an exercise, we encourage you to interact with the student whenever you can. Our involvement has paid dividends in three ways.

1. It encourages participation from our students. When they see that we are willing to discuss our own experiences, they seem to be encouraged to do the same. Student comments support this assertion.
2. Giving something of ourselves seems to increase our interaction with the group. Although it may sound paradoxical, we've found that we have been most successful when we've taken the risk of participating and making mistakes.
3. Our participation gives us a good perspective on the student's experience in the class. We sometimes discover that what appears to be a simple exercise to us is actually quite challenging; and on the other hand, activities that appear valuable in theory may prove to be dismal failures in practice.

STUDENT FEEDBACK

So that you may discover how students perceive the class, we suggest that you ask your students to make periodic formal evaluations of the course. We found that using a form encourages more specific responses that are the most useful to us. You will probably find that allowing students to respond anonymously works best, although you might allow students to sign their names if they wish. You can design the form to fit your particular situation.

Here is a sample form we have found useful:

1. What expectations did you have for this course (unit)? Has the course (unit) met your expectations? If not, why not?
2. Do you find the workload too light, too heavy, or just right? Were there any specific assignments on which you'd like to comment?
3. Do you think that the grading has been fair? If not, why not?
4. What do you think of the classroom atmosphere? How would you like to see it change?
5. Have the readings (text and outside) been satisfactory? Please give specific examples.
6. Is the teaching style satisfactory? What do you like about your instructor's style? What do you think should be changed?
7. Please make any other comments you feel might be helpful. Do you have any suggestions for improvements? Is there anything you feel we ought to continue doing?
8. What was one thing you learned today?
9. What thing(s) were unclear?
10. What question(s) do you have?
11. What would you like to discuss next time?
12. Do you have any relevant examples or experiences you'd like to share?

THE IMPORTANCE OF EXERCISES

Our unshakable belief is that complete learning takes place only when the student understands a concept on an affective as well as a cognitive level. For example, we consider ourselves to have failed if by the end of the semester a student can list all the factors necessary for effective listening but cares no more about being attentive or understanding than when he or she began our class.

This commitment to encouraging our readers to examine everyday behavior explains the number of exercises you find in *Looking Out/Looking In* and the *Student Activities Manual*. We have purposely supplied more than you'll need for a one-semester course. Our hope is that you can find exercises that work for you for each unit you cover in your interpersonal communication course. We've taken this extra step because we expect that participating in exercises, both group and individual, will make a personal application of the subject almost inevitable. Each activity is designed to lead the reader beyond talking about how people communicate and to ask the question "How do I communicate?"—and further, "How can *I* make my communication more satisfying?"

This emphasis on self-examination necessarily involves asking your class to examine (individually and as a group) feelings and behaviors that often aren't revealed in academic settings. Although we've found that very little growth comes without this kind of examination, it's absolutely essential not to push too hard, not to demand more self-disclosure or risk than the group is ready to volunteer. And always, we respect a student's right to pass or to carry out an alternate task in place of a given exercise. Despite our best efforts, we are often unaware of the personal anguish that some of our students suffer that they would prefer to keep private.

You'll find that the text exercises start by asking for very simple contributions and progress gradually to relatively greater amounts of self-disclosure. We hope that this pacing will prevent any anxiety on the part of your students; but in any doubtful cases, we urge you to move at whatever pace seems right for your situation.

STUDENT ACTIVITIES MANUAL USE

The *Student Activities Manual* is a valuable student aid for the course.

Student Activities Manual

In addition to the many exercises in the text, the *Student Activities Manual* has 80 individual and group skill builders and invitations to insight that focus on written and oral interpersonal communication skills. A new addition to the eleventh edition of the *Student Activities Manual* is *Dear Professor—Relational Responses*. These exercises model application of text material to real life problems, and then invite students to play the role of communication advice giver. In the last edition, short case studies for each chapter were added. They focus on ethics, competence and adaptation to situation; they are referred to as *Your Call*. Technology influences on interpersonal communication are analyzed in each chapter of the *Student Activities Manual*; they are referred to as *Mediated Messages* and invite students to adapt their knowledge of interpersonal communication to mediated situations.

Study Guide

The Study Guide section contains over 500 puzzles and test questions with answers that enable students to test themselves on the many concepts and skills contained in the text. In addition, extensive outlines help students check their reading or follow classroom lectures. Students using the Study Guide aids in the *Student Activities Manual* should understand class material more readily, guide themselves through skill development more easily, and score higher on exams.

CLASSROOM ENVIRONMENT

Although many of the exercises and activities in this book suggest particular arrangements, we feel that some general notes on the design of the classroom may be in order. If we expect our students to interact with each other, it becomes very important to create the best environment possible to promote this development. Knowing that we all work within certain limitations, we'd like to mention some of the items we have found helpful. Chapter 6 speaks directly to this subject.

1. Arrange the classroom seating so that all members of the group can see each other. If the room plan will allow it, a circle is the most useful arrangement.
2. If possible, choose comfortable chairs or small table-armed desks that can be easily rearranged into large groups, small groups, and dyads. Vary the arrangement of the classroom to meet the needs of lecture, discussion and group work.
3. Regroup students frequently. This allows them to get to know many more people and to get new perspectives on communication behavior.

Another way to set up a good classroom environment is to set up expectations about attitude and behavior in one of the first classes. Two methods that address this are the "contract" and the "standards for student success."

Bill Edwards of Columbus State University in Georgia offers this version of an instructor/student "contract" that he and his students adapted from Melanie Booth-Butterfield at West Virginia University.

I divide my class into two groups. One group will re-write the contract for the professor and the other group will re-write the contract for the students by accepting, revising, adding, and omitting contract items.

Instructions: Read the following contract. Revise the contract in any way you see fit. Your goal is to design a good contract which each party will sign. You can omit, revise, or accept any item. You can create new items.

INTERPERSONAL COMMUNICATION *PROFESSOR'S OATH*

As your professor I pledge that I will do the following appropriate teacher behaviors:

I will strive to be on time for class and to dismiss the class in a timely fashion when I have finished, so that you don't have your time wasted.

I will offer you an opportunity to ask questions and make observations.

I will respect you and treat you as an adult.

Box continued

I will try to always be fully prepared and well-organized in class.

My material will be up-to-date and contemporary in hopes that it will apply to your life.

I will attempt to be unbiased and reasonable in my approach to the material.

I will always be available to talk to you during my office hours.

I will try to be energetic, encouraging, and enthusiastic, because I like the material and I hope you do too.

None of the assignments will be busy work. Each will have direct relation to class goals.

I will prepare you for assignments and exams.

I will provide quick feedback on written assignments and exams.

I will put forth effort in teaching this class.

Signature: ___·_____

INTERPERSONAL COMMUNICATION *STUDENT'S OATH*

As a student in this course I pledge to do these appropriate student behaviors.

I will be actively involved with the class and its activities, asking questions, providing examples, etc.

I will smile and nod at my professor at lot, because I know this encourages the teacher to do his/her best.

I will not read newspapers, have side conversations, wear my headset, have my beeper turn on, pack up early during class because I know that it hurts my learning and my teacher"s feelings.

I will be on time for class on a regular basis.

I will not attempt to cheat on exams, copy others" assignments, turn in others" work as my own, etc. All work that I do in this class will be my own, original work.

I will be polite and cooperative with my teacher and classmates. I won"t try to put anything over on them, or ask them to make exceptions for me.

I will try to always stay awake during class.

I will endeavor to keep my mind open to the ideas presented and really consider how they affect my life.

I will put forth effort in taking this class.

Signature: _____

A second way of setting up a positive classroom environment comes from the Communication faculty at Santa Barbara City College. They put the following "Standards for Student Success" in all course packets and review the expectations at the outset of each semester:

STANDARDS FOR STUDENT SUCCESS IN COMMUNICATION DEPARTMENT COURSES

To Our Students:

Welcome to the Communication Department! Your instructor may choose to share the ten expectations below with you. These standards or norms for success address attitudes and behaviors beyond the good practices you have already acquired in your years of experience in educational environments. Some of these are givens that fall under the heading of routine but sometimes unstated premises that operate in healthy classrooms. We believe that noting expectations early in the semester will help you to be a successful learner, provide benefits for other students in the class, save time, and assist your instructor in conducting effective class sessions that offer every student the opportunity to be heard and acknowledged as a productive course participant.

Your instructor will discuss variances in the expectations with you. We are, after all, individuals whose standards may differ. We hope you will talk to your instructor about your expectations as well. The most constructive classroom environment will be one that encompasses the best that everyone—instructor and students alike—can offer to produce a positive learning experience... and that is what Santa Barbara City College is all about.

The Communication Faculty at Santa Barbara City College

1. **Attend classes regularly, be on time, and stay for the entire class period.** .In most courses, students receive attendance credit/points but the points are less important on a day-to-day basis than what you will miss by unnecessary absences and what your classmates will lose in not having your discussion contributions. Late-comers are a distraction to everyone. Anticipate challenges and try to plan for them. For example, it is well known that finding a parking spot at 10:00 a.m. is difficult. Plan your schedule with enough flex time to accommodate circling the lots until you find a slot.

2. **Participate in class discussion.** Some courses have participation points and others do not. Your discussion contributions are important in either case. Be a positive force in your classroom interaction. Ask questions, express your opinions, and make yourself known as someone who is actively involved.

3. **Use the instructor's office hours.** This time is set aside explicitly for you to talk with your teachers. You don't have to come with a monumental issue or problem (although these are good times to drop by). Students often use office hours to:
    a. introduce themselves to the instructor.
    b. provide important information about unique challenges such as learning disabilities, child care issues, and potential conflicts with work responsibilities outside the college. Crucial factors known in advance are likely to be better accommodated than last-minute surprises.
    c. ask questions about course material and/or discuss individual problems. In many cases, the instructor will never know your concerns unless you speak up.
    d. pass the time of day sharing insights and observations. The office hour is yours. A casual and non task-oriented visit may produce positive results on both sides.

4. **Avoid speaking with your instructor about significant issues immediately before and after class** as s/he is trying to either get everything ready for one class or prepare for the one starting in 10 minutes. Use office hours, e-mail, or telephone messages to contact the instructor on important items. The SBCC voice mail allows you 24-hour access. We will return calls promptly if we are not in when you call. (Leave your name and phone number.)

5. **Understand that instructional memory is not flawless.** Many of us have 150 students and more. It is hard to recall all the details of your class performance without help. If you want to discuss, for example, your progress from one assignment to the next, bring along instructor critiques and any other helpful notes to the meeting with your instructor. Be prepared to explain your issue or complaint. If videotape is available, review it before discussion with your instructor. If you have questions about a grade, write out your reasons so your teacher can see the specifics.

6. **Take notes in class.** Informed discussion is far more likely to arise from documented notes than hazy recall. Notes will also aid study for exams.

7. **Read assignments in the text and comply with homework expectations on the dates assigned.** Bring materials required (Scantron answer sheets, pencils, etc.) when needed. Don't expect others to bail you out if you neglect your responsibilities.

8. **Review the syllabus periodically.** Ask questions if you have them. Know what is expected. If you don't know, ask.

9. **Participate in class activity appropriately.** This involves such disparate behaviors as listening to others and acknowledging opposing viewpoints, choosing language that avoids uselessly antagonizing others (obscenity, personal attacks, hostile or sarcastic comments, etc.), blatantly reading *The Channels* or some other non-course-related text while class matters are in progress, talking with other students while someone else (who has the floor) is trying to speak, and taking a nap during class. Some of these negative behaviors may seem barely worth mention but they do occur and they do influence classroom interaction. Most of the courses in the Communication Department are relatively small. One person's distracting behavior can have a larger impact than you might imagine. For the student or students trying to present a speech, a group project, a review of the literature, and so forth, audience members who appear to be dozing or paying no attention whatever, present an extremely bothersome problem. Your responsibility as a student of Communication theory and practice includes being an open, alert, courteous, and receptive listener, as well as a competent presenter.

10. **Take responsibility for your education.** Excuses and rationalizations should be eliminated from your academic repertoire. Know that your instructors are human and predisposed to trust rather than doubt you. If you get away with a faked illness or fabricated emergency, you may find that the inevitable result hurts you more than anyone else. In one recent course, the instructor distributed a take-home quiz with instructions to use the text as a resource but work alone in discovering the answers. A student inquired, "How will you know if we cheat?" The teacher responded, "I probably won't ever know... but you will."

Learning is not a game or a contest to discover who is most adept at bending/breaking the rules to suit individual needs. It is an opportunity to prepare for life, professional requirements, and individual success—both as a singular human being and a contributing member of an enduring social network. You are attending Santa Barbara City College in the interest of your own professional advancement and the enhancement of the society in which you live. We are here to help you give both of these aims your best shot. Help us, and we will do our best to help you.

METHODS OF EVALUATION

A good evaluation system should serve at least two purposes:

1. It should give the student feedback on his or her mastery of the skills under study to answer the question, "How well do I understand the subject?"
2. It should give the instructor feedback on how successful he or she has been in communicating the subject matter to the students to answer the question " Which areas have I taught successfully and which do I need to cover in greater depth or in a different way?

At the same time, a good system of evaluation should avoid the trap of inviting and rewarding unproductive behaviors—busy work, deceit, and "shooting the bull."

At first, we despaired of finding a useful system of grading that would help rather than hinder students and teachers. But experience has shown that there are several good alternatives. In addition, we have found that no matter which grading system we used, it was very important to delineate clearly the method of grading, the student assignments, and the assignment due dates at the outset of the course. We've also found it important to collect work on the assigned date. These practices seem to reinforce the seriousness of the work involved, increasing respect for the instructor and the course.

A number of grading alternatives follow, which can be used either singly or in combination. For each, we have listed both advantages and disadvantages.

Traditional Examinations

The biggest advantage of traditional examinations is the greater likelihood that students will read and study the text with care. We have found that giving a quiz before the discussion of each chapter works well. Test questions are for checking comprehension after the unit has been studied. We have included over 1100 questions in true/false, multiple choice, matching, and essay formats. The questions appear in print in this manual, and on computer disk (in either PC or MAC formats) for adopters of *Looking Out/Looking In*.

The principal disadvantage of a grading system based only on tests is that it may not actually measure the most important goals of the class, namely improving the student's everyday communication behavior. For example, it is entirely possible for a student to describe in writing a number of effective listening behaviors, but he or she may never practice any of them. Thus, tests may measure skill in taking tests about communication and little else.

Practice tests can be a good study aid for students. With the large number of test items available in this test bank, it is relatively easy to create short exams for practice. Whether you do it in class or a laboratory situation, students can grade themselves and review items to prepare for the graded exam.

Student-Planned Examinations

In this procedure, students split into small groups, each of which submits several possible examination questions. All questions are then displayed to the entire class, with the understanding that the instructor will select several of them for the actual test.

Although this method carries the same disadvantage as the traditional method just described, students do study the material more intensively as they select and draw up questions. Another challenge is students' unfamiliarity with writing exam questions; it can take some time before items of quality emerge.

Written/Oral Skill Assignments

In this approach, the emphasis is placed on performance of the skills introduced in *Looking Out/Looking In*. After the presentation of material in class, students use many of the exercises from the *Student Activities Manual* to practice the concepts in class. Then written and/or oral exercises are assigned as tests of the skills introduced.

A major advantage of this approach is that instructors can evaluate the student's ability to operationalize the skills introduced. Both written and oral abilities are assessed, and students who score poorly on objective tests can often demonstrate their knowledge in essay and oral formats. Another advantage is the amount of involvement students feel in the class when they see one another performing the skills they have studied; this also serves to help students to individualize the skills, to make them realistic by noting real-life situations in which they are used, and to move toward integrating the communication skills into their everyday lives.

A disadvantage of this approach is that it can take a lot of class time. Any videotaping facility on campus can help here by allowing students to practice oral skills and tape them for playback in class. A communication laboratory with videotape cameras and communication tutors can ease the burden on the instructor.

Student-Instructor Contracts

In this system, students and instructor develop a specific program of study that the students agree to undertake, in return for which they receive a predetermined grade. Contracts can cover work corresponding to units of study, or they can be written for term projects, which may take the place of a final examination. Projects can take many forms—research papers, interviews, dramatic productions, surveys, journals.

There are two advantages to such a plan. First, it demands student initiative in proposing a course of study—a pleasant contrast to more passive types of assignments in which students play less creative roles. Also, such a format allows students some latitude in choosing how to channel their energies. Research and experience show that the quality of work and motivation are higher when students work on subjects with a high degree of personal interest.

Two disadvantages often occur in the contract method. First, some tasks that students choose may not focus on concepts that the instructor deems most important. However, this difficulty can be remedied by defining acceptable areas of study—for example, "Develop a project demonstrating three factors influencing perception and communication." The second disadvantage lies in the inability of some students to be self-motivated scholars. After being trained for twelve or more years in the passive art of test taking, it is difficult to suddenly have to define and pursue one's own course of study.

Journal (Diary) Assignments

In place of examinations, some instructors substitute journal assignments in which students reflect on how topics under study apply to their personal lives. Journals may either be graded or returned to the student for revisions until they are satisfactory.

The advantage of such an approach to evaluation lies in extending the concepts discussed in the classroom into the student's everyday relationships. The value of such applications is obvious in a course designed to improve the participant's communication skills.

One potential disadvantage lies in the failure of journals to focus clearly on key concepts discussed in class. We think this problem can be remedied by assigning journals that concentrate on specific topics, for example, "Record the number and types of destructive styles of conflict you use during the next week." Many assignments in the *Student Activities Manual* follow this method; a collection of these from each chapter would make a substantial journal. Most of the exercises labeled *Invitation to Insight* in the *Student Activities Manual* are useful as journal entries.

Book Reports/Exercises

Book reports may be assigned to students to encourage more in-depth study of a particular subject.

The greatest disadvantage of book reports as a method of evaluation is that students often prepare reports that only regurgitate what was said in the book. To overcome this disadvantage, when assigning book reports, we have asked students to create an activity from the book they have read. The activity should be designed to teach others in the class one important thing (cognitive or affective) that the student gleaned from the book. We suggest that students look in the text for model exercises. Then we periodically set aside a class session for students to work out their activities with their classmates. Class members are asked to give feedback evaluating each student's exercise. The book report/exercise method seems to reinforce learning of the basic tenets of each book, and most students seem to enjoy sharing discoveries with their classmates.

Self-Evaluation

This method operates on the assumption that in many respects, the student is in the best position to judge his or her own progress in the course. Instructors who use self-evaluation systems ask each student to select a grade that reflects that person's effort and gain in understanding key ideas. Usually, the student is asked to write an explanation for the chosen grade.

The first advantage of this approach is its emphasis on self-judgment. It demonstrates that the student is responsible for his or her own growth and that whatever grade appears on the transcript is merely a symbol of that growth. Second, asking a student the question "What grade do you deserve?" often generates much more self-reflection about effort expended than any other system of evaluation.

The most obvious disadvantage is the potential for abuse. There is no guarantee that a lazy student will not take a high grade. A second shortcoming is the absence of any feedback from the instructor, who presumably has some valuable information about the student's progress. A remedy is to have the instructor reserve the right to give the final grade.

Peer Evaluation

In this system, the students assign each other individual grades based on the assumption that in a communication course, the perceptions of one's peers are a good indication of improvement and mastery of skills. The most efficient method of peer evaluation we've discovered involves reproducing the names of every class member, four to six names to a page. The names are equally spaced down the left side of the paper, and horizontal lines are drawn to separate the area on the paper that will be used to write comments to the student named there. (The back side of each student's space may also be used if the writer needs more room.)

Copies of this special evaluation roster are then distributed to everyone in the class. Each student records a grade and a statement of specifics that supports the assigned grade for each classmate. Ample time should be allowed for this assignment. In-class time seems to result in the best feedback.

The completed pages are collected. Like pages are stapled together and then cut with a paper cutter into individual packets. At the first opportunity, these packets are returned to the individual student. If all has gone well, the student will receive a sheaf of papers containing a grade and an evaluation from every member of the class.

The greatest advantage of peer evaluation is the feedback each student receives. If the class has been successful, students should know each other well enough to make many valuable comments. Assuming that class members are a representative sampling of the general population, the comments should be a fair reflection of the way a student is perceived outside of class.

The biggest disadvantage of this method is the desire of students to be nice to avoid any negative feedback—thus turning the exercise into an experience reminiscent of signing high school yearbooks. On the other hand, there is always the danger (although experience shows it to be extremely rare) that some unfavorable feedback can be psychologically damaging to the student.

GRADING SYSTEMS

Recognizing the strengths and weaknesses of each method of evaluation, you may want to combine several of them to suit your needs. Several possible grading systems follow as illustrations. We have successfully used each of these systems. You'll find that we have personalized each system by choosing to emphasize different areas. In addition, each grading system also posits a slightly different type of student-teacher relationship.

Grading System Option 1: *Student Activities Manual* Emphasis (Examinations, Quizzes, Attendance, Written and Oral Exercises)

Objective This grading system places added emphasis on the individual student's involvement with the various units covered in the course. It asks that students demonstrate their knowledge on traditional exams and quizzes and also in written exercises or oral skill checks from the *Student Activities Manual*. The philosophy underlying this approach is that communication skills should be studied and practiced and then performed orally to demonstrate knowledge of the material. It is believed that students will be more likely to use communication skills in their personal lives that they have practiced in a number of ways in class.

Examinations	35% of the final grade
Quizzes	10% of the final grade
Oral/Written Assignments	40% of the final grade
Attendance	10% of the final grade
Participation/Extra Assignment	5% of the final grade

Here are the points you will need to earn the grade of your choice:

A	=	900–1000
B	=	800–899
C	=	700–799
D	=	650–699

Here are the activities that will earn you points:

100 points. Attendance. Everyone will start with 100 points. You are entitled to a certain number of absences without penalty (3 for classes that meet 3 times a week, 2 for classes that meet 2 times, and 1 for a class that meets only once). Beyond these, each missed meeting will cost you points (correspondingly 6, 9, and 18), on the assumption that you need to be present to learn and practice the skills introduced in the course. Anyone who drops below 75 points in this area may be dropped.

50 points. Class Activities. Fifty points are available here for quality of class participation, extra assignments, or other activities assigned by the instructor.

100 points. Quizzes. There will be ten brief quizzes, designed to check your reading of the text. These quizzes are simple recall quizzes and are aimed only at being sure you've read the assigned pages. To take the quizzes, you'll need a packet of Scantron quiz-strips—the 15-question size. (10 quizzes x 10 points = 100 points)

350 points. Tests. There will be two 100-point midterms and a 150-point final exam. These exams will consist of objective questions (multiple choice, true/false and matching). For the exams you will need a packet of 100-item Scantron test strips. (100 + 100 + 150 = 350 points)

200 points. Written Exercises. Written exercises from the *Student Activities Manual* will help you apply course information to your own life. Entries will be assigned periodically, and selected assignments will be collected and graded. Exercises turned in late will be penalized for each class session they are overdue. (5 exercises x 40 points = 200 points)

200 points. Oral Skill Demonstrations. These dyadic exercises from the *Student Activities Manual* will help you orally practice the skills covered in class by applying them to your experience and receiving feedback from a partner. Anyone not in class when these exercises are conducted forfeits the points. (5 exercises x 40 points = 200 points)

NOTE: Some exercises may need to be videotaped in class or in the communication laboratory. You will be able to review videotaped oral skills after they are graded by the instructor.

Grading System Option 2: Attendance, Tests, Quizzes, Papers, Projects, Book Reports

The grade you earn in this class will depend on the amount of work you choose to do as well as its quality. Following is a list of activities, each of which will earn you a number of points. None of these activities is required. You choose the grade you want and pick the tasks that look most appealing that will earn you that grade.

Here are the points you will need to earn the grade of your choice:

A = 420–500

B = 340–419

C = 220–339

D = 180–219

Here are the activities that will earn the points:

100 points. Attendance. Everyone will start with 100 points. You are entitled to a certain number of absences without penalty (3 for MWF classes, 2 for TTh classes, 1 for evening classes). Beyond these, each meeting you miss will cost you points (10 for MWF classes, 15 for TTh classes, 30 for evening classes), on the assumption that you need to be present to learn and practice the skills introduced in this course. Anyone who drops below 50 points in this area will be dropped from the class.

150 points. Tests and Quizzes. There will be seven brief 10-point quizzes, designed to check your reading of the chapters of *Looking Out/Looking In*. These quizzes will be simple and are aimed only at being sure you've read the assigned pages.

In addition, there will be a 40-point midterm and a 40-point final examination, designed to test your understanding and your ability to apply the information discussed in this class.

150 points. Papers. You will be given a number of opportunities to write papers throughout the semester. You may write on up to six of the topics presented. Each paper will be worth 25 points.

These papers aren't tests. Their purpose is to help you see how the ideas we discuss apply to your everyday life. They will lead you to think about the way you presently communicate, offer you some alternatives, and invite you to try these alternatives to see if they help.

100 points. Projects and Book Reports. The project gives you an opportunity to focus on whatever area of interpersonal communication especially interests you. It might take the form of an experiment in which you try out different behaviors to see which work best, a research paper in which you explore an area of personal interest, or a questionnaire or survey to learn how other people see you or deal with a situation similar to yours. You may want to keep a journal to record certain kinds of communication, which you will then analyze.

In any case, if you are interested in doing a project, you will need to complete and turn in a contract form by _____. It will include a description of the area you want to explore, why that area interests you, how you plan to work on that area, and what you will hand in. In addition, it will indicate how many points you want to work for on your project. The instructor will look over your contract and either sign it or negotiate revisions with you. After signing it, the contract becomes the standard against which the quality of your work will be measured. All projects must be typewritten and are due no later than _____.

Book reports may be done on any book in the bibliography you will receive in class or on any title you clear with the instructor in advance. You may write up to two reports, each of which will be worth up to 50 points.

Your reports must be typewritten and should include a chapter-by-chapter discussion of the book in which you (1) describe the author's ideas in the chapter and (2) discuss how these ideas relate to your life.

Finally, you should write a conclusion in which you summarize your opinions of the book and how it relates to your own life.

Optional Paper Topics. The following paper topics are designed to help you see how the ideas discussed in class apply to your own life. These papers aren't tests. Their purpose is to help you think about the way you presently communicate, offer you some alternatives, and invite you to try out these alternatives to see if they help.

You can earn up to 25 points for each paper you write, and you may write as many as six papers. (In addition to the papers described on this sheet, you may propose in writing any other paper assignment that you believe will help you apply the concepts discussed. With the instructor's approval, such assignments will substitute for one or more of the papers.) In each case where there is more than one paper described for a chapter, you may do only one of the papers described. The last dates each paper will be accepted will be announced in class, and no work will be accepted after those dates.

The format for each paper involves:

1. Following the instructions in the text.
2. Writing a summary that describes
   a. What (if anything) you learned about yourself in following the instructions.
   b. How you feel about this learning (satisfied, indifferent, depressed, resolved, etc.).
   c. Anything you want to say about the exercise (suggest changes, describe difficulties, etc.).

Paper Topics

Chapter 1: A First Look at Interpersonal Relationships
1. Expanding your Communication Effectiveness (1.2 in *Student Activities Manual*)

Chapter 2: Communication and Identity: The Self and Messages
2. Who Do You Think You Are? (2.1 in *Student Activities Manual*)
3. Reevaluating Your "Can'ts" (2.4 in *Student Activities Manual*)

Chapter 3: Perception: What You See Is What You Get
4. Pillow Method (Shifting Perspectives, 3.3 in *Student Activities Manual*)
5. Your Call—Perception (3.8 in *Student Activities Manual*)

Chapter 4: Emotions: Thinking, Feeling, and Communicating
  6. Recognizing Your Emotions (text, p. 137)
  7. Disputing Irrational Thoughts (4.5 in *Student Activities Manual*)

Chapter 5: Language
  8. Effective Language (5.5 in *Student Activities Manual*)
  9. Your Call—Language (5.7 in *Student Activities Manual*)

Chapter 6: Nonverbal Communication: Messages Beyond Words
  10. Evaluating Ambiguity (6.3 in *Student Activities Manual*)

Chapter 7: Listening: More than Meets the Ear
  11. Listening Choices (7.4 in *Student Activities Manual*)

Chapter 8: Communication and Relational Dynamics
  12. Discovering Dialectics (8.1 in *Student Activities Manual*)
  13. Relational Stages (8.2 in *Student Activities Manual*)

Chapter 9: Improving Communication Climates
  14. Understanding Your Defensive Responses (9.1 in *Student Activities Manual*)
  15. Your Call—Climate (9.7 in *Student Activities Manual*)

Chapter 10: Managing Interpersonal Conflicts
  16. Understanding Conflict Styles (10.1 in *Student Activities Manual*)
  17. Win-Win Problem Solving (10.4 in *Student Activities Manual*)

Grading System Option 3: Instructor, Peer, and Self-Evaluations

Objective
To give each student as much control over his or her grade as possible while dealing with the responsibility this control demands.

Overview of Policy
To be successful and receive credit for this class, the following requirements must be met:

  1. Attendance in class must be satisfactory.
  2. All homework assignments must be completed and satisfactory.
  3. Participation in class activities must be satisfactory to peers, self, and instructor.

  If these requirements are met satisfactorily, you will receive a C grade.

  The B-grade requirement may be met by reading two books, twelve articles, or a combination of one book and six articles.

  If you wish to receive an A grade, you must complete satisfactorily the C and B requirements and, in addition, design and carry out a project concerning some aspect of interpersonal communication.

Details on Option 3 System

Attendance Requirement. The student's attendance will account for 30 percent of his or her grade. Each student will receive a notice of attendance requirements at the beginning of the course. To illustrate, here is a set of regulations for an MWF class:

0 to 1 class period missed	=	A for attendance part of grade
2 class periods missed	=	B for attendance part of grade
3 class periods missed	=	C for attendance part of grade
4 class periods missed	=	D for attendance part of grade
5 or more class periods missed	=	F for attendance part of grade

Adjustments would be made for classes meeting twice (TTh) a week or once a week. Students should be reminded that attendance governs only part of the grade and that missing four class periods doesn't necessarily mean that a semester grade of D will result. It would depend on the grades in the other areas and the amount of work the student completes.

Homework Requirements. There will be nine to twelve homework assignments. They will consist of journals, inventories, self-observation, and so on. There will be no letter grades on these assignments. Each assignment will be evaluated as satisfactory, unsatisfactory, or incomplete. To fulfill this requirement, the student must have all assignments handed in, completed, and satisfactory. Opportunity may be given to bring unsatisfactory homework up to a satisfactory level.

Quizzes. Quizzes will be given on the first class meeting after the class has been assigned to complete the reading of a chapter in the text. These quizzes will be graded but will be counted only to help the student achieve a higher grade. In other words, you will be rewarded if you have done the assigned reading and scored well on the quiz. You may take the quiz only when it is given to the entire class—no make-ups of quizzes.

Participation Requirements. You are already aware that attendance is extremely important in this class. There is a considerable amount of student participation during each class meeting. There is no available way to make up the activities and exercises that involve the class. However, just being present in the classroom will not satisfy the participation requirement. It is necessary for you to take an active part because you will be evaluated by fellow classmates, instructor, and yourself. Heading the listed criteria for these evaluations will be class participation.

Instructor's Evaluation. The instructor's evaluation will account for 30 percent of your grade. In arriving at that grade, your homework and classroom participation (with particular attention to improvement and attitude) will be reviewed. All class participants are expected to cooperate with the various activities and exercises in class and to be supportive of classmates. You should realize that some of the instructor's grade will come from impressions formed of your actions and reactions in the class. In other words, the instructor will form a subjective opinion of your effort in the class.

Peer Evaluation. This will account for 20 percent of the final grade. Each student is required to grade all the other students in the class. This evaluation will be done with criteria that have been published and in most cases developed by the class.

In this feedback process, students should place special emphasis on improvement that has been observed and improvement that needs to be made.

To make this process manageable, we will use the following method. Twice during the term, you will be asked to give feedback to your classmates—at about the halfway point and again at the end of the semester. The second evaluation will include a grade from each member of the class. You will arrive at your final peer-evaluation grade by finding the average of all the grades you receive.

Self-Evaluation. This will count for 20 percent of your final grade. At the end of the course, you will assign yourself a grade, which you must be able to justify in terms of criteria worked out before this assignment. Should there be any question about the self-grade assigned, the instructor will confer with the student so that they may reach an understanding.

B Grade. Attendance, instructor's and peer evaluation, and self-evaluation must be satisfactory before a student is eligible for a C grade. If a student wants to pursue a B grade, he or she must complete the previous requirements plus the following:

Select from the book list provided two books, read them, and write reports on the forms provided and/or give an oral report to a small group of classmates. In either case, the student must demonstrate that he or she has read the book, from the information given in the report.

or

Select twelve articles from a list of articles that have been collected and placed on reserve in the library by the instructor. These articles are to be read and reported on by completing an Article Report Form that will be provided for each article. The student may also be required to give oral reports to small groups in class.

or

Do a combination reading assignment of one book and six articles. Article and book reports that are not written in acceptable form—complete sentences, correct spelling, sensible paragraphs, and so on will be returned as unsatisfactory. They may be corrected and resubmitted, provided there is enough time for the instructor to review them a second time.

A Grade. If a student expects to receive an A grade, he or she must demonstrate the capacity to do superior work.

In this class, this will take the form of some kind of project concerned with interpersonal communication.

This project will earn an A grade only if it is of excellent quality and both the B and C grade requirements are met.

The A project must follow this schedule:

Within the first ten class hours, a plan must be submitted to the instructor. Remember, designing your own individual project is part of the assignment. Under no circumstances will the instructor give you a project to complete.

At the halfway mark, the instructor will meet with each student attempting an A project. It will be determined at that time if the project is of a kind that will be informative for all the class. If this is the case, it would be presented during a class period. If not, it would be submitted in written form. The specific written form will be agreed on at this time.

As soon as the projects are finished, they should be presented in class or submitted in writing. No project will be received for credit during the last two class meetings.

Some projects that have been attempted in the past follow.

Research Papers

How to Break Up and Remain Friends

Giving and Receiving Criticism Effectively

Interpersonal Communication in Personnel Management

A Study in How We Learn to Be Parents

An Investigation into the Language of Men and Women

Methods for Improving the Handling of Human Conflict.

Personal Projects

Improving my relationships with my coworkers

Becoming a better partner in my marriage

Improving the quality of communication with my fourteen-year-old daughter

Increasing my participation in class

Improving my relationship with my stepfather

Showing more positive independence around my parents

Other Projects

Do T-shirts communicate? (presented as a slide show to the class)

How conditioned are we to our sex roles? (class participation)

How do married couples want their mates to say, "I love you"?

How much does another's expectations of me influence my actions?

Establishing effective family meetings.

All of the projects were acceptable. Not all of them, however, earned their designer an A—not because of the subject matter but rather because of an insufficient amount of effort on the student's part.

SUGGESTED COURSE SYLLABUS

The following course syllabus is a sample outline that uses *Looking Out/Looking In* as the basic text. You may find a part or all of this syllabus useful in designing your own course outline. Since the lengths of semesters vary, we have arbitrarily assumed a 15-week duration for this course with classes meeting three times a week for 50-minute sessions.

Week 1

Class 1

Topic: Getting Started

> The instructor explains the nature of the course and completes normal beginning-of-course housekeeping chores. Particular emphasis should be made on the classroom participation that will be expected from each student.
>
> To reinforce the participation dimension of the course, begin at once with the exercise Name Calling, wherein each member of the group learns the names of all the others.

Exercise: Name Calling

> (Find under Chapter One Notes following this section of *Instructor's Resource Manual.*)

Assignment: Obtain your own copy of *Looking Out/Looking In* and the *Student Activities Manual*. Begin Chapter One.

> NOTE: Students should read all the material presented in each chapter, including the poetry, quotations found in the page margins, pictures and cartoons, exercises, and the regular text. All the material in each chapter is part of the message.

Class 2

Topic: Getting to Know One Another

Activity: Explain the importance of knowing one another in a communication skills class. It is important that students feel as comfortable as possible to experience less anxiety in trying out new communication behaviors.

Exercise: Introductions

> (Find under Chapter One Notes following this section of *Instructor's Resource Manual.*)

Assignment:

> Complete your communication skills inventory (1.1 in *Student Activities Manual*).
> Read Chapter One (quiz to verify reading—next class session).
> Complete the *Study Guide* section of the *Student Activities Manual* for Chapter 1.

Class 3

Quiz: Chapter 1

Topic: The Importance of Human Communication

Activity: Encourage discussion of basic human needs and how communication is necessary to obtain them. Use the student's Communication Skills Inventory to identify goals for the class.

Assignment: Expanding Your Communication Effectiveness (1.2 in *Student Activities Manual*)

Week 2

Class 1

Topic: Effective Communication

Exercise: Mediated Messages – Channels (1.4 in *Student Activities Manual*) and Your Call – Communication Basics (1.5 in *Student Activities Manual*).

Assignment: Read Chapter Two of text. Complete the *Study Guide* section of the *Student Activities Manual* for Chapter 2.

Class 2

Quiz: Chapter Two

Topic: The Self-Concept

Activity: Instigate discussion of the different ways in which our self-concept may have developed.

Exercise: Who Do You Think You Are? (2.1 in *Student Activities Manual*)

Assignment: Self-Concept Inventory (2.2 in *Student Activities Manual*)

Class 3

Topic: Characteristics of Your Self-Concept

Exercise: Discuss Self-Concept Inventory (2.2 in *Student Activities Manual*).
 Ego Boosters and Busters (2.3 in *Student Activities Manual*)

Assignment:
 Reevaluating Your "Can'ts" (2.4 in *Student Activities Manual*)

Week 3

Class 1

Topic: Self-fulfilling Prophecies/Changing the Self-Concept

Exercises: Dear Professor—Relational Responses (2.8 in *Student Activities Manual*)

Assignment: Prepare Mediated Messages –Identity Management (2.6 in *Student Activities Manual*) for the next class.

Class 2

Topic: Managing Impressions

Exercise:
> Discussion groups compare their prepared responses to Mediated Messages—Identity Management (2.7 in *Student Activities Manual*)
> Success in Managing Impressions (2.5 in *Student Activities Manual*)

Assignment: Read Chapter Three for quiz. Complete the *Study Guide* section of the *Student Activities Manual* for Chapter 3.

Class 3

Quiz: Chapter Three

Topic: The Process of Perception

Activity: Discuss the process of perception; students give examples and discuss in groups how perception influences communication. Relate to concept of self and how clear messages are or are not given. Use Your Perceptual Filters (text, p. 95).

Assignment: Guarding Against Perceptual Errors (3.1 in *Student Activities Manual*)

Week 4

Class 1

Topic: Accuracy and Inaccuracy of Perception

Exercise: Discuss Guarding Against Perceptual Errors (3.1 in *Student Activities Manual*) in class. Compare and discuss in groups physiology and perception. In the same groups, discuss New Body, New Perspective (text, p. 103) and compare group findings with class.

Assignment:
> Examining Your Interpretations (3.2 in *Student Activities Manual*)
> Observation and Perception (3.4 in *Student Activities Manual*)

Class 2

Topic: Role of Culture and Society in Perception

Activity: Discuss physiological influences, social roles, and cultural influences in the perceptual process. Use the Perception-Checking Stimulus games in this Instructor's Resource Manual (see E. Perception-Checking Stimuli in section 4 of Notes on Class and Student Activities in this Instructor's Resource Manual) or 3.6—Perception Checking in *Student Activities Manual*.

Assignment: Prepare perception-checking statements to deliver in class based on today's activity (3.5 and 3.6 in *Student Activities Manual*)

Class 3

Topic: Empathy

Activity:

Deliver perception-checking statements (3.5 and 3.6 in *Student Activities Manual*).

Discuss differences between understanding someone and agreeing with that person.

Exercise: Punctuation Practice (text, p. 98)

Assignment: Shifting Perspectives (3.3 in *Student Activities Manual*)

Week 5

Class 1

Topic: Broadening Perception

Activity: Group discussions of Mediated Messages—Perception (3.7 in *Student Activities Manual*) and Your Call—Perception (3.8 in *Student Activities Manual*).

Assignment: Read Chapter Four for quiz. Complete the *Study Guide* section of the *Student Activities Manual* for Chapter 4.

Class 2

Quiz: Chapter Four

Topic: Emotions: Thinking and Feeling

Exercise: Recognizing Your Emotions (text, p. 137)

Discuss difficulty we have in expressing our emotions. Explore benefits resulting from being able to express our emotions and the variations in expression due to culture and gender.

Assignment:

The Components of Emotion (4.1 in *Student Activities Manual*)

Your Call—Emotions (4.7 in *Student Activities Manual*)

Class 3

Topic: Emotions and Thought/Talking to Yourself

Exercise:

Talking to Yourself (text, p. 153)

Discuss overcoming irrational thinking.

How Irrational Are You? (text, p. 158)

Assignment:
>Find the Feelings (4.2 in *Student Activities Manual*)
>Self-Talk (4.4 in *Student Activities Manual*)

Week 6

Class 1

Topic: Expressing Feelings

Exercise: Stating Emotions Effectively (4.3 in *Student Activities Manual*)
>Discuss minimizing debilitative emotions and when and how to share feelings.

Assignment: Disputing Irrational Thoughts (4.5 in *Student Activities Manual*)

Class 2

Topic: Disputing Irrational Thoughts

Exercise: Compare and correct student assignments to Disputing Irrational Thoughts (4.5 in *Student Activities Manual*)

Assignment: Read Chapter Five for quiz. Complete the *Study Guide* section of the *Student Activities Manual* for Chapter 5.

Class 3

Quiz: Chapter Five

Topic: Words and Meanings

Exercise: In groups, students discuss Your Linguistic Rules (text, p. 178).
>Discuss meanings people have for words and their emotional reaction to words.

Assignment: Complete Misunderstood Language (5.1 in *Student Activities Manual*).

Week 7

Class 1

Topic: Abstraction and Language

Activity: Discuss the nature of language (a symbol system) and abstraction. Introduce and have class members work with the abstraction ladder and the assignment exercises from the last class.

Assignment: Behavioral Language (5.2 in *Student Activities Manual*)

Class 2

Topic: Responsibility in Language

Activity: Discuss communication issues involved with the Language of Responsibility. Complete Responsible Language (5.3 in *Student Activities Manual*).

Assignment: Prepare "I" Language (Oral Skill) (5.4 in *Student Activities Manual*) for next class.

Class 3

Topic: "I" Language

Activity: "I" Language (Oral Skill) (5.4 in *Student Activities Manual*)

Assignment: Down-to-earth Language (text, p. 175)

Week 8

Class 1

Topic: Language in action

Activity: Effective Language (5.5 in *Student Activities Manual*)

Assignment: Record at least ten examples of language that is gender- or culture-related for the next class.

Class 2

Topic: Language, Gender, and Culture

Activity: Discuss how gender and cultural variables affect language use. Discuss in groups Mediated Messages—Language (5.6 in *Student Activities Manual*) and Your Call—Language (5.7 in *Student Activities Manual*).

Assignment: Read Chapter Six for quiz. Complete the *Study Guide* section of the *Student Activities Manual* for Chapter 6.

Class 3

Quiz: Chapter Six

Topic: Nonverbal Communication

Exercise: Reading "Body Language" (text, p. 220)
    Discuss awareness of nonverbal communication.

Assignment: Nonverbal Description (6.1 in *Student Activities Manual*)

Week 9

Class 1

Topic: Characteristics of Nonverbal Communication

Exercise: Nonverbal How-To's (6.2 in *Student Activities Manual*)

Assignment: Evaluating Ambiguity (6.3 in *Student Activities Manual*)

Class 2

Topic: Nonverbal Functions/Congruency

Activity: Discuss the six functions of nonverbal communication and relate them to the congruency and incongruency of verbal and nonverbal messages. Use Evaluating Ambiguity (6.3 in *Student Activities Manual*) to build upon the text.

Assignment: Your Call—Nonverbal Behavior (6.5 in *Student Activities Manual*)

Class 3

Topic: Types of Nonverbal Communication

Exercise:

>   Pralanguage and Accent (text, p. 234)
>
>   Distance Makes a Difference (text, p. 238)
>
>   Discuss proxemics, kinesics, paralanguage, clothing, territoriality, chronemics and environment.

Assignment: Observe nonverbal behaviors in a number of contexts. Take notes for discussion next class. Complete Mediated Messages—Nonverbal (6.4 in *Student Activities Manual*)

Week 10

Class 1

Topic: Applying Your Knowledge of Nonverbal Communication

Activity: Dear Professor—Relational Responses (6.6 in *Student Activities Manual*).

Assignment: Read Chapter Seven for quiz. Complete the Study Guide section of the *Student Activities Manual* for Chapter 7.

Class 2

Quiz: Chapter Seven

Topic: Listening versus Hearing

Exercise: Your Call – Listening (7.8 in *Student Activities Manual*)

>   Discuss types of ineffective listening and why we don't listen. Discuss benefits of talking less and listening more.

Assignment: Listening Diary (7.1 in *Student Activities Manual*)

Class 3

Topic: Becoming a More Effective Listener

Exercise: One-Way and Two-Way Communication (Chapter Seven notes following this section in the Instructor's Resource Manual)

Assignment: Listening Choices (7.4 in *Student Activities Manual*)

Week 11

Class 1

Topic: Listening Responses

Exercise: Compare and correct 7.4 Listening Choices. Effective Questioning (7.2 in *Student Activities Manual*)

Assignment:

> Paraphrasing (7.3 in *Student Activities Manual*)

Class 2

Topic: Paraphrasing

Activity: Compare and contrast paraphrasing with other listening styles discussed in the text.

Assignment: Complete Informational Listening, 7.5 in *Student Activities Manual*.

Class 3

Topic: Listening Effectiveness

Exercise:

> Discuss types of listening and when to use each.
>
> Listening and Responding Styles (oral skill) (7.6 in *Student Activities Manual*)

Assignment: Read Chapter Eight for quiz. Complete the *Study Guide* section of the *Student Activities* Manual for Chapter 8.

Week 12

Class 1

Quiz: Chapter Eight

Topic: Interpersonal Attraction/Building Positive Relationships. Discuss characteristics of relational communication, breadth and depth of relationships.

Exercise: Your IQ (text, p. 291).

Assignment: Breadth and Depth of Relationships (8.3 in *Student Activities Manual*)

Class 2

Topic: Relational Dialectics

Exercise: Discuss characteristics of relational dialectics. Your dialectical tensions (text, p. 304)

Assignment: Discovering Dialectics (8.1 in *Student Activities Manual*)

Class 3

Topic: Developmental Stages in Intimate Relationships

Exercise: Your Relational Stage (text, p. 300)

Assignment: Relational Stages (8.2 in *Student Activities Manual*)

Week 13

Class 1

Topic: Self-Disclosure and Risk in Interpersonal Communication

Exercise:
> Have class discuss Johari Window and self-disclosure. Appropriate Self-Disclosure (text, p. 316)
> Reasons for Nondisclosure (8.4 in *Student Activities Manual*)
> Degrees of Self-Disclosure (8.5 in *Student Activities Manual*)
> Discuss alternatives to self-disclosure.

Assignment: Read Chapter Nine for quiz. Complete the *Study Guide* section of the *Student Activities Manual* for Chapter 9.

Class 2

Quiz: Chapter Nine

Topic: Confirming and Disconfirming Communication

Exercise:
> Discuss Gibb Categories
> Evaluating Communication Climates (text, pp. 338-339), and Defensive and Supportive Language (9.2 in *Student Activities Manual*)

Assignment: Understanding Defensive Responses (9.1 in *Student Activities Manual*).

Class 3

Topic: Building Clear Messages

Exercise: Clear Messages (9.3 in *Student Activities Manual*)

Week 14

Class 1

Topic: Handling Defensiveness

Exercise:

Discuss defensiveness and defense mechanisms and ways to cope with defensiveness.

Defense Mechanism Inventory (text, p. 342), and Nondefensive Responses to Criticism, 9.4 in *Student Activities Manual*)

Assignment: Prepare Coping with Criticism (9.5 in *Student Activities Manual*) for next class.

Class 2

Topic: Coping with Criticism

Activity: Coping with Criticism (9.5 in *Student Activities Manual/* Study Guide)

Assignment: Read Chapter Ten for quiz. Complete the *Study Guide* section of the *Student Activities Manual* for Chapter 10.

Class 3

Quiz: Chapter Ten

Topic: Conflict Is Natural and Normal for All Persons

Activity: Discuss attitudes we're learning concerning conflict. Encourage personal testimony. Discuss how we behave in avoiding conflict and how these behaviors tend to drive us crazy.

Assignment:

Understanding Conflict Styles (10.1 in *Student Activities Manual*)
Your Conflict Styles (10.2 in *Student Activities Manual*)

Week 15

Class 1

Topic: Types of Conflict Resolution

Activity: Discuss win-lose, lose-lose, compromise, and win-win problem solving.

Assignment: The End vs. the Means (10.3 in *Student Activities Manual*)—prepare this to provide background for win-win problem solving next class.

Class 2

Topic: Effective Problem Solving

Exercise: Win-Win Problem Solving and Conflict Resolution Dyads (10.4 and 10.5in *Student Activities Manual*)

Use these to role-play the resolution of conflicts. Discuss effectiveness.

Assignment: Review for final exam.

Class 3

Topic: Conclusion of course

Activity: Give final examination and remarks.

USING INTERNET LINKS IN THE INTERPERSONAL COMMUNICATION COURSE

Making use of the Internet to enrich classroom instruction is easy. We provide a number of links below that we have found useful. They connect you to journals, publications, collections, bibliographies, teaching strategies, and other course-related materials such as audiotapes and videotapes. You will want to use some of the information yourself, but others can provide a valuable supplement to reading, lecture, discussion, and other activities in the classroom. Many thanks to **Heidi Murphy** from Albuquerque Technical Vocational Institute for the following.

Chapter 1: A First Look at Interpersonal Relationships

What Employers Want Vs. What They See in Job Candidates
This article explains that communication skills are among the top qualities employers seek in job candidates.

http://www.jobweb.com/joboutlook/2004outlook/outlook5.htm

Applications of an Interpersonal Model to Educational Environments
In this scholarly article, an interpersonal communication model is applied to the field of education.

http://www.wlu.ca/~wwwpress/jrls/cjc/BackIssues/22.1/donalds.html

Establishing and Maintaining Interpersonal Relationships
This page describes one theory of interpersonal needs.

http://www.comsci.co.za/acii01/establish120303.htm

Making Friends in Cyberspace
A 1996 academic journal article entitled "Making Friends in Cyberspace."

http://www.ascusc.org/jcmc/vol1/issue4/parks.html

What Makes a Good Communicator?
This article gives tips to police officers about conveying appropriate relational messages.

http://www.communitypolicing.org/publications/exchange/e25_99/e25kidd.htm

Interpersonal Competence Resources
A brief definition of interpersonal competence and links to many sites related to interpersonal competencies.

http://novaonline.nv.cc.va.us/eli/spd110td/interper/relations/relationsscomp.html

Human Communication is "The Answer!"...or is it?
A speech professor discards several communication-related myths.

http://www.ccp.uwosh.edu/whatsnews/Fall2002/Communication.html

Focus on Feelings Rather Than Content
Read about the content and relational dimensions of interaction.

http://www.coping.org/communi/model.htm

Interpersonal Communication Links

A comprehensive list of text-related links.

http://staff.gc.maricopa.edu/~dbrenner/InterpersonalCommLinks.html

Interpersonal Communication Workbook

A comprehensive interpersonal communication course workbook that includes articles, quizzes, and class exercises.

http://www3.shastacollege.edu/communication/rsaunders/workbooks/10workbook/pd fworkbook/SP10WBF02.pdf

The Seven Challenges: Communicating More Cooperatively

This site features an excellent, comprehensive online book that explores seven challenging interpersonal communication skills.

http://www.coopcomm.org/workbook.htm

Models of Communication

See many of the various communication models developed over the years in the communication discipline.

http://web.sfc.keio.ac.jp/~masanao/Mosaic_data/com_model.html

Communication Skills for School Leaders

This digest provides practical suggestions for school leaders who want to increase the effectiveness of their communication interactions. Suggestions focus on the following skills covered in the textbook: improving understanding, listening advice, perception checking, giving feedback, describing behavior, "I" messages, expressing feelings, and improving nonverbal communication.

http://eric.uoregon.edu/publications/digests/digest102.html

Communication Skills Test

Self-test: Evaluate your general level of communication skill ability. A comprehensive score interpretation requires a fee.

http://www.queendom.com/tests/relationships/communication_skills_r_access.html

Communication Characteristics and Causes of Miscommunication

This site provides a detailed explanation of the transactional model of interpersonal communication and variables that can cause miscommunication.

http://communication.utsa.edu/leblanc/courses/2061-1-1.htm

Web Exercise 1.1: Illustrating Miscommunication

Visit the Transactional Model website at *http://communication.utsa.edu/leblanc/ courses/2061-1-1.htm*. Read the explanations of communication variables and the possible causes of miscommunication in Table 1. Using as many of the communication variables as possible, visually illustrate a "miscommunication" for each of three contexts (work, school, and home). Illustrate the situation with arrows, pictures, words, and dialogue or thought balloons. Explain which of the variables contribute to the "miscommunication" and why.

Web Exercise 1.2: Comparing and Contrasting Communication Models

Visit the Models of Communication Web site [*http://web.sfc.keio.ac.jp/~masanao/ Mosaic_data/com_model.html*]. This list of links provides you with visual access to the many various communication models developed over the years in the communication discipline. Choose two communication models to compare and contrast. In your own words, describe the similarities and differences between the two models. Referencing the models described in your textbook, what elements are included and left out of the models you chose? Finally, describe how the models you chose are similar or different to the linear and transactional models described in your textbook.

Web Exercise 1.3: Why Communicate Cooperatively?

Visit the Cooperative Communication Skills Internet Resource Center [*http://www .coopcomm.org/w7a2intr.htm*]. The author lists 7 benefits/reasons for learning and adopting a more cooperative communication style. What are these 7 reasons? Which of these 7 reasons apply to your own life? Give specific, concrete examples of how these reasons apply in your own life (i.e. if one reason you agree with is "more respect," state that you would like to have more respectful relationships with your children, or with your co-workers, and explain what that "respect" might look like). What are the barriers to success? What steps can you take to overcome these barriers?

Web Exercise 1.4: What are Your Communication Strengths and Weaknesses?

This article gives basic hints for reducing misunderstandings and achieving competent communication outcomes: *http://www.selfgrowth.com/articles/Menechella12.html*. Read the 5 steps for improving communication competence at the address above. According to these suggestions, where do your strengths lie and where do you feel you need to improve?

Web Activity 1.5: Your Communication Style

Take the quiz and follow the directions at this site *http://www.cyberparent.com/talk/quiz.htm*. Did you detect a pattern in your answers? What, if any, insight did you gain about yourself from this activity? Describe the communication style of a person you admire. Why do you admire this style? How is it different from your style? What relational goals can you achieve with this style?

Web Activity 1.6: A Personal Communication Inventory

Print and complete the worksheet at *http://www.stepfamilyinfo.org/02/evc-strengths .htm*. Write a short essay describing any insights you gained from this activity.

Chapter 2: Communication and Identity: The Self and Messages

Self-Monitoring: Do You Censor What You Say?

Self-test: Are you a low or high self-monitor?

http://www.outofservice.com/self-monitor-censor-test/

Identity Management in Cyberspace

Read about five interlocking factors that are useful in understanding how people manage identities in cyberspace.

http://www.rider.edu/~suler/psycyber/identitymanage.html

Self-Esteem Self-Evaluation Survey

Evaluate your self-esteem by responding to a brief survey.

http://www.self-esteem-nase.org/jssurvey.shtml

How Can We Strengthen Our Children's Self-Esteem?

An expert in early childhood education explains what adults can do to help strengthen children's self-esteem.

http://www.kidsource.com/kidsource/content2/strengthen_children_self.html

Symptoms of Low Self-Esteem

An employment seekers' manual lists 19 symptoms of low self-esteem.

http://www.jobbankusa.com/lowse.html

Shaping Body Image

Read about how theories of *social comparison* and *reflected appraisal* play roles in shaping negative body image.

http://www.hc-sc.gc.ca/hpfb-dgpsa/onpp-bppn/leaders_image_e.html

US/Chinese Memories Show Impact of Culture on Self-Concept

Read a college newspaper article entitled "US/Chinese memories show impact of culture on self-concept."

http://www.news.cornell.edu/Chronicle/01/6.28.01/memory-culture.html

Face: It Just Depends on Your Perspective

Learn more about the concept of "face" and how it is managed differently in individualistic and collectivistic cultures.

http://content.monster.com.sg/experts/curran/library/6213/

Developing Self-Esteem Through Interactions With Others

A list of annotated citations for academic and popular articles about the relationship between communicating with others and building self-esteem.

http://novaonline.nv.cc.va.us/eli/spd110td/interper/self/linksdevselfesteem.html

Self-Fulfilling Prophecy: The Penny and Nancy Story

A unique story dialogue that illustrates a self-fulfilling prophecy between teacher and students in the classroom.

http://dana.ucc.nau.edu/~tlp24/t5.htm

A Diagram of a Self-Fulfilling Prophecy

Through description and diagram, business consultants feature a specific example of how initial beliefs can influence behavioral outcomes in an organization.

http://www.outsights.com/systems/theWay/sss/ssx01.htm

Methods for Changing Our Thoughts, Attitudes, Self-Concept, Motivation, Values and Expectations

As part of a self-help online book, this skill-based chapter takes a comprehensive look at communication and self. Sub-topics include: changing your self-concept and building self-esteem; increasing self-awareness; challenging irrational ideas; determinism; trying a new lifestyle; paradoxical intention; increasing motivation; straight thinking, common sense and good arguments; developing attitudes that help you cope; and self-hypnosis and mental imagery.

http://mentalhelp.net/psyhelp/chap14/

Increasing Self-Awareness

As part of a self-help online book, this page provides an excellent description of several chapter concepts including: self-monitoring, perceived self, and resisting self-concept change.

http://mentalhelp.net/psyhelp/chap14/chap14e.htm

Changing Our Self-Concept and Building Self-Esteem

As part of a self-help online book, this page describes a step-by-step procedure to analyzing the self and taking steps to change the self-concept and improve self-esteem.

http://mentalhelp.net/psyhelp/chap14/chap14b.htm#a

Self-Esteem Test

Take a comprehensive quiz to find out your level of self-esteem. Score and interpretation provided.

http://www.queendom.com/tests/personality/self_esteem_r_access.html

Strategies for Building Self-Esteem

This page provides 12 suggested tips for building self-esteem.

http://www.vivaconsulting.com/counselling/selfesteem.html

Web Activity 2.1

Based on the example at *http://www.outsights.com/systems/theWay/sss/ssx01.htm*, create your own labeled diagram and explanation of a self-fulfilling prophecy that has played out in your own life.

Web Activity 2.2

Based on the descriptions at *http://mentalhelp.net/psyhelp/chap14/chap14e.htm,* speculate about your level of self-awareness (high, low, medium). Explain your answer using information from this Web page and/or your textbook. Read the information on self-deception. Analyze your own level of self-deception. Give specific examples of times you have been guilty of these defensive deceptions.

Web Activity 2.3

Examine the list of suggested tips [*http://www.vivaconsulting.com/counselling/selfesteem.html*]. Which of these might be relevant to your life situation? Select strategies that relate to you and elaborate on the specific steps you could take to proceed with building self-esteem. For example, are your life goals realistic and achievable? If you believe there are any irrational "shoulds" in your life, what are they? Can you dispute them? How? Do you have a "cruel inner critic?" If so, what does he/she say? Can you argue with this critic? What would you say?

Presenting the Off-Line Self in an Everyday Online Environment

Read a scholarly research article entitled "Presenting the off-line self in an everyday online environment."

http://les1.man.ac.uk/cric/Jason_Rutter/papers/Self.pdf

Good or Bad, What Teachers Expect From Students They Generally Get!

An education scholar explains the mechanisms of the self fulfilling prophecy as it applies to teachers and students.

http://www.kidsource.com/education/good.bad.expect.html#credits

Self-Monitoring Test

Self-test: Assess your levels of interpersonal (public) and intrapersonal (private) self-monitoring.

http://www.queendom.com/tests/personality/self_monit_access.html

How High is Your Self-Esteem?

Self-test: Rate your self-esteem and compare it with the average score of other quiz-takers.

http://www.rateyourself.com/poll.cfm/Subject_ID/3/Poll_ID/2241

Chapter 3: Perception: What You See Is What You Get

The Accuracy and Power of Sex, Social Class and Ethnic Stereotypes

http://www.psychology.iastate.edu/faculty/madon/accuracy.sex.socialclass.pdf

This lengthy research article examines the accuracy and power of sex, social class and ethnic stereotypes in person perception. A comprehensive and useful list of related references follows the article.

Basic Self-Controls to Interact Effectively With People

http://www.motivator-on-call.com/selfcontrol2.htm

This article reviews skills of self-control, including perception checking, that can help us enhance our business and career success.

Empathy and Listening Skills

http://www.psychological-hug.com/listeningskills.htm

Authored by a retired clinical psychologist, this site provides information about the power of using empathy and listening skills to promote productive relationships.

Different Drummers

http://keirsey.com/Drummers.html

This essay by personality theorist David Keirsey provides an explanation of how and why people are different. Keirsey emphasizes that relational harmony comes from understanding and accepting differences, rather than trying to change another person to your ways of thinking.

Typical Stereotypes and Misconceptions

http://www.pbs.org/wgbh/globalconnections/mideast/questions/types/index.html

This page explains some typical stereotypes and misconceptions Westerners hold about Islam and people in the Middle East and vice-versa. In addition, find links to other sites with accurate information about the Middle East.

Test Your Hidden Racial Biases

http://racerelations.about.com/library/weekly/aa102699.htm

A unique site that allows you to test your hidden biases towards race, gender, age, disability

Discover Your Emotional Empathy Profile

http://moodware.com/basic_page.cfm?page=tests

Click on "Emotional Empathy" to take a test that determines your degree of emotional empathy. Submit your answers and receive a lengthy analysis of what your score can mean for your career. The authors also suggest possible careers based on your score.

Experiencing Empathy Online

http://www.ifsm.umbc.edu/~preece/paper/17%20ricekatz11.pdf

This book chapter outlines a recent study that explored the presence of empathy in online communities.

The Difference Between Jurors' Perception of Self and Others

http://www.lawcommerce.com/litigation/art_jurors_perception.asp

This article, entitled "The Difference between Jurors' Perception of Self and Others: Why So Many Plaintiffs Get the Benefit of the Doubt," illustrates the *self-serving bias* in the courtroom.

Checking Out Our Interpersonal Hunches

http://mentalhelp.net/psyhelp/chap13/chap13k.htm

As part of an online psychological self-help book, this article suggests specific strategies for clarifying our interpersonal assumptions.

The Empathy Belly

http://www.empathybelly.org/expectant_fathers.html

Read about the "Empathy Belly," which is a product that helps men understand what it's like to be pregnant.

Empathy and Emotional Intelligence

Read about empathy and its connection to emotional intelligence.

http://www.eqi.org/empathy

Influence of Stereotyping on Guilty Verdicts

A scholarly research article describes the effects of stereotyping in a study where race seemed to influence guilty verdicts.

http://web.nwe.ufl.edu/~jdouglas/8.pdf

Web Activity 3.1 Differing Interpretations: Misunderstandings between Men and Women

Read the article about gender communication differences at *http://www.jou.ufl.edu/rolemodels/studentissues/understand-opposite-sex.shtm*. How does perception play a role in misunderstandings between men and women? Give examples from the article. Can you think of additional examples where men and women might interpret each other's behavior in different ways? What suggestions do you have that might help men and women understand each other more accurately?

Web Activity 3.2: Walking in My Shoes: Empathy Building

Read the information about the "empathy belly" at *http://www.empathybelly.org/expectant_fathers.html*. This product helps men build empathy and understand a bit of what it's like to walk in someone else's shoes. Create a "suggestions for building empathy" guide that includes your own creative and helpful ideas about how one might understand more about what it's like to walk in the shoes of others. For example, if I want to understand what it's like to be homeless, what are some ways I could go about doing that? Could I dress like a homeless person and walk through the streets? Could I volunteer at a homeless shelter? Interview a homeless person? If I want to understand what it's like to be blind, what could I do? As a class, share your guides with each other and pick suggestions to act on. After participating in and carrying out one of your suggestions, write an essay about what it's like to "walk in the shoes of another."

Web Activity 3.3: Inaccurate Stereotypes and Cultural Misconceptions

Read the information at *http://www.pbs.org/wgbh/globalconnections/mideast/questions/types/index.html*. As you read at this site, we often inaccurately prejudge other people, cultures and places until we actually meet someone or experience something for ourselves. See if you can find 4-5 people who have traveled to other countries and realized that their prejudgments were inaccurate. Interview them and ask how their views have changed, how their communication has changed, and how their own lives have changed as a result of experience. Write an essay summarizing your interview answers and draw your own conclusions using concepts from the chapter.

Chapter 4: Emotions: Thinking, Feeling, and Communicating

EQ International Site

A useful and comprehensive site that provides a list of over 2,000 feeling words in addition to detailed explanations of primary and secondary emotions, causes behind emotions, tips for managing negative emotions, history and explanation of "emotional intelligence," and links to other resources on emotions.

http://eqi.org/index.htm

Advice for Couples: How to Control Anger

This article makes suggestions for couples on how to control anger and problem-solve.

http://www.sensiblepsychology.com/improving_anger.htm

How Do You Feel Today?

See if you can describe how you are feeling today by looking at 65 faces representing a variety of emotions.

http://www.theoaktree.com/feelings.htm

Thinking Quiz

Take this true/false quiz to explore what you know about how our emotional responses are controlled by our thought processes.

http://www.helpself.com/thinker.htm

Who is the Only Person in the World Who Can Make You Angry?

The author of this article, entitled "Who is the Only Person in the World Who Can Make You Angry?" diagrams and explains how our thoughts cause our emotions, not people or events. She also gives suggestions for anger control.

http://members.aol.com/AngriesOut/grown1.htm

Using Rational-Emotive Therapy to Control Anger

Learn how to use rational emotive therapy to control anger. The examples given are perfect for illustration of the process, and are very accessible for the young college-age student.

http://www.palace.net/~llama/psych/ret.html

Rational-Emotive Behavior Therapy

At this site, a clinical psychologist gives the reader tools for identifying and overcoming the source of emotional difficulties.

http://www.threeminutetherapy.com/rebt.html

An Introduction to Rational Emotive Therapy

This lengthy and comprehensive article gives an extensive description of the REBT process, and provides a useful list of references related to the topic.

http://www.rational.org.nz/prof/docs/intro-rebt.htm

Understanding Yourself

This page describes four purposes emotions can serve in your life, and gets you ready to begin expanding your emotion-vocabulary.

http://www.region.peel.on.ca/health/commhlth/selfest/emotions.htm

Expressing Emotions by Expanding Your "Feelings" Vocabulary

Use the "feelings vocabulary" and practice being expressive with your emotions by responding to hypothetical situations.

http://www.region.peel.on.ca/health/commhlth/selfest/vocab.htm

Managing Emotions

Read about six ways to help you begin to understand, interpret and manage your feelings.

http://www.region.peel.on.ca/health/commhlth/selfest/2emotion.htm

"Cool-Down" Strategies

Expand your list of "cool-down" strategies.

http://www.region.peel.on.ca/health/commhlth/selfest/cooldwn.htm

Emotional Intelligence Quotient Self-Test

Take a non-scientific self-test of your emotional intelligence quotient. Results and analysis are provided.

http://www.utne.com/interact/test_iq.html

Managing Emotions as a Part of Conflict Resolution

Read a series of questions you might ask yourself when learning to manage and express emotions.

http://crnhq.org/freeskill6.html

Albert Ellis Institute

Read more about Albert Ellis and rational emotive therapy at the Albert Ellis Institute homepage.

http://www.rebt.org

Methods for Coping with Depression

As part of a self-help online book, this section reviews several methods for coping with depression. The methods relate to: behavior, emotions, skills, cognition and unconscious factors.

http://mentalhelp.net/psyhelp/chap6/chap6s.htm

Challenging Irrational Ideas

As part of a self-help online book, this section provides helpful exercises on how to challenge irrational ideas.

http://www.mentalhelp.net/psyhelp/chap14/chap14i.htm

Producing Desired Emotions: How to Be Happy

As part of a self-help online book, this section provides lengthy advice on producing desired emotions and includes a section on "how to be happy."

http://www.mentalhelp.net/psyhelp/chap12/chap12e.htm

Methods for Handling Our Own Aggressions/Anger

As part of a self-help online book, this section provides lengthy advice on how to handle our own anger and aggression.

http://www.mentalhelp.net/psyhelp/chap7/chap7n.htm

Directory of Emotional Intelligence Internet Sites

A comprehensive clearinghouse of sites, resources and organizations dedicated to the study and practice of "EQ" (emotional intelligence quotient).

www.eq.org

Web Exercise 4.1: Practicing the ABCs of Rational Emotive Therapy

The author of Using Rational Emotive Therapy to Control Anger [*http://www.palace.net/~llama/psych/ret.html*] expands on the textbook description of rational emotive therapy. Using the ABC approach described at this site, create an example problem of your own and practice applying rational emotive therapy to the problem. Be sure to include all steps A-G. After you finish, describe your usual the

possible consequences that may result in this relationship from choosing to apply this approach.

Web Exercise 4.2: Express Your Emotions

Using the structure at Expressing Emotions by Expanding Your 'Feelings' Vocabulary: A Practice Exercise [*http://www.region.peel.on.ca/health/commhlth/ selfest/vocab.htm*], practice expressing your emotions with a wide range of word choices For suggestions, see the table of feelings in chapter 4 of *Looking Out/Looking In*, or click on "feeling word possibilities" at the bottom of the web page. Review the guidelines for expressing emotions in your textbook, and practice describing your feelings by writing statements for each of the hypothetical situations listed at the web site.

Web Exercise 4.3: Challenging Irrational Thoughts

As part of a self-help online book, Methods for Coping With Depression [*http://mentalhelp.net/psyhelp/chap6/chap6s.htm*], this section reviews several methods for coping with depression. The methods relate to: behavior, emotions, skills, cognition and unconscious factors. After reading the chapter, list some negative thoughts you hold about yourself. Next to each thought, make a list of the external forces that you blame for these negative qualities. Now, as the author says, challenge any faulty perceptions, irrational ideas, automatic ideas, faulty conclusions, and excessive guilt. Review the fallacies in the textbook and change any irrational self-talk. Did you change any of your original thoughts? If so, why? If not, why not? How might changes influence communication and relationships with others?

Chapter 5: Language: Barrier and Bridge

Gender Differences in E-mail Communication

An academic research article examines the implications of gender differences on language use in electronic mail discussion groups.

http://iteslj.org/Articles/Rossetti-GenderDif.html

Basic Differences Between Men and Women

Scroll down to "Basic Differences between Men and Women." The author describes many types of gender differences and makes skill recommendations for improving relationships.

http://www.familycare4u.com/male_female.htm

Gender Differences in Communication

Read more about gender differences in communication and access a lengthy list of online links related to the topic.

http://www.geocities.com/Wellesley/2052/genddiff.html

Styles of Communication: Direct and Indirect

Read more about high- and low-context communication styles, and test your knowledge with a quiz.

http://www.peacecorps.gov/wws/culturematters/Ch3/stylescommunication.html

Why Men and Women Don't Always Understand Each Other

Get more information about how gender differences can prevent men and women from understanding each other.

http://www.mediatraco.com/interper.html

More About High- and Low-Context Communication Styles

This academic research article provides information about high- and low-context communication styles and their relationships to individualism, collectivism and self-concept.

http://www.communication.ilstu.edu/activities/CSCA2002/High_Low_Context_CSCA _2002.pdf

Language: Say What You Mean

Click any link under "Language: Say What You Mean" to read humorous examples of equivocal language.

http://www.coping.org/write/percept/language1.htm

How Much Do You Know About How Men and Women Communicate?

Test your knowledge of gender communication differences. Detailed answers follow the quiz.

http://www.glc.k12.ga.us/pandp/guidance/schoices/sc-f20.htm

Gender Styles in Computer-Mediated Communication

This article briefly reviews the current state of research on gender communication styles in computer-mediated communication.

http://www.georgetown.edu/faculty/bassr/githens/cmc.htm

Gender Differences in Communication

An informative article describing gender differences in communication.

http://pages.towson.edu/itrow/wmcomm.htm

Avoiding Emotive Language in Writing

See examples of how to avoid emotive language in academic writing.

http://unilearning.uow.edu.au/academic/2diq2_feedback.html

Direct and Indirect Communication Styles

Read a description of and examples of low and high context communication styles.

http://www.pierce.ctc.edu/tlink/general/context.html

Getting Along With Americans

For an outsider perspective on U.S. American styles of communication, read the information at this site for international students.

http://www.rit.edu/~306www/international/handbook/verbalcommunication.html

Expressing Yourself More Clearly and Completely

An excellent, comprehensive online book that explores seven challenging interpersonal communication skills. This chapter expands on "I" statements and offers a step-by-step methodology for assertively expressing yourself clearly and completely (also a variation on the clear message format explained in chapter 10 of your textbook).

http://www.coopcomm.org/w7chal3.htm

Rethinking "I" Statements

The author of this page suggests a revision to the traditional format of "I" messages, in order to further reduce defensiveness.

http://www.state.oh.us/cdr/schools/contentpages/Istate21.htm

Gender Communication Differences in Business

Read what business educator and speaker Candy Tymson says about gender communication differences and about how to deal effectively with the opposite gender in business.

http://www.tymson.com.au/articles.html

"I" Messages

As part of a self-help online book, this page takes a comprehensive look at accepting responsibility for your feelings and developing "I" messages to express yourself. The author discusses several reasons for using "I" messages and suggests comprehensive steps for creating effective "I" messages.

http://mentalhelp.net/psyhelp/chap13/chap13g.htm

The Power of Language

Scroll down to "The Power of Language" to see information about how language reflects attitudes and feelings about what and whom we are describing. Specific examples are given.

http://www2.magmacom.com/~sneiman/df.htm

Gender Differences in Communication: An Intercultural Experience

This scholarly article argues the appropriateness of viewing gender communication as a form of intercultural communication. The author includes a primer on gender differences in communication, and provides suggestions for applying effective intercultural communication skills to the situation of gender communication.

http://www.cpsr.org/cpsr/gender/mulvaney.txt

The Linguistic Relativity Hypothesis

A lengthy academic explanation and review of linguistic relativity and the Sapir-Whorf hypothesis.

http://plato.stanford.edu/entries/relativism/supplement2.html

Linguistic Relativity: Does Language Shape Thought?

An accessible article with good examples of how having different ways of describing the world leads speakers of different languages also to have different ways of thinking about the world.

http://www.mit.edu/~lera/papers/ECS-proofs.pdf

Linguistic Relativity and Linguistic Determinism

This essay explains and compares linguistic relativity and linguistic determinism using very specific examples from the Turkish and American Indian languages.

http://www.lsadc.org/fields/index.php?aaa=lang_thought.htm

What Happens When Japanese and U.S. Americans Meet

Read an account of what often happens when Japanese and U.S. Americans meet. Japanese translator Ueda writes about the differences between Japanese and U.S. American culture and communication styles, and emphasizes intercultural understanding for sake of the global economy.

http://fly.hiwaay.net/~eueda/japguest.htm

Web Exercise 5.1: Identifying Direct and Indirect Communication Styles

At Direct and Indirect Communication Styles [*http://www.pierce.ctc.edu/tlink/ general/context.html*], several examples are given that illustrate the differences between direct (low-context) and indirect (high-context) communication styles. Which style is being illustrated in the last example about the late teacher? How do you know? Create 2-3 additional communication situations in which you illustrate both direct and indirect styles by writing and labeling thoughts, dialogue or actions.

Web Exercise 5.2: Personalizing "I" Statements

The author of Rethinking 'I' Statements [*http://disputeresolution.ohio.gov/schools/ contentpages/Istate21.htm*] makes a point about how the traditional structure of "I" statements do not always work in students' cultural climates. In addition, the author mentions that the traditional "I" statements include several "you"s that could potentially be interpreted defensively. The author makes suggestions for how to revise "I" statements to fit personal communication styles and to further reduce defensiveness. Follow the example on this web page and create several traditional "I" statements for your own real-life situations. Then revise them according to the author's suggestions. Give your opinion about which structure might work best for you and explain why.

Web Exercise 5.3: Practicing "I" Messages

Read the information and examples on I-Messages [*http://mentalhelp.net/ psyhelp/chap13/chap13g.htm*]. Think of a situation from your own life for which the use of an "I" message might be useful. State at least two reasons for why an "I" message might be effective in this situation. Write 5-7 "you" statements that apply to your situation, and label them according to the names given on this page. Now, turn these "you" statements into effective "I" statements.

Web Exercise 5.4: Linguistic Relativity & Linguistic Determinism

Question: Read the essay on Language and Thought [*http://www.lsadc.org/fields/ index.php?aaa=lang_thought.htm*]. According to this author, what is the hypothesis of linguistic determinism? What evidence is given in support of and against the argument for determinism? What questions might you ask a bilingual in order to test this hypothesis? Carry out an experiment by interviewing one or more bilingual persons to determine how language and thought are related.

Web Exercise 5.5: High Context & Low Context Cultures

This page is an account of what often happens when Japanese and U.S. Americans meet. Japanese translator Ueda writes about the differences between Japanese and U.S. American culture and communication styles, and emphasizes intercultural understanding for sake of the global economy. Read the portion of the article entitled "The art of communication" at Your Japanese Guests

[*http://fly.hiwaay.net/~eueda/japguest.htm*].

Are the Japanese high-context communicators or low-context communicators? Using 2-3 examples from the article, explain the differences between high-context and low-context communication styles.

Web Exercise 5.6: Intercultural Misunderstandings

http://www.peacecorps.gov/wws/culturematters/Ch3/stylescommunication.html

Based on your understanding of high- and low-context communication from your textbook and this web page, create two short role plays that illustrate a potential misunderstanding that occurs as a result of these style differences. For example, in #8 on the quiz, if "yes" can mean "I hear you" to high context communicators, but it means simply "yes" to low context communicators, what might happen if a low context communicator asks a high context communicator if he/she accepts her price offer in a business deal? Your dialogues should illustrate: 1) a U.S.—Japanese business deal negotiation gone bad; 2) an embarrassing incident with your high-context in-laws. Label the speech parts with "high" or "low" context and demonstrate your role plays in class.

Web Exercise 5.7: Gender Communication Differences

http://www.glc.k12.ga.us/pandp/guidance/schoices/sc-f20.htm

Read the research on gender communication differences summarized in the quiz answers on this page. Think of some common difficulties between men and women in both personal and work relationships. Do you think any of these difficulties can be explained by the gender communication differences explained in either the textbook or the quiz answers on this page? Explain your answer and give examples.

Chapter 6: Nonverbal Communication: Messages Beyond Words

Nonverbal Communication in Japan

Prepare for travel to Japan with this article that describes some of the nonverbal "norms" and customs in the following areas: silence, facial gestures, touching, showing respect to objects, gestures, dress, Tatami rooms, seating and standing protocol, being on time, rank, elevators, table seating, cars, table manners, slurping, dishes, toasting, and smoking.

http://www.shinnova.com/part/99-japa/abj17-e.htm

Nonverbal Communication in Text-Based Virtual Realities

An academic Master's thesis investigates the functions of nonverbal communication in MUDs (multi-user dimensions), similar to chat rooms on the Internet.

http://www.johnmasterson.com/thesis/

An Overview of Nonverbal Communication in Impersonal Relationships

A scholarly article, written by a graduate student, summarizes many theories and facts related to the study of nonverbal communication with strangers.

http://hamp.hampshire.edu/~enhF94/kinesics.html

Dress for Success

http://getcustoms.com/articles/dress.html

Tips on the specifics of appropriate business dress in five countries.

Nonverbal Communication in Asian Cultures

Read a lengthy and comprehensive explanation of the differing meanings behind American and Asian gestures.

http://www.csupomona.edu/~tassi/gestures.htm

Nonverbal Communication Abstracts

A useful listing of nonverbal communication-related abstracts (short summaries) for scholarly articles published in academic journals. You may find this list useful when searching for research paper resources.

http://www.faculty.ucr.edu/%7Efriedman/nvcabstract.html

Nonverbal Communication Helps Us Live

Read a variety of brief anecdotes and news items about nonverbal communication.

http://www.csun.edu/~vcecn006/nonverb.html

Chinese Emotion and Gesture

An excellent article explaining and illustrating (with photos) Chinese gestures.

http://www.ling.gu.se/~biljana/gestures2.html#neg

Gender Differences in Nonverbal Communication

A brief bulleted listing of the major differences in nonverbal communication behaviors between males and females.

http://www.colostate.edu/Depts/Speech/rccs/theory20.htm

Gender Differences in Nonverbal Communication

A brief summary of the results of a study conducted to examine student's perceptions of gender differences in several areas of nonverbal communication.

http://www.bvte.ecu.edu/ACBMEC/p1999/Griffin.htm

The Nonverbal Dictionary of Gestures, Signs and Body Language Cues

A comprehensive resource for understanding human nonverbal behaviors. This site offers an extensively researched dictionary of nonverbal communication terms and illustrations.

http://members.aol.com/nonverbal2/diction1.htm#The%20NONVERBAL%20DICTIO NARY

How's Your Personal Distance—Watch This Space

An excellent article aimed at exploring perceptions of nonverbal behavioral norms between the U.S. and Russian cultures.

http://www.friends-partners.org/oldfriends/spbweb/lifestyl/122/how.html

The Body Language of Proxemics

A concise essay about how spatial relationships and territorial boundaries directly influence our daily encounters.

http://members.aol.com/katydidit/bodylang.htm

Cross-Cultural Job Interview Tips

Scroll down to "The Handshake" to read a brief section offering tips on how to greet someone from another part of the world.

http://www2.magmacom.com/~sneiman/df.htm

Lack of Nonverbals: How Can Email Communication Affect Your Business?

Read about problems that can occur in email communication because of the lack of body language, voice tones and shared environments.

http://www.pertinent.com/articles/communication/chrisCom1.asp

Are Poor Nonverbal Skills Slowing You Down?

This site gives tips to family physicians about the importance of using good nonverbal skills with patients.

http://www.aafp.org/fpm/970900fm/suite_3.html

Nonverbal Negotiation Skills

A sales consultant gives advice about using nonverbal skills in the negotiation of sales.

http://www.everyonenegotiates.com/nonverbalnegotiation.htm

I'm Running Late: The Silent Signals of Time

What does being late communicate to others? Find out in this article.

http://www.expertmagazine.com/articles/late.htm

Links, Links, and More Links to Information on Nonverbal Communication

A virtual clearinghouse of nonverbal communication links!

http://www3.usal.es/~nonverbal/introduction.htm

Emoticons

Link to sites with emoticon galleries.

http://novaonline.nv.cc.va.us/eli/spd110td/interper/message/Linkscmcemoticons.html

Nonverbal Communication Travel Guide

Read this travel guide advice about nonverbal communication norms in Japan.

http://athene.riv.csu.edu.au/~hnampo01/travelguide.html

Body Language Quiz

Test your understanding of body language.

http://www.janhargrave.com/quizes.htm

More Nonverbal Communication Links

More links to a variety of nonverbal communication-related websites.

http://novaonline.nv.cc.va.us/eli/spd110td/interper/message/linksnonverbal.html

Use Nonverbal Communication to Improve Relationships

Ten brief pieces of advice on using nonverbal behavior to improve relationships.

http://www.selfgrowth.com/articles/Albright2.html

More About Nonverbal Communication

Definitions, examples and activities are provided.

http://www.coping.org/communi/nonverbal.htm

Quiz: Hidden Aspects of Communication

Take a college practice quiz on "hidden aspects of communication."

http://anthro.palomar.edu/language/quizzes/langqui6.htm

Paralanguage

http://www.esl-lab.com/para.htm

Hear sound-byte examples of vocalizations and test your knowledge of their meanings.

Nonverbal Library

A virtual library of information about nonverbal behavior and related topics. Subject headings include: proxemics, kinesics, gestures, touch, paralanguage, smell, attractiveness, light and colors, and applications of nonverbal studies.

http://digilander.libero.it/linguaggiodelcorpo/biblio/

How Do Attractiveness and Stereotypes Affect Development?

A summary of study findings on how facial attractiveness and associated stereotypes affect development.

http://homepage.psy.utexas.edu/homepage/students/DAVISD/test/paanddev.html

Turkish Body Language

Read about the meaning behind Turkish gestures and other body language.

http://www.business-with-turkey.com/guia-turismo/turkish_body_language.shtml

Social Perception and Physical Attractiveness

A research article summarizes findings from a study that explores how individuals make personality judgments based on facial attractiveness.

http://www.personal.psu.edu/users/m/r/mra134/realindex.htm

Quiz: Gestures Around the World

Test your knowledge of gestures around the world.

http://www.isabellemori.homestead.com/questionsgestus.html

Quiz: Brazilian Gestures

Test your knowledge of Brazilian gestures.

http://www.forusers.com/forme/brazil/GestureQuiz.htm

Quiz: General Knowledge of Nonverbal Communication Concepts

Test your knowledge of nonverbal communication.

http://www.quia.com/pop/1704.html

Quiz: Recognizing Emotions

Take this quiz to see if you accurately read facial expressions.

http://condor.depaul.edu/~lcamras/images/recogexp.htm

Russian and English Nonverbal Communication

A lengthy and detailed explanation (in two languages) of nonverbal communication differences between the Russians and the English.

http://www.bilingua.ru/r_b_nc.htm

Web Exercise 6.1: Gender Differences in Nonverbal Communication

Read the information at *http://www.colostate.edu/Depts/Speech/rccs/theory20.htm.*

Develop a research strategy to observe nonverbal behaviors in males and females. Using the information at this site, develop a research question or a hypothesis and an instrument that you can use to keep track of your observations. Observe nonverbal behaviors in a public place (shopping mall, restaurant, bus station). Analyze and write up your results in a report describing observed differences and similarities between males and females. Do your results match those in stated in this web page? Do they match what the textbook says?

Web Exercise 6.2: Asian and American Nonverbal Differences Can Lead to Misunderstandings

First, read the article Gestures: Body Language and Nonverbal Communication *[http://www.csupomona.edu/~tassi/gestures.htm]* and then complete the exercise. Using Table 6-2 on p. 228 of your textbook as a model, create a table with the following columns. In column A, describe 5-6 gestures. In column B, list the American interpretation of the gesture. In column C, explain how the gesture might be interpreted by an Asian culture (be specific as to which culture: Korea, China, Japan, all Asian cultures, etc.). In column D, explain any misunderstandings that could occur as a result of the different interpretations. For discussion: How different is Asian nonverbal communication from American nonverbal communication? Why is it different at all? How can we prevent misunderstandings when traveling or doing business with other cultures?

Web Exercise 6.3: Nonverbal Communication Quiz: Types and Functions

Click on Quiz *[http://www.janhargrave.com/]* and make guesses about nonverbal behaviors and meaning. Submit and check your answers. How well did you do? Refer to true answers 4, 6, 7, 9 and 10, and describe the *type* of nonverbal communication that is being described in each question (according to your textbook). Also for each question, describe the *function* of the nonverbal behavior being described.

Web Exercise 6.4: Cultural Differences in Nonverbal Communication

Based on the differences you read about at: Analysis of Cultural Communication and Proxemics *[http://www.unl.edu/casetudy/456/traci.htm]*, create specific examples of potential misunderstandings that could occur as a result of interpreting nonverbal behaviors differently.

Web Exercise 6.5: Exploring Cultural Differences in Nonverbal Communication: An Interview

After reading the article How's Your Personal Distance—Watch This Space, and the paper at *http://www.odu.edu/webroot/orgs/ao/ip/ip.nsf/files/S_Imai.pdf/$FILE/ S_Imai.pdf*, interview several people who have recently spent some time living in another country. Find out what that person observed and learned about differences in the 12 areas of nonverbal communication discussed in your textbook. Also ask participants to give examples of nonverbal misunderstandings they have experienced. Write up a report on your findings.

Web Exercise 6.6: Guide to Effective Nonverbal Communication

Synthesizing information from your text and any of the Chapter 6 Web Links, create a "Nonverbal Communication Advice Guide" in one of the following areas: Improving Male-Female Relationships, Successful Intercultural Travel, Nonverbal Essentials for the Workplace, Nonverbal Communication Online.

Chapter 7: Listening: More Than Meets the Ear

Be All Ears

An article about how listening is more important than talking.

http://www.redding.com/currents/feature/past/20020526cu055.shtml

Active Listening Skills

Read specific examples of paraphrasing and other listening strategies.

http://www.taft.cc.ca.us/lrc/class/assignments/actlisten.html

Quiz: The Listening Quiz For Couples

Find out how well you listen to your partner, and get tips for improving your listening skills.

http://www.marriagesupport.com/quiz/1ds_intro.asp?id=2

Quiz: What is the Speaker Feeling?

Test your ability to listen for feelings.

http://www.gov.mb.ca/agriculture/homeec/cba20s04.html

Improving Listening Skills

Read more about effective listening and practice improving your own skills with the suggested activities.

http://www.coping.org/communi/listen.htm

Improving Responding Communication Skills

Read more about effective responding and practice improving your "listening to give help" skills with the suggested activities.

http://www.coping.org/communi/response.htm

Quiz: Are You a Really Good Listener?

A self-test.

http://www.stand-deliver.com/column/article_050503.shtml

Quiz: Rate Your Listening Skills

A self-test.

http://webhome.crk.umn.edu/students/ubar002/tutortraining/ListeningTest.htm

Quiz: How Well Do You Really Listen?

A self-test.

http://www.powercommunicator.com/test1a.asp

Quiz: How Well Do You Listen to Your Children?

A self-test.

http://www.powercommunicator.com/test2a.asp

Quiz: Measure Your Listening Abilities

A self-test.

http://www.careerjournal.com/myc/climbing/20021224-raudsepp.html

Quiz: Evaluate Your Listening Skills and Your Perception of Your Partner's Listening Skills

A self-test.

http://www.positive-way.com/listenin.htm

Quiz: Where Do You Stand on the Listening Scale?

A self-test.

http://www.caucusnj.org/adubato/starledger/listening.asp

Empathy and Listening Skills

A retired clinical psychologist provides information about the power of using empathy and listening skills to promote productive and positive relationships.

http://www.psychological-hug.com/

Listening Skills: A Key Element to Learning to Communicate Well

Click on "Listening Skills" to read about the importance of and strategies for listening with "understanding", which allows us to see an idea and attitude from another person's point of view or frame of reference.

http://www.itstime.com/aug97a.htm

Listening—With Your Heart As Well As Your Ears

Read about the following topics: 1) why being a good listener is important, 2) how listening affects family and work life, 3) some styles of poor listening, and 4) ways to improve listening skills.

http://www.ianr.unl.edu/pubs/family/g1092.htm

Men Do Hear—But Differently From Women

A report on the brain research study mentioned in your textbook revealing that men use only one side of their brain while listening.

http://www.medicine.indiana.edu/news_releases/archive_00/men_hearing00.html

International Listening Association

This home page belongs to the International Listening Association, a professional organization that promotes the study, development, and teaching of listening and the practice of effective listening skills and techniques. Links provide the following information about: membership; organization calendar; members, board and staff; conferences, seminars and workshops; discussion group; exercises; resources; quotes and factoids about listening.

http://www.listen.org/index.html

Quiz: Check Your Own Listening Skills

Check your own listening competency in the areas of: attention, empathy, respect, response, memory, and open-mindedness.

http://www.highgain.com/SELF/index.php3

Listening: Recommended Reading

A training organization that specializes in listening offers an excellent annotated bibliography of resources related to listening and communication.

http://www.highgain.com/html/recommended_reading.html

Sssh! Listen Up! How to Bring the Critical Skill of Listening Into Your Business

A free monthly online newsletter provided by a professional training organization specializing in listening and other communication skills. Articles feature advice and tips about the importance of listening skills for success in business.

http://www.highgain.com/newsletter/hg-enews-current.html

Back issues of Sssh! Listen Up!

http://www.highgain.com/newsletter/back-issues/back-issues-main.html

Listening More Carefully and Responsively

Read this chapter from an excellent, comprehensive online book that explores seven challenging interpersonal communication skills. The chapter addresses the practice of responsive listening, and focuses on the practice of separating the acknowledgement of the thoughts and feelings that a person expresses from approving, agreeing, advising, or persuading.

http://www.coopcomm.org/w7chal1.htm

How Do You Rate Your Listening?

A self-test.

http://www.facetofacematters.com/pages/qlistenc.htm

Listening and Empathy Responding

As part of an online psychological self-help book, this page provides a detailed, step-by-step methodology for developing listening and empathic response skills.

http://mentalhelp.net/psyhelp/chap13/chap13c.htm

Web Exercise 7.1: Practice Listening to Help

Practice Listening to Help *[http://www.adv-leadership-grp.com/programs/ evaluations/listening.htm]* provides several case scenarios in which a person describes a problem he/she is dealing with in his/her life. Assume these people are your friends or people who are important to you. Using the space provided, respond to each person with words you might normally use. Be honest about how you would normally respond. Now, submit your responses and read the results. Analyze and label your response with terms from the text (advising, judging, analyzing, minimizing significance of situation). Next, rewrite your statements and create additional dialogue between you and the friend, using suggestions from the "results" section and from the textbook section on "listening to help." Be sure to label your revised response. How did your responses change? Speculate about how the outcomes of each listening situation might change by using advice from the textbook.

Web Exercise 7.2: Assessing and Improving Communication Between You and Your Partner

Take the Listening Skills *[http://www.positive-way.com/listenin.htm]* self-evaluation quizzes and then click on "ratings discussion and listening advice." If you find there is room for improvement in your relationship, develop a dialogue between you and your partner that resembles a recent conflict where neither partner practiced good listening skills. However, revise the dialogue to include the suggested advice on this page. Label your responses with the following terms: paraphrasing, clarification, effective feedback, awareness of body language. Did the outcome of the conflict change? If so, why? Practice using these listening skills during your next conflict.

Web Exercise 7.3: Identifying Barriers to Listening

Choose a story topic from the dozens of listening quizzes in the Cyber Listening Lab *[http://www.esl-lab.com/]*. Listen to the whole story and then take the comprehension quiz. If you did not score 100%, try to identify which listening barriers might have interfered. Repeat this exercise with other stories. Which barriers might be more prevalent in your life and why? Explain. What could you do to reduce ineffective listening? Apply some of the tips for informational listening from your chapter and see if your retention and recall improves. Practice these listening techniques in your next lecture class.

Web Exercise 7.4: Practicing Empathic Responding

Read the information and examples on Listening and Empathy Responding *[http://mentalhelp.net/psyhelp/chap13/chap13c.htm]*. As the author suggests, get together with 2 classmates and practice listening to each other tell about a problem from your past or present. One of you should rate your empathy responses on the scale provided by the author. How did you do? Take turns speaking, listening/responding, and rating. Discuss your ratings. What were common problem areas? Did any low rated responses relate to the barriers discussed in the beginning of the chapter? If so, which ones? What concrete steps can each of you take to improve your empathy responses?

Web Exercise 7.5: Learning to Acknowledge What you Hear

Read Challenge One: Listen First & Acknowledge *[http://www.coopcomm.org/ w7chal1.htm]*. With another classmate, discuss a topic that is fairly controversial (a current news event usually works best). Be sure that the topic is one in which you take opposing sides. Decide which one of you will speak first (person 1) and which one of you will listen (person 2). Give person 1 two minutes to present his/her take on the issue. After two minutes, person 2 must accurately summarize and state what the other person said without approving, disapproving, agreeing, disagreeing, advising or persuading. Start this statement by saying "I hear you saying that...." Use the skills suggested in this chapter to listen more responsively. Person 1 must agree that this statement is an accurate reflection of what was said before person 2 can take a turn. Now person 2 takes a turn giving his/her side of the issue and person 1 listens, summarizes and states what the other person said in a similar manner. How did you do? How difficult was the task of summarizing and acknowledging? How is this type of conversation different from what you are used to? Can you think of a personal example of a situation where someone could have benefited from using this technique?

Web Activity 7.6: Ineffective Listening Styles

Read about ten types of ineffective listening. *http://topten.org/public/BN/BN153.html*
Compare and contrast the 10 ineffective listening styles at this site and the 7 styles in your textbook. Which ones are similar? Write 5 scenarios that illustrate a situation in which one person demonstrates an ineffective listening style. Trade scenarios with your classmates and try to guess which styles are being illustrated.

Web Activity 7.7: Payoffs for Effective Listening

http://www.ianr.unl.edu/pubs/family/g1092.htm

Read over the 9 payoffs for effective listening at this site. Which ones can you relate to specifically? Give *specific* examples of positive payoffs that might result in *your life* if you improved your listening skills.

Web Exercise 7.8: Empathy & Listening Skills in a Conversation

Read the conversation between two friends at: Empathy and Listening Skills *[http://www.psychological-hug.com/listeningskills.htm]*. Find and describe 2-3 examples of Anita's ability to empathize with Tanya. Summarize the end result. Create your own situation and dialogue: Respond to a friend in need using similar empathic responses. Speculate about the possible consequences of empathizing in a variety of contexts.

Chapter 8: Communication and Relational Dynamics

Honesty and Intimacy

A scholarly article (also published in the *Journal of Social and Personal Relationships*) analyzes and argues the importance of honesty in developing and sustaining intimate relationships.

http://www.etsu.edu/philos/faculty/hugh/honesty.htm

Battle of the Genders

Read about the intimacy factor in the battle of the genders.

http://www.cyberparent.com/gender/battle3.htm

Intimacy: Recommended Reading for Men

A comprehensive listing of books for men on the topic of intimacy.

http://www.menstuff.org/books/byissue/intimacy.html

Interpersonal Perspectives and Theories

Scroll down to find the following links to useful analyses, in-depth explanations, and concrete examples of the following chapter-related theories: interpersonal deception, relational dialectics, social exchange, social penetration, Knapp's stages of relationship development, and uncertainty reduction.

http://www.uky.edu/~drlane/capstone/interpersonal/

Equivocal Communication

A book review includes a brief summary, explanation of and examples of equivocal communication.

http://oak.cats.ohiou.edu/~sa102596/ITResearch.htm

Quiz: Self-Disclosure

Take a self-test (small fee required) to determine your willingness to self disclose to family members, friends, acquaintances and strangers. Submit your answers and obtain a detailed analysis of your results in addition to tips on "how to get closer."

http://www.queendom.com/tests/relationships/self_disclosure_general_access.html

The Johari Window Model: Brief Explanation

A sample diagram and brief explanation of the Johari Window model of self-disclosure.

http://www.knowmegame.com/Johari_Window/johari_window.html

The Johari Window Model: Lengthy Explanation

This page provides a sample diagram and lengthy explanation and interpretation of the Johari Window model of self-disclosure.

http://www.noogenesis.com/game_theory/johari/johari_window.html

Johari Window and Self-Disclosure Discussion

A diagram, explanation and brief discussion of the benefits and risks of self-disclosing.

http://www.cultsock.ndirect.co.uk/MUHome/cshtml/psy/johari.html

Excuses, Emotions and In-Between

A scholarly essay about excuse-making that addresses the question: what makes us view a message as an excuse, and what are the emotional consequences of doing so?

http://research.haifa.ac.il/~benzeev/excuses.htm

Self-Disclosure and Openness

As part of an online self-help book, this section gives comprehensive skill advice for expressing yourself clearly and giving useful feedback.

http://mentalhelp.net/psyhelp/chap13/chap13i.htm

Common Interpersonal Problems and Needed Skills

As part of an online self-help book, this section discusses many of the problems associated with making and keeping friends, including: fear (risk) of approaching someone, fear (risk) of rejection, hints for becoming a good conversationalist, and the importance (benefits) of self-disclosure.

http://mentalhelp.net/psyhelp/chap9/chap9m.htm

Social Penetration Theory

This student-created site introduces and briefly explains Altman & Taylor's Social Penetration Theory. Also provided are links to student-created pages relating to research, application and critique of the theory.

http://oak.cats.ohiou.edu/~bz372497/socpenbz.htm

Interpersonal Attraction

A chapter outline explaining the following factors of attraction: competence, proximity, physical attractiveness, similarity, reciprocity, and cooperation. Results of scholarly studies are also listed and help explain and support each factor.

http://www.psych.purdue.edu/~ben/iuk-p320/ch7.html

Can Marital Success Be Predicted and Improved?

As part of an online self-help book, this chapter comprehensively reviews the topic of marital relationships and focuses on: stages in the development of a relationship; factors of success in marriage; unconscious factors, needs and motives in mate selection; and types of "love stories."

http://mentalhelp.net/psyhelp/chap10/chap10e.htm

Relational Dialectics

An introduction and brief explanation of Baxter & Montgomery's theory of Relational Dialectics. Also provided are several links to student-created pages relating to research, application, and critique of the theory.

http://oak.cats.ohiou.edu/~pc406097/rd.htm

Social Exchange Theory

This student-created site introduces and briefly explains Thibaut & Kelley's Social Exchange Theory. Also provided are links to student-created pages relating to research, application and critique of the theory.

http://oak.cats.ohiou.edu/~al891396/exchange.htm

Compatibility and Interest Guide

Take this quiz with your partner to determine and communicate about how compatible you are.

http://www.positive-way.com/compatibility.htm

Quiz: What's Your New Couple Quotient?

A self-test.

http://www.newcouple.com/couplequiz.html

Quiz: A Self-Disclosure Test for Couples.

A self-test.

http://www.queendom.com/tests/minitests/self_disclosure_couples_abridged_access.html#h

Are You an Open Person?

A self-test.

http://members.fortunecity.co.uk/siukaice/openness.htm

Social Exchange Theory

A comprehensive explanation of social exchange theory.

http://www.afirstlook.com/archive/socialexchange.cfm?source=archther

Do Opposites Attract? Not Really.

A study suggests that when finding a mate "likes" may attract better than opposites.

http://my.webmd.com/content/article/70/80965.htm

Sexual Intimacy and Emotional Intimacy

A scholarly article examines the relationship between sexual intimacy and emotional intimacy.

http://elysa.uqam.ca/Revue/Vol3no1/Shaughnessy%20M.html

Web Exercise 8.1: Draw Your Own Johari Window

Take this online questionnaire to determine your scores for "soliciting feedback" (or receptivity to feedback) and for "willingness to self-disclose." With your knowledge of the Johari Window quadrants, draw an intuitive model of your own Johari Window with the size of the panes reflecting your scores. Justify the sizes of your window panes with detailed explanations. How receptive are you to feedback from others? How willing are you to know and learn things about yourself from others? How willing are you to self-disclose to others? What do these results and answers say about your level of self-awareness? Do you feel that there is anything about your communication style that you want to change? If so, why? If not, why not?

Web Exercise 8.2: Factors of Attraction in Your Own Relationships

Read the lecture Interpersonal Attraction *[http://www.nd.edu/~rwilliam/ xsoc530/attraction.html]*. Make a list of people you are attracted to (people you like). Review the factors of attraction and make a list of which factors apply to the people on your list. In other words, why are you attracted to the people you listed? Because they are physically attractive? Similiar to you? Comptent? Which factors appear most on your list? Which factors appear least?

Web Exercise 8.3: Evaluating Relational Outcome in a Movie Relationship

Read a student's application of Social Exchange Theory *[http://www.nd.edu/ ~rwilliam/xsoc530/attraction.html]* to the movie "Jerry Maguire." Think of another movie relationship and write a similar short essay in which you apply the theory to determine the rewards and costs. Evaluate the decision that was made to stay together or break apart using the following concepts: rewards, costs, outcome, comparison level (CL) and comparison level of alternatives (CLalt).

Web Activity 8.4: Blocks to Trust and Effective Communication

http://crs.uvm.edu/gopher/nerl/group/b/j/Exercise18.html

As a small group, read the list of 23 blocks to developing trust and effective communication. Add your own ideas and then try to reach consensus about the 5 most serious blocks. Share reasons for making your choices and discuss ways to overcome these blocks. Include a discussion of self-disclosure and how it is connected to trust and effective communication.

Web Activity 8.5: A Relationship Diagram

http://www.uky.edu/~drlane/capstone/interpersonal/reldev.html

Read the section in the text on relational development, and then read the example dialogue in the relational stages at this site. Think of a relationship you that you are no longer involved in (romantic or platonic). Diagram your relationship using your perceptions of what occurred at each stage and include sample dialogue. Did your relationship proceed through all 10 stages? If not, which ones were missing? How much time did you spend at each stage? What insight, if any, did you gain about your relationship through this exercise?

Chapter 9: Improving Communication Climates

Life Skills: Being Nice

Read about the power of being nice.

http://www.pamf.org/teen/parents/emotions/lifeskills/lifesks3.html

Quiz: Evaluate Your Relationship

Take a self-test to assess the level of effective and positive communication in your relationship with a partner. Then, read the explanations that follow for suggestions on how to more effectively communicate in your relationship.

http://www.positive-way.com/communic.htm

Criticism Doesn't Have to Hurt

Read suggestions about how to avoid experiencing criticism as an "attack."

http://www.marriagesupport.com/qc005/theme.asp

Handling Criticism With Honesty and Grace

Read useful and practical suggestions for responding to another's criticism with honesty and grace. The focus is on how to actually gain new insights about yourself and the other person in the process.

http://www.pertinent.com/articles/communication/kareCom8.asp

Know Yourself and the Communication Climate

Scroll down to the section titled "Predicting the weather or setting the stage for a positive communication climate." This section offers brief explanations and concrete examples of indicators and strategies for positive communication climates.

http://www.allenshea.com/knowyourself.html

Open Communication Climate

Read about supportiveness, defensiveness and communication barriers as they as they relate to open and closed communication climates in organizations.

http://cyber.bentley.edu/faculty/wb/printables/opencomm.pdf

Assertiveness Training: Responding to Criticism

As part of an online self-help book, this section reviews strategies for responding to criticism with assertive responses.

http://mentalhelp.net/psyhelp/chap13/chap13f.htm

Expressing More Appreciation, Gratitude, Encouragement and Delight

A chapter in an excellent, comprehensive online book that explores 7 interpersonal communication skills. The chapter addresses research on the relational power of expressing appreciation and gratitude. The author also gives a step-by-step methodology for fully expressing appreciation (similar to the steps involved in the clear message format).

http://www.coopcomm.org/w7chal6.htm

Translating Complaints and Criticisms Into Transformative Requests

A chapter in an excellent, comprehensive online book that explores 7 interpersonal communication skills. In order to gain more cooperation from others, learn how to ask for what you want by using specific, action-oriented requests rather than generalizations.

http://www.coopcomm.org/w7chal4.htm

Keeping Cool While Under Fire

Here are some "tools" to add to your "toolbox" for the next time someone is upset and is taking it out on you.

http://www.pertinent.com/articles/communication/kareCom.asp

Invalidation—The Opposite of Empathy

This article about empathy and communication provides some excellent examples of disconfirming responses.

http://www.selfgrowth.com/articles/winnett2.html

Acknowledgement While Talking and Communicating

Read examples of confirming communication in this article.

http://www.cyberparent.com/talk/acknowledge.htm

A Personal Guide to Defense Mechanisms

Read more about defense mechanisms at this site.

http://www.strangephilosophy.com/defenses/

Quiz: Defensive?

Take this self-test to determine which defense mechanisms you rely on most.

http://www1.excite.com/home/health/diet_center_article/0,20766,420,00.html

Quiz: Are You Too Critical?

Take this self-test to determine how critical you are of others.

http://www.lovingyou.com/content/engaged/content.shtml?ART=critical

Quiz: How Critical Are You of Others?

Take this self-test to find out how critical you are of others and compare your ratings with the average ratings of other quiz-takers.

http://www.rateyourself.com/poll.cfm/Subject_ID/3/Poll_ID/4001

Non-Defensive Exercises

This series of exercises can help you understand your non-defensive strengths and the areas that need improvement.

http://www.pndc.com/exercises/NonDefensiveExercises.htm

Defensive Exercises

This series of exercises can help you understand your own defensive patterns, a vital step in the process of change.

http://www.pndc.com/exercises/DefensiveExercises.htm

The Power of Non-Defensive Communication

A collection of stories about the power of using non-defensive communication in real-life situations.

http://www.pndc.com/stories/index.php

How Does One Handle Negative Criticism? It's Your Choice!

An educator offers his perspective about how to handle negative criticism:

http://home.earthlink.net/~bmgei/educate/docs/aperson/thinking/negative.htm

Transforming a Defensive Climate

Read more information about responding non-defensively and transforming a defensive climate.

http://www.aligningaction.com/climate.htm

Non-Defensive Communication Tools

Read a summary of non-defensive communication tools suggested by the author of a book entitled "Taking the War Out of Our Words."

http://www.mediate.com/articles/ford7.cfm

Accepting Criticism

An organizational psychologist describes three common emotional reactions we experience in the face of criticism. He also explains how these emotional reactions can prevent us from learning from feedback and using constructive problem-solving methods.

http://www.innerself.com/Behavior_Modification/warren03203.htm

Communication Climate

Read more about Gibb's pairs of defensive and supportive behaviors, and about creating positive communication climates.

http://www.bsu.edu/classes/flint/climate.html

Dealing With People You Can't Stand

In these online sample chapters and in fun, interactive exercises, learn methods that help us deal more effectively with difficult people.

http://www.thericks.com

Web Exercise 9.1: Translating Your Criticisms and Complaints into Clear Requests

After reading Challenge Four: Translating Criticisms and Complaints into Requests *[http://www.coopcomm.org/w7chal4.htm]*, make a list of 5 common complaints that you might make in your own life (i.e. clean up this house; do this correctly next time; you'll never amount to anything). Using the suggestions from the chapter, revise these complaint statements into specific action requests and/or clear explanatory clauses. According to the chapter, what are the benefits of communicating in this manner?

Web Exercise 9.2: Expressing Appreciation in Your Own Life

Read Challenge Six: Expressing More Appreciation *[http://www.coopcomm .org/w7chal6.htm]*, list 5 things you are grateful to other people for. Using the three-part method for expressing appreciation mentioned in this chapter, develop clear statements for each thing on your list. Be sure to describe behavior, feelings and consequences. What are the benefits of expressing appreciation to others? How does expressing appreciation relate to communication climates?

Web Exercise 9.3: Analyzing Communication Climate in Your Own Relationship

After obtaining the results from your self-assessment quiz *[http://www.positive-way.com/communic.htm]*, write a short essay describing a relationship you have or have had with someone. Use terms from the chapter such as: communication climate, defensiveness, supportiveness, spirals, responding to criticism, Gibb's behavior pairs, confirming and disconfirming communication. Describe problems as well as specific skills or behaviors that could be used to improve the relationship.

Web Activity 9.4: Non-defensiveness: A Growth Opportunity

Read the article at *http://home.earthlink.net/~bmgei/educate/docs/aperson/thinking/negative.htm* and reflect on your own defensiveness. Think of a recent time in which you were actually at fault, but you chose to respond defensively. Which of the nine defensive reactions mentioned in the textbook best describes your reaction? Why do you suppose you chose to react defensively instead of non-defensively? Replay the incident in your head and change your reaction to a non-defensive one. What would you say? Which of the non-defensive strategies mentioned in your textbook would allow you to best understand and acknowledge your error? What personal and relational outcomes do you envision in this replay?

Chapter 10: Managing Interpersonal Conflicts

Family Life Skills

This site for teens contains three links to useful and practical information related to conflict resolution. The links (on the left in the orange box) are entitled: Beyond the Blame Barrier; Being a Skilled Negotiator; Family Problem Solving.

http://www.pamf.org/teen/parents/emotions/lifeskills/

Conflict: An Essential Ingredient for Growth

A trainer/educator makes a point about how growth in an organization is limited without conflict. The article also briefly explains five conflict styles.

http://www.pertinent.com/articles/communication/spilgrim4.asp

Managing Conflict Successfully

This comprehensive article describes the differences between conflict and disagreement, and provides procedures for resolving both successfully.

http://www.ianr.unl.edu/pubs/family/heg181.htm

Resolving Everyday Conflicts Sooner

Get practical "tips" for resolving conflict such as: Ten Ways You Can Stop a Conflict From Escalating; Ten Approaches for Offering Your Solution; and The Roundtrip to Resolution.

http://www.pertinent.com/articles/communication/kareCom91.asp

Interpersonal Relationships and Conflict Resolution

A comprehensive article containing many useful suggestions for how to resolve conflicts and manage personality differences in groups.

http://www.ic.org/nica/Process/Relation.html

Gender, Conflict and Conflict Resolution

A conflict resolution practitioner discusses the role of gender in conflict.

http://www.mediate.com/articles/birkhoff.cfm

There Is No Such Thing As a Relationship Without Conflict

A clinical psychologist/marriage & family therapist discusses conflict styles, conflict resolution styles, attitudes needed for conflict resolution and stages of conflict resolution.

http://www.drnadig.com/conflict.htm

Getting to Yes: Negotiating Agreement Without Giving In

This page contains a summary of a popular book, written by two negotiation experts, on the subject of negotiating.

http://www.colorado.edu/conflict/peace/example/fish7513.htm

The Conflict Resolution Information Source

An extremely comprehensive database of links related to conflict resolution and conflict research.

http://www.colorado.edu/conflict/

The Win-Win Method of Settling Disagreements

Read a step-by-step discussion of the win-win conflict resolution method.

http://mentalhelp.net/psyhelp/chap13/chap13m.htm#a

Mediation

A database of links to conflict-related articles, news briefs and discussion forums.

http://www.mediate.com/

Win-Win Approach to Conflict Resolution

Read a brief explanation of the win/win approach to conflict resolution.

http://crnhq.org/freeskill1.html

Expressing Yourself More Clearly and Completely

An excellent, comprehensive online book that explores 7 challenging interpersonal communication skills. This chapter expands on "I" statements and offers a step-by-step methodology for assertively expressing yourself in a clear and complete manner (a variation on the clear message format explained in the textbook).

http://www.coopcomm.org/w7chal3.htm

Conflict Prevention and Conflict Resolution in the Workplace

Read articles about conflict prevention in the workplace. Scroll down to access free articles.

http://www.work911.com/conflict/index.htm

Conflict Styles: What Are You Like?

Read a brief explanation of five different conflict styles. Also included is a brief self-test to determine your own conflict style.

http://jeffcoweb.jeffco.k12.co.us/high/wotc/confli1.htm

Quiz: How Self-Assertive Are You?

A self-test.

http://www.theoaktree.com/assrtquz.htm

Quiz: Assertiveness Inventory

Determine your scores on passiveness, aggressiveness and assertiveness.

http://www.humanlinks.com/manskill/assertiveness_inventory.htm

Quiz: How Do You Deal With Problems in Your Relationships?

A self-test.

http://www.positive-way.com/communic.htm

Quiz: Adult Personal Conflict Style Inventory

Calculate your preferred method for dealing with conflict.

http://peace.mennolink,org/cgi-bin/conflictstyle/inventory.cgi

Quiz: How Well Do You Handle Conflict?

A self-test.

http://www.rateyourself.com/poll.cfm/Subject_ID/3/Poll_ID/1202

Quiz: Do you confront? Deny? Or run away screaming?

A self-test.

http://www.pallotticenter.org/SharedVisions/Vol9%20No1/confront.htm

Quiz: How Assertive Are You?

A self-test.

http://www.queendom.com/tests/minitests/assertiveness_abridged_access.html

Quiz: Are You a Creative Problem-Solver?

A self-test.

http://www.queendom.com/tests/career/create_ps_access.html

Quiz: Are You Assertive?

This lengthy self-test generates only brief results—more explanation requires a fee.

http://www.testcafe.com/sert/

Passive Aggressiveness Resources

A comprehensive collection of links to information on passive aggressiveness.

http://www.passiveaggressive.homestead.com/Links.html

Life Would Be Easy...If It Weren't For Passive-Aggressive People

The author of this article suggests that the first step to dealing with a passive aggressive person is to take a close look at yourself and your own communication style.

http://www.conniepodesta.com/articles_life9.htm

Quiz: Fighting Fair Evaluation Guide

Gain insight into how fair your disagreements might be and what the implications might be for your relationship.

http://www.positive-way.com/wqfightingfarepage.htm

12 Skills for Conflict Resolution

The Conflict Resolution Network details 12 skills necessary for solving any conflict, including the "win-win approach" and "appropriate assertiveness."

http://www.crnhq.org/twelveskills.html

Understanding Your Communication Style

Detailed descriptions of the aggressive, assertive and passive communication styles.

http://www.sba.gov/manage/comm_style.html

How Do You Handle Conflict In Your Marriage?

Read the list of "dirty fighting techniques" for a humorous look at ineffective methods for dealing with conflict in a marriage. Which methods have been used in your relationships?

http://www.geocities.com/lmft_99/conflict.html

A Communication Model of Problem-Solving

Helpful hints for relational problem-solving.

http://www.coping.org/communi/probsolv.htm

Conflict in Cyberspace: How to Resolve Conflict Online

Explanations for how heightened conflict and misunderstandings occur in online communication, and suggestions for how to effectively resolve conflict online.

http://www.rider.edu/~suler/psycyber/conflict.html

Communication and Conflict-Related Articles

Scroll down to "Communication and Conflict-Related" to access articles that relate to managing conflict and building effective relationships in the workplace.

http://work911.com/articles.htm

Avoiding Conflict Online

A description of five key attributes to online communication and hints for avoiding conflict online.

http://www.fullcirc.com/community/avoidingconflict.htm

What Does Win-Win Problem-Solving Sound Like?

This detailed dialogue illustrates a win-win outcome in a family problem-solving situation.

http://www.stepfamilyinfo.org/02/win-win.htm

Ineffective Couple's Communication

This detailed dialogue illustrates a lose-lose outcome in a marriage conflict.

http://www.stepfamilyinfo.org/02/lose-lose.htm

Quiz: Conflict Resolution Strategy Style

A unique self-test that helps you identify your dominant conflict style by indicating your opinions of proverbs.

http://cotton.uamont.edu/~roiger/write/conflict.html

Web Exercise 10.1: Delivering Your Own Clear and Complete Messages

Carefully follow the steps and suggestions provided in Challenge Three: Expressing Yourself More Clearly and Completely *[http://www.coopcomm.org/w7chal3.htm]* to develop 3 of your own clear and complete messages. Use all five steps and label your messages. What communicative results can a person achieve by using this method?

Web Exercise 10.2: What is Your Conflict Style?

Take the self-test Conflict Styles: What Are You Like? *[http://jeffcoweb .jeffco.k12.co.us/high/wotc/confli1.htm]* and determine which conflict style best represents you. Do you agree with the outcome of this test? Why or why not? Give specific examples of conflict situations in which you demonstrated characteristics of a particular style.

Web Exercise 10.3: Win-Win Conflict Resolution

Read the section in the textbook on win-win problem solving and the online chapter Conflict Resolution: The "Win-Win" or "No Lose" Method of Settling Disagreements *[http://mentalhelp.net/psyhelp/chap13/a]*. Apply the steps to win-win conflict resolution to the following conflict situations: 1) Sarah and Desidra have lived together harmoniously for a year. One day, Desidra brings home a new puppy, and Sarah is upset because she does not want to deal with the care of or mess from this new animal. Sarah decides to approach Desidra about the problem. 2) Pedro and Roxanne are married and just had a new baby. Pedro is a smoker, and Roxanne is worried about Pedro smoking around the baby. She decides to approach Pedro about the problem. Pedro states that he is not willing to quit smoking. 3) Malik and Mario have been good friends and employees of equal status, until recently when Malik was promoted to a supervisor position. Malik is now in charge of supervising Mario's work. Recently Malik has been frustrated with Mario because Mario brings his input and revisions to Malik a few hours before a deadline. Malik is feeling pressure from his boss to turn in good work on time, and he wants to confront Mario. However, he is also worried about ruining their friendship. For each situation, work through the steps of the win-win process until you reach a win-win solution. Show your work for each step. What might each character think, say or do in each situation, assuming each character is willing to apply the win-win approach. Give examples of specific dialogue that might occur in the process. If necessary, make up details about each person or about the situation. How is the win-win approach and outcome different from other conflict management methods? Which parts of the process were easy? Difficult? Did you experience any blocks? Were you satisfied with the win-win process? If not, how could it be improved? Would you be likely to use this method of problem-solving in your own life? Why or why not?

Web Activity 10.4: One Story, Five Endings

Read the descriptions of the five conflict management styles at *http://www.state.oh.us/cdr/schools/contentpages/styles.htm*. Scroll down to "Activity 1" and read the story and its five endings. Write your own story illustrating a conflict in an interpersonal relationship (family, friend, coworker, classmate). You may make up a story or write one that is based on a real-life conflict. Similar to the example, write (and label) five different endings based on the five styles described here. Finish the story illustrating the relational outcomes that you think might occur in each scenario as a result of using different conflict styles. Relate the styles at this site to the methods of conflict resolution described in your textbook. What are the similarities and differences?

Web Activity 10.5: Problem Solving Mix and Match

Read the section on "win-win problem solving" in the textbook and the "steps for two people in solving a problem" at *http://www.coping.org/communi/probsolv.htm*. With a partner, choose one of the "ten role play situations" at this site. Write the following phrases on separate slips of paper: accommodation, avoidance, aggressive, assertive, passive-aggressive, win-win outcome, win-lose outcome, lose-lose outcome, compromise. Put the conflict style scripts into one pile and the outcome slips into a separate pile. With your partner, choose two slips from the conflict style pile and one slip from the outcome pile. Develop a 4-5 minute role play script in which each of you adopts one of the conflict styles and together you reach the chosen outcome. Role-play your script for the class and see if your classmates can guess which conflict styles and outcome you're illustrating.

USING FEATURE FILMS IN THE INTERPERSONAL COMMUNICATION COURSE

"Are we going to see a movie today?" In most cases the sight of a video cassette or DVD player in the classroom results in this kind of question. Conditioned by the sophisticated production techniques and high entertainment value of many films and television programs, students often welcome the break of routine provided by video programming. When they learn that the "show" will be a feature film, their interest level goes up even more. Beyond entertainment, however, feature films provide a valuable supplement to the reading, lecture, discussion, and other activities more common in the classroom.

Uses of Film and Television

To Model Desirable Behaviors By providing positive models of skillful communication, instructors can capitalize on the power of the media to further their instructional goals. The empathic listening of Judd Hirsch in *Ordinary People*, t he positive communication climate created by Robin Williams in *Dead Poets Society*, or the family values illustrated in *Running on Empty* help students understand how they can behave more effectively in their own lives.

To Illustrate Ineffective Communication In addition to providing positive models, film and television can provide illustrations of ineffective or counterproductive types of communication. The controlling behavior of Nurse Ratched in *One Flew Over the Cuckoo's Nest* provides a vivid portrait of the abuse of power. Valmont's manipulative strategies in *Dangerous Liaisons* offers a cautionary tale of the evils of deceit. Bull Meecham's autocratic domination of his family in *The Great Santini* can help future parents avoid the same sort of alienation he suffered from his children and wife.

To Provide Material for Description and Analysis Films are not only useful in skills-oriented parts of the interpersonal communication course; they can also provide outstanding examples when the goal is to illustrate or analyze communication behavior. Consider, for example, the subject of stages in relational development and deterioration. A good text and lecture can introduce various models of relational trajectories, but dramatic illustrations can make them real. Students who watch the rise and fall of the romance between Woody Allen and Diane Keaton in *Annie Hall* gain an understanding of relational stages that goes far beyond what they gain in a lecture that is not supported with illustrations. Likewise, the way a single incident can appear different from the perspectives of various observers and participants is illustrated dramatically in Akira Kurosawa's classic film *Rashomon*.

Advantages of Film and Television The value of film becomes clear when the medium is compared to the alternatives. Lecturing about how to communicate more effectively is important, but it is clearly a different matter from illustrating the actual behavior. Describing appropriate self-disclosure or ¹ise of "I" language, for instance, is no substitute for providing examples of how this behavior looks and sounds in common situations.

Films also can have advantages over students sharing their own personal experiences. While this sort of involvement can demonstrate the relevance of ideas introduced in a course, some topics do not lend themselves to personal examples. For example, it is unlikely that students or instructors will feel comfortable discussing their own experiences with deceptive communication, remediating embarrassment, or sexual involvement. With topics like these, films and television provide an ideal way to illustrate people realistically handling the issues without invading the privacy of students.

Role-playing appropriate behaviors has its advantages, but this sort of impromptu acting is often simplistic, artificial, and only remotely linked to how interactions occur in the "real" world beyond the classroom. Every instructor who has tried to demonstrate principles like self-disclosure or conflict management skills by staging a scene in the classroom knows that this approach can fall flat as often as it can succeed. Student actors are self-conscious, situations are often contrived, and the whole activity often lacks the spontaneity and dynamism that occurs in real life.

Nothing in this argument should be taken to suggest that all films or television programming can be legitimately or productively used to support instruction. Works with unrealistic plots or dialogue, poor acting, and shabby production values are likely to be unusable. Furthermore, some programming may be too upsetting or otherwise inappropriate for classroom use. But well-chosen examples, supported with commentary by an instructor, can be a legitimate and uniquely effective means of enhancing principles introduced by more traditional means.

Film is never likely to replace more traditional methods of instruction. The clarity of a good textbook, the lectures and commentary of a talented instructor, and the contributions of motivated students are all essential ingredients in successful instruction.

But the addition of dramatizations from television and film provide a complement to these elements.

Advantages of Videotaped Films

Availability Not too many years ago, screening films for students was a time-consuming and expensive task. With the VCR, DVD and film rental sources, literally thousands of titles are available quickly, easily, and inexpensively.

Flexibility In addition to their availability, another benefit of videotaped examples from film and television is their flexibility. They can be edited in advance, played repeatedly for examination and analysis, and they are highly portable. As the following section illustrates, they can be used in a number of ways.

What Film to Use? How to Use It?

Films should be selected and used carefully in the interpersonal communication course to avoid trivializing the subject matter or confusing students. The text has suggestions for films at the end of each chapter. Look for thorough descriptions of the following films in the text:

Chapter 1
About Schmidt (the importance of interpersonal communication)
Erin Brockovich (communication competence)

Chapter 2

Boyz in the Hood (influences on the self-concept)
Catch Me if You Can (identity management)
Stand and Deliver (self-fulfilling prophecy)

Chapter 3

White Man's Burden (multiple perspectives)
The First Wives Club (shared narratives)
Waiting to Exhale (shared narratives)
The Doctor (building empathy)

Chapter 4

Monster's Ball (the significance of expressing emotions)
Riding in Cars with Boys (expressing emotions (ir) responsibly)

Chapter 5

Nell (the importance of language)
The Miracle Worker (the importance of language)
When Harry Met Sally (gender and language)

Chapter 6

The Birdcage (masculine and feminine nonverbal behavior)
Mrs. Doubtfire (masculine and feminine nonverbal behavior)
Tootsie (masculine and feminine nonverbal behavior)
Life as a House (the power of touch)

Chapter 7

Jerry McGuire (ineffective listening and its alternatives)
Dead Man Walking (supportive listening)

Chapter 8

About a Boy (the need for intimacy)
Bend It Like Beckham (dialectical tensions)
Liar Liar (risks and benefits of self-disclosure)

Chapter 9

Changing Lanes (communication spirals)
Antwone Fisher (confirming communication)
Stolen Summer (defensiveness)

Chapter 10

American Beauty (dysfunctional conflict)
The Joy Luck Club (culture and conflict)

Widely available films and topics illustrated

In addition to those films highlighted in the text, many more film summaries and applications are available at the **Film in Communication Database** on the Book-Companion Web site, accessible through the *Looking Out/Looking In* CD-ROM. Following is a list of all the films available, the chapter most closely associated with the film, and the general context of the film (e.g., friendships, work relationships, family, couple, etc.). Please see the website for more thorough descriptions.

Chapter 1: A First Look at Interpersonal Relationships

The Accidental Tourist (couple)
The Anniversary Party (friendship/acquaintances)
A Beautiful Mind (strangers)
The Breakfast Club (friendship/acquaintances)
Cast Away
Children of a Lesser God (work/organizations)
Dad (medical)
Dangerous Liaisons (couple)
Denise Calls Up (friendship/acquaintances)
Dominick and Eugene (family)
Gung Ho (work/organizations)
Intimacy (family)
Italian For Beginners (couple)
Joy Luck Club (family)
Kramer vs. Kramer (friendship/acquaintances)
Life Lessons (in New York Stories) (couple)
My Family (Mi Familia) (family)
Nothing in Common (friendship/acquaintances, family, work/organizations)
An Officer and a Gentleman (work/organizations)
One Flew Over the Cuckoo's Nest
On Golden Pond (friendship/acquaintances)
Rain Man (family)
Ordinary People (family)
Parenthood (work/organizations)
Shrek (friendship/acquaintances)
Swept Away (couple)
Terms of Endearment (work/organizations)
The Unbearable Lightness of Being (couple)
Waking Life (friendship/acquaintances)
When a Man Loves a Woman (couple)
When Harry Met Sally (couple)
You've Got Mail (couple)

Chapter 2: Communication and Identity: The Self and Messages

Antz (work/organizations)
All About Eve (couple)
The Breakfast Club (friendship/acquaintances)
Bridget Jones's Diary (couple, work/organizations)
The Closet (work/organizations)
Clueless (school)
Children of a Lesser God (work/organizations, friendship/acquaintances)
The Color Purple (couple)
Dad (medical)
Finding Forester (strangers)
First Wives Club (friendship)
Grease (couple)
The Great Santini (family, work/organizations)
Gung Ho (work/organizations)
Kramer vs. Kramer (friendship/acquaintances)
Mr. Holland's Opus (family, school)
Parenthood (family, friendship/acquaintances, work/organizations)
Pay It Forward (family)
Pretty Woman (couple)
Riding in Cars with Boys (family)
The Right Stuff (work/organizations)
Shallow Hal (couple)
Shirley Valentine (school)
Stand and Deliver (school)
Stand By Me (friendship/acquaintances)
The Story of Us (couple)
The Truth about Cats and Dogs (couple)

Chapter 3: Perception: What You See Is What You Get

Annie Hall (family)
At First Sight
Being There (strangers)
Children of a Lesser God (couple)
The Doctor (work/organizational)
The Outrage (strangers)
Rashomon (strangers)
Trading Places (friendship/acquaintances)
Waiting to Exhale (friendship/acquaintances)
White Man's Burden (friendship/acquaintances)

Chapter 4: Emotions: Thinking, Feeling, and Communicating
About Last Night (couple)
The Accidental Tourist (couple)
Annie Hall (couple)
The Big Chill
Broadcast News (couple; friendship/acquaintances)
Bull Durham (work/organizations)
Casablanca (couple)
Children of a Lesser God (couple)
High Fidelity (couple)
Intimacy (couple)
Remains of the Day (couple)
Shall We Dance? (couple)
Smoke (friendship/acquaintances)
Tootsie (couple; work/organizational; friendship/acquaintances)

Chapter 5: Language: Barrier and Bridge
Being There (couple)
Big (couple)
Gone with the Wind (couple)
Shirley Valentine (couple)
Meet the Parents (family)
The Miracle Worker (school)
My Fair Lady (strangers)
Nell (strangers)
Pushing Tin (couple)
Quest for Fire
Stand By Me (friendship/acquaintances)
A Thousand Clowns (friendship/acquaintances)

Chapter 6: Nonverbal Communication: Messages Beyond Words
About Last Night (couple)
Alice (family)
Baby Boom (couple)
Beaches (friendship/acquaintances)
The Big Chill (friendship/acquaintances)
The Birdcage (couple)
Broadcast News (couple)
Life as a House (family)
Meet the Parents (friendship/acquaintances)
An Officer and a Gentleman (work/organizations)
The Paper Chase (school)

Philadelphia (work/organizational)
Sea of Love (friendship/acquaintances)
Tootsie (work/organizational)
Two Guys and a Girl (friendship/acquaintances)

Chapter 7: Listening: More Than Meets the Ear

Children of a Lesser God (friendship/acquaintances)
Dead Man Walking (friendship/acquaintances)
Good Will Hunting (friendship/acquaintances)
Grosse Pointe Blank (friendship/acquaintances)
Kramer vs. Kramer (couple; work/organizations)
Office Space (work/organizational)
Rain Main (medical; couple)
Shirley Valentine (couple; family)

Chapter 8: Communication and Relational Dynamics

About a Boy (couple)
About Last Night (couple)
Almost Famous (friendship/acquaintances)
Annie Hall (couple)
Beaches (friendship/acquaintances; couple)
Before Sunrise (couple)
Broadcast News (couple)
The Brothers McMullen (family)
Dad (family)
Diner (couple)
Dominick and Eugene (family)
Down and Out in Beverly Hills (family)
The Fabulous Baker Boys (family)
Gone with the Wind (couple)
He Said, She Said (friendship/acquaintances)
Jerry McGuire (couple)
Liar Liar (work/organizational)
Magnolia (couple)
Meet the Parents (friendship/acquaintances)
My Fair Lady (couple)
My Life (couple)
Parenthood (family)
Reality Bites (couple)
Romeo and Juliet (couple)
secrets and lies (family)
sex, lies, and videotape (couple)

Chapter 9: Improving Communication Climates

Annie Hall (couple)
Beaches (friendship/acquaintances)
Broadcast News (work/organizational)
Children of a Lesser God (school)
Dead Poets Society (friendship/acquaintances; school)
The Fabulous Baker Boys (couple)
Ghost World (friendship/acquaintances)
Gone with the Wind (couple)
My Fair Lady (couple)
One Flew Over the Cuckoo's Nest (medical)
One True Thing (family)
Parenthood (family)
Patch Adams (medical)
Tin Men (strangers)
Welcome to the Dollhouse (school)
When Harry Met Sally (couple)

Chapter 10: Managing Interpersonal Conflicts

American Beauty (friendship/acquaintances)
The Anniversary Party (couple)
Dangerous Minds (work/organizational)
Good Morning Vietnam (work/organizational)
Joy Luck Club (family)
Lost in America (couple)
Mississippi Masala (couple)
On Golden Pond (friendship/acquaintances; school)
Shirley Valentine (couple)
War of the Roses (couple)
Who's Afraid of Virginia Woolf (couple)

In every case, it is important for the instructor to view a film in advance of a class screening to become familiar with the material and determine how it can best be used to further instructional goals. Once a film has been identified as having instructional value, it can be used in one of several ways:

In class Segments or complete films may be shown in class to illustrate points about a single topic (e.g., defense-arousing communication, self-disclosure) or to preview and/or review the entire course or major units.

In the college media center Most campuses have a media center where students can view segments or entire films, and if desired complete workbook assignments.

As homework Class members can all view the same film on their own time, or they may choose a variety of titles from a pre-approved list in order to complete an analytical assignment.

Available to Adopters of *Looking Out/Looking In,* Eleventh Edition

A film guide, *Communication in Film III: Teaching Communication Courses Using Feature Films*, prepared by Russ Proctor, describes how a wide array of movies can be used to illustrate how concepts from *Looking Out/Looking In* appear in realistic situations. This guide takes advantage of students' inherent interest in the medium of film, showing them how movies can be both entertaining and educational.

PART THREE

NOTES ON CLASS AND STUDENT ACTIVITIES

CHAPTER 1

A FIRST LOOK AT INTERPERSONAL RELATIONSHIPS

OBJECTIVES

After studying the material in Chapter One of *Looking Out/Looking In,* you should understand:

1. The types of needs that communication can satisfy.
2. The elements and characteristics of the transactional communication model.
3. The principles and misconceptions of communication
4. The differences between impersonal and interpersonal communication.
5. The content and relational aspects of messages.
6. The concept of metacommunication.
7. The characteristics of effective communicators.

You should be able to:

1. Identify the needs you attempt to satisfy by your interpersonal communication and the degree to which you satisfy those needs.
2. Use the transactional model to
   a. diagnose barriers to effective communication in your life.
   b. suggest remedies to overcome those barriers.
3. Identify the degree to which your communication is impersonal and interpersonal.
4. Improve your effectiveness as a communicator by using models to
   a. broaden your repertoire of behaviors and your skill at performing them.
   b. identify the most appropriate communication behaviors in a variety of important situations.
5. Discover how satisfied you are with the way you communicate in various situations.
6. Identify the content and relational aspects of
   a. messages you deliver to others.
   b. messages that are sent to you.

NOTES ON CLASS AND STUDENT ACTIVITIES

A. Name Calling

1. Assemble your group, including instructor, so that everyone can see each other; a circle works well.

2. The first person (ask for a volunteer) begins by giving his or her name to the whole group, speaking loudly enough to be heard clearly by everyone. (" My name is Sheila.") Instructors may want to repeat what they've heard to check whether the speaker has been heard correctly. If you're not sure of a name, ask to have it repeated.

3. The group member seated on the first speaker's left will then give his or her own name followed by the first speakers. (" My name is Gordon, and this is Sheila.")

4. Now the person to the left of the second speaker gives his or her name, followed by the second and first speaker's names. (" My name is Wayne, this is Gordon, and that's Sheila.") This procedure is followed around the whole group so that the last person names everyone in the class. It sounds as if it will be impossible for the last few people, but when you try it, you'll be surprised at how many names are remembered.

5. Things to watch for:
   a. If you forget a name, don't worry; that person will help you after you've had a little time to think.
   b. If you don't catch the speaker's name, ask to have it repeated.
   c. You may want the person who begins the activity to end it also. After that, anyone who wants to should try to " name them all."
   d. Above all, keep the atmosphere informal. As you know, personal comments and humor have a way of lessening pressure.

Objectives
1. To learn the names of all the group members, thus forming a foundation for future interaction.
2. To achieve immediate participation from every class member.
3. To demonstrate that making mistakes is an acceptable, normal part of learning.
4. To provide an activity that calls for a minimal contribution with relatively little threat.

Note: WE STRONGLY RECOMMEND THAT THIS BE THE FIRST CLASS ACTIVITY! Over many semesters, it has proved to be one of the activities most often reported by the students as being of extreme value.

Variations

Use first names only, or work with both first and last. Both approaches have their advantages. Try both methods to see which works best for you.

Have each person attach a descriptive word to his or her name, for example: Gardening (or Digger) Dan, Patient Cindy, and so on. The variety of names is good for several laughs, thus making the exercise an even better icebreaker.

Discussion Questions
1. Was remembering all the names as difficult as you expected?

   The answer is usually no, and you can make the point that what was true here will likely hold true for other activities, both in and out of class. Taking risks isn't always as dangerous as it seems.

2. What will you do if you can't remember someone's name the next time you see him or her?

   This is a good time to talk about a common problem. Is it better to pretend you remember a person's name, or come right out and tell the person you forgot? Just how valuable is "tact" in social situations?

3. How did you feel as your turn approached? How did you feel after you were done?

   This question invites the students to reveal the feelings of anxiety they had and to discover that their fears in social situations are not unique but are rather like their classmates".

4. Which name(s) do you think you'll remember easily? Why?

   This question invites discussion on what factors make names or people stand out in our memories. It is the differences that make individuals unique. This question leads into the next activity very naturally.

B. Introductions

1. Form dyads (groups of two). If possible, pair up with someone you've not known previously. The instructor or facilitator should use himself or herself to even out the dyads if necessary. In any event, someone should introduce the instructor.

2. Each member of a dyad will interview the other. Try to allow about 20 minutes for this activity.

   a. You should find three unique things to tell the group about the person you're introducing. These may be actions, characteristics, or experiences that set your partner apart from other people. (For example, the fact that your partner graduated from Lincoln High School probably isn't as important as the fact that he or she is thinking about getting married, quitting school, or planning an interesting career.) Remember that most people feel uncomfortable talking about themselves, so you'll have to probe to get those unique aspects from your partner.

   b. Use the name of the person you're introducing instead of the pronoun he or she. This will help everyone learn names.

3. Back in the large group, students introduce their partners to the class until everyone has been introduced.

Objective

To assist the students further in becoming acquainted by having them learn some personal characteristics of their classmates.

Discussion Questions (in addition to those found in the text)

1. Did you feel scared or threatened during any of the steps in this exercise? When?

   This question may encourage group members to discover something about beginning acquaintances.

2. How successful were you in finding out unique things about your partner? Why?

   Students may shed some light on the difficulty we seem to have in getting most persons to talk about themselves. The group may also discover the prevalence of clichés in our conversation.

3. This experience was different from the usual way you get to know someone. What parts of it did you like? Were there parts that you didn't like? Why?

4. Now that you know more about each other, have your feelings changed about any of the individuals? How? Have your feelings changed in regard to the group? How?

C. Autograph Party

Objective

This exercise in getting to know others in the group is outstanding as an icebreaker.

Purpose

To help you become acquainted with others in the group.

Instructions

Your task is to find someone who fits each of the descriptions below, and get his or her signature on this sheet. Try to find a different person for each description.

Find someone who

is an only child _____

skipped breakfast today _____

drives an imported car _____

was born east (west) of the Mississippi _____

isn't getting enough sleep _____

plays a musical instrument _____

is a parent _____

is left-handed _____

is taller than you _____

has an unusual hobby _____

is married _____

goes to church regularly _____

knows someone you know _____

has schedule problems _____

writes poetry _____

has traveled overseas _____

has read a book you've read _____

is in love _____

speaks a language besides English _____

knows some information helpful to you _____

is self-employed _____

D. Making Models Meaningful (Text, p. 16)

Objectives
1. To apply the transactional communication model to communication challenges.
2. To formulate steps to address these challenges.

Discussion Questions
1. In which elements of the transactional model are you likely to experience difficulties?
2. How do the experiences of others in your group compare to yours?

E. How Personal Are Your Relationships (Text, p. 25)

Objectives
1. To enable the student to classify communication relationships along the impersonal-interpersonal spectrum.
2. To evaluate the relationship according to the characteristics of interpersonal communication.

Discussion Questions
1. What are the unique qualities of your relationships?
2. How irreplaceable are your relationships?
3. How much interdependence characterizes your different relationships?
4. Compare the amounts of self-disclosure present in your relationships along the, p. –00impersonal-interpersonal spectrum.
5. Distinguish the rewards (extrinsic and intrinsic) in your different relationships.

F. Expanding Your Communication Effectiveness
(1.2 in *Student Activities Manual*)

Objectives
1. To develop awareness of a personal range of communication behaviors with people important to the student.
2. To evaluate the effectiveness of the current range of behaviors.
3. To propose effective communication behaviors that might widen the range of personal communication behaviors.

Discussion Questions
1. Relate the range of behaviors observed to your own evaluation of your skill. Comment specifically on how a communicator can choose appropriate behaviors.
2. How accurate do you think you are in identifying effective models? Is there any reason why you might be inaccurate?
3. What behaviors that you don't engage in currently would you like to develop? Why?

G. Recognizing Relational Messages (1.3 in *Student Activities Manual*)

Objectives
1. To identify relational messages.

2. To compare the relational messages of affinity, respect, and control sent in an important interpersonal relationship.

Discussion Questions

1. How do the needs for relational messages of affection, respect, and control vary in relationships?
2. What bad outcomes can occur as a result of these relational messages? What good outcomes?

CHAPTER 2

COMMUNICATION AND IDENTITY:
THE SELF AND MESSAGES

OBJECTIVES

After studying the material in Chapter Two of *Looking Out/Looking In,* you should understand:
1. How the self-concept is defined.
2. How the self-concept develops.
3. Two characteristics of the self-concept.
4. Four reasons why the self-concept is subjective.
5. Differences between public and private selves.
6. The role of self-fulfilling prophecies in shaping the self-concept and in influencing communication.
7. Four requirements for changing the self-concept.
8. The ethics of impression management.

You should be able to:
1. Develop a self-concept that enhances your communication by
   a. identifying the key elements of your self-concept.
   b. identifying the people who have had the greatest influence on your self-concept.
   c. describing the ways in which your self-concept may be inaccurate, and suggesting ways of improving its accuracy.
   d. identifying the differences between your public and private selves.
   e. recognizing and giving proper credit to your personal strengths.
2. Describe the ways in which you influence the self-concept of others.
3. Avoid destructive self-fulfilling prophecies that affect your communication and create positive self-fulfilling prophecies that can improve your communication.
4. Manage impressions of yourself to meet your relational goals.

NOTES ON CLASS AND STUDENT ACTIVITIES

A.   Take Away (Text, p.47)

Objectives

To demonstrate that the concept of self is perhaps our most fundamental possession.

Discussion Questions
1. What types of descriptors seem most fundamental to your self-concept?
2. What descriptors do you see as the most vulnerable to change?
3. Do you think others would describe you as you have yourself?

B.   Ego Boosters and Busters
(Text, p. 50-51 and 2.3 in *Student Activities Manual*)

Objectives
1. To enable the student to see how his or her self-concept developed.
2. To enable the student to understand how his or her communication affects the self-concept of others.

Discussion Questions
1. What sorts of things were "busters"? Why did they affect your self-concept negatively? What sorts of things were "boosters"?
2. Are there any differences of opinions among class members about what indicates a booster or buster? Why might that occur? Are there any universal boosters and busters?
3. Is it possible to always send booster messages and avoid sending intentional and unintentional busters? If not, how can one deal with this state of affairs?

C. Recognizing Your Strengths (Text, p.59)

Objectives
1. To illustrate the disproportionate emphasis we place on negative parts of the self-concept.
2. To demonstrate the value of feeling positive about oneself.
3. To build class cohesiveness and morale.
4. To further develop the acquaintance of group members.

D. Reevaluating Your "Can'ts"
(Text, p. 69 and 2.4 in *Student Activities Manual*)

Objective
To demonstrate how an obsolete self-concept becomes a self-fulfilling prophecy that keeps the student from growing.

Note: This is one of the most effective exercises in the book, for it clearly demonstrates many ways in which students can change and develop their communication habits.

E. Your Personal Coat of Arms

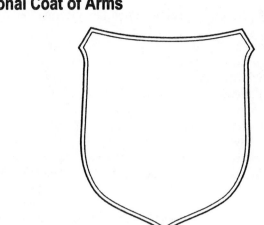

Objectives
1. To help the group members search out some of the positive aspects of their lives.
2. To further acquaint the class members with each other.

Note: If the instructor wishes, he or she may assign this as an out-of-class activity. All students may be supplied with an enlargement of the shield outline provided in the Student Workbook and allowed to use pictures from magazines, snapshots, or their artistic talents to complete their own "coats of arms."

Our groups seem to like to have their coats of arms displayed without names in the classroom for a few days so that they can see all of them. They like to try to guess the owners.

Discussion Questions
1. When you have seen the coats of arms of your whole group, do you find any similarities?
2. In what ways are the coats of arms most alike? What could be an explanation?
3. In what ways are the coats of arms most different? Explain.

There are no set answers to these questions, but they usually promote good discussion, and the search for explanations leads students to the areas of their lives that they share with most others and also those in which they differ.

Purpose

To help you identify the important parts of yourself and to become better acquainted with other group members.

Instructions

1. Create a personal coat of arms that represents important information about you, such as
   a. people who are important to you.
   b. locations that are significant to you.
   c. activities with which you are associated.
   d. personal traits that characterize you.
   e. your ambitions.
   f. physical features that identify you.
   g. talents and skills you have.
   h. anything else you think is an important part of you.
2. Remember that you needn't be a professional artist to complete this activity. This is a getting-acquainted activity, not a contest.
3. In addition to pencil or pen, you might use other materials to construct your coat of arms: photos, crayons, felt-tip pens, rub-on letters, paint, and newspaper or magazine clippings.
4. After completing your coat of arms, explain it to other class members.

F. Interpersonal Interviews

If you haven't done Introductions (B in this manual) in Chapter One, a good, nonthreatening way to help all class members begin to talk to one another and in front of the class is to conduct interpersonal interviews.

Pair class members and ask them to exchange information about themselves (biographical, interests, values, family, school, work, etc.). Allow them about 15-20 minutes to interview one another, and ask them to take brief notes about the other person.

Stop the interviews and allow about 2-3 minutes for all persons to organize the information they have about their partners so that they can introduce their partners to the class.

Sitting in a circle so that everyone can see everyone else, ask class members to introduce their partners. After the introduction, other class members may ask questions of their partners or the partners may clarify or correct any information given about them to the class.

Variations

Do shorter interviews on a number of days, using one topic at time (e.g., only biographical information one day, only interests another, and only future goals another). Or, after the interviews have occurred, ask students to analyze how they have presented their self-concept to the partner (different from the way they present to others?) and how they would change the way they interacted if they could. Another idea is to have class members go around the circle after the interviews, using one positive adjective to describe each of the persons introduced.

G. Your Many Identities (Text, p. 74 and Success in Managing Impressions, 2.5 in *Student Activities Manual*)

Objectives
1. To recognize how manner, appearance, and setting affect identity management.
2. To illustrate the appropriateness of different presenting selves.

H. Self-Monitoring Inventory (Text, p. 77)

Objectives
1. To recognize your level of self-monitoring.
2. To consider the appropriate level of self-monitoring in different situations.

Discussion Questions
1. What are the advantages of high self-monitoring? The disadvantages?
2. How can we balance paying attention to our own behavior with focusing on that of others?

CHAPTER 3

PERCEPTION: WHAT YOU SEE IS WHAT YOU GET

OBJECTIVES

After studying the material in Chapter Three of *Looking Out/Looking In,* you should understand:

1. How the processes of selection, organization and interpretation operate in the perception process.
2. The physiological, cultural, social roles, gender roles, occupational roles, and self-concept variables that influence the perceptual process.
3. Five common tendencies that influence the accuracy and inaccuracy of our perceptions.
4. Requirements for developing empathy to improve the accuracy of perceptions.

You should be able to:

1. Identify
   a. the physiological influences which cause your perceptual differences.
   b. the cultural and social factors which cause your perceptual differences.
   c. common perceptual errors which contribute to your opinions of others.
2. Engage in perception-checking by
   a. using appropriate nonverbal behaviors (eyes, voice).
   b. describing clearly and accurately the behavior you observed.
   c. posing at least two possible interpretations of the behavior you described.
   d. requesting feedback from your partner about the accuracy or inaccuracy of your observation and interpretations.
3. Communicate empathy by
   a. using appropriate nonverbal behaviors (eyes, proximity, touch, voice).
   b. describing the correct or understandable elements of your position and/or the position of your partner.
   c. describing the incorrect or difficult elements of your position and/or the position of your partner.
   d. describing at least two different ways these elements might affect your relationship.

NOTES ON CLASS AND STUDENT ACTIVITIES

A. Your Perceptual Filters (Text, p. 95)

Objectives
1. To recognize the perceptual, physical, role, interaction, psychological, and membership constructs that help us categorize others.
2. To consider the validity of our constructs.

Discussion Questions
1. How do constructs limit our perceptions of others?
2. How do constructs help us relationally?

B. Punctuation Practice (Text, p. 98)

Objective

To appreciate the importance of punctuation in our perceptual organization.

Discussion Question

How can you use the concept of punctuation to appreciate the perception of others?

C. New Body, New Perspective (Text, p. 103)

Objective

To enable students to understand how perception can be changed by different physiological conditions.

Discussion Questions
1. How did the situation you chose differ when you changed the physiological "symptoms"?
2. Is it difficult to understand how someone else would "see" in each of those conditions? Why?
3. Did any of the people of your group foresee differences of opinion, problems, or conflicts when under any of the different conditions?

D. Role Reversal (Text, p. 112)

Objective

To give the student firsthand experience with an orientation different from his or her own.

NOTE: This can be an outstanding assignment, well worth the time and effort necessary to make it work.

An effective warm-up is to have the class members name a person, group, or philosophical position they do not understand at all—which should provide each student with at least one target for the assignment.

An alternate approach is to stage debates in which students are required to defend positions opposed to their own. You might even want students actually to assume the role they're playing, that is, have conservatives pretend they're radicals, children play parents, and so on.

In many cases, you'll need to become the director to help students get into their roles. You may need to goad them into acting out contrasting positions, play alter ego, or just plain put words into their mouths until they get the idea.

E.   Perception-Checking Stimuli

Objectives

To enable students to take on the perceptions of others.

To provide situations where perceptions can be aired, discussed and "perception checked." Here are two activities designed for group interaction.

1. The Gender Game. Divide the class into men and women. Each group is to come up with 5-10 questions they have always wanted to ask the opposite gender but, for some reason or another, never have. They are to rank their questions in importance because the class may not get to all the questions. Two simple rules govern the limits here: (1) you may not ask a question of the opposite gender that you are unwilling to answer yourself, and (2) you should avoid questions that are insulting (i.e., specific sexual behaviors that might embarrass some class members) or that tend to group all members of a gender together (e.g., " Why do women always go to the bathroom in pairs?").

    Groups meet face to face after about 20 minutes allotted to question-generation, and the instructor acts as moderator as one "side" and then another asks one question at a time; each time the opposite side can " put the question back to them. The instructor should encourage all members of the class to answer the question put to the group, but no one should be pressured if he or she feels uncomfortable.

2. The Intercultural Game. Using the same format as The Gender Game, this activity makes good use of any diverse population your institution may have. If your class has members of many cultures, you can divide them that way. Or, make use of foreign language classes or English as a Second Language (ESL) classes, and coordinate your activity with another instructor. In addition to providing a forum for perception checking, you can further interdisciplinary relationships at the same time.

Note: Both of these activities can be used as the stimulus for the oral perception-checking skill in the *Student Activities Manual*. Ask students to keep track of perceptions they have during the course of the activity and prepare 2-5 perception-checking statements to be delivered to specific individuals during the next class. (Examples: "Shelley, when you said that men didn't take enough responsibility for birth control in relationships, I didn't know if you meant that men should bring up the subject of birth control first or if you thought that men should just take it upon themselves more to be the ones that actually use protection. Did you mean either of those two things or something else?" Or "Jose, when you said most white people in the U.S. made no effort to understand you, I wondered if you were referring to just your language, or if you meant more than that—like trying to understand what you think and feel. What did you mean?")

F.   Perception-Checking Practice
(Text, p. 118 and 3.5 and 3.6 in *Student Activities Manual*)

Objective

To apply perception checking to a variety of situations

Discussion Questions

What aspects of perception checking are most/least useful? How can you use perception checking most effectively in your life?

G.   Pillow Talk
(Text, p. 125 and Shifting Perspectives, 3.3 in *Student Activities Manual*)

Objective

To provide students with a systematic tool for exploring the perceptions of those who differ from them on important issues.

Notes:
1. The pillow method is a culmination of the entire chapter. The measure of a student's success in understanding perceptual variability is the ability to move through the steps on a personal problem.
2. Working through the pillow becomes more difficult with the immediacy of the issue. You will most likely want to work through several cases in class. You may need to suggest to students some possible reasons for position 2, in which the "opponent" is right.
3. We urge you not to become discouraged when students say they "can't" understand a position different from their own. Although this kind of understanding is difficult, the reward of increased empathy is well worth the effort.

H. Empathy Skills

Objective

To give students practice in demonstrating their abilities to build common ground and express empathy.

Name _____ Class day/time _____ Date

Goals

This assignment will allow you to demonstrate your ability to build common ground and empathy.

Instructions
1. Choose an interpersonal issue with a person who is important to you. This person may be a friend, family member, fellow student or worker, instructor, or any other person who matters to you. This person must be available to you for feedback during the time you are completing this assignment.
2. Compose a draft paper, describing the issue from the other's point of view. Write your description in the first person as if you were the other person. (You may choose

to meet with the other person before writing your description to understand his or her perspective better.)

3. Show your completed draft to the other person to verify its accuracy. Based on the comments you receive, revise your description.

4. Show your revised description to your partner. If you have represented his or her thoughts and feelings accurately, have this person verify its correctness by signing the paper. If your description is still not accurate, keep revising it until the other person is willing to sign it.

Note: As you write your description, remember that you are not required to agree with the other person's position—only to understand it.

5. Add a written summary to your paper describing the following dimensions of the issue:

   a. There are understandable reasons for the behavior of both parties in the issue.

   b. Both parties have engaged in at least some erroneous thinking and behavior with regard to this issue.

   c. In at least one way the issue may be seen as less important than the parties have perceived it to be.

CHAPTER 4

EMOTIONS:THINKING, FEELING,
AND COMMUNICATING

OBJECTIVES

After studying the material in Chapter Four of *Looking Out/Looking In,* you should understand:
1. The four components of emotions.
2. The seven influences on emotional expression.
3. The characteristics of facilitative and debilitative emotions.
4. The relationship between activating events, thoughts, and emotions.
5. Seven fallacies that result in unnecessary, debilitative emotions.
6. Four steps in the rational-emotive approach to coping with debilitative feelings.

You should be able to:
1. Identify the components of the emotions you experience.
2. Recognize the emotions you experience and the circumstances and consequences surrounding them.
3. Distinguish true feeling statements from counterfeit expressions of emotions.
4. Distinguish between debilitative and facilitative emotions and label the emotions.
5. Express facilitative emotions you experience clearly and appropriately by using the guidelines for sharing feelings.
6. Minimize your difficult/debilitative emotions.

NOTES ON CLASS AND STUDENT ACTIVITIES

A. How Would You Feel?

Objective

To provide situations involving emotions that will prompt an examination of students' feelings.

Notes:
1. In groups, have students generate situations in which they or their friends or family get emotional (e.g., weddings, funerals, birthdays, promotions, failures). They should write down specific situations.

2. Once the list is made, groups should discuss what emotions are felt in each situation. They should note how different people are likely to feel differently in each situation.
3. Next the group should report back to the class about their discussion.
4. Discussion of each group's situations and responses will allow them to compare their individual reactions and group reactions.

B.   Recognizing Your Emotions (Text, p. 137)

Objective

To further the student's awareness of his or her feelings and how these feelings register themselves physically in the body.

Notes:
1. We find that when we provide a duplicated form for the diary/journal, the students tend to take the assignment a bit more seriously. Design a form to fit your situation.
2. Another way of adding importance to the assignment is to collect the diaries and take a number of the better entries and publish them for the whole group. It goes without saying that this is done without disclosing the individual's name.
3. You'll find that this diary technique is used on many occasions in the text. Our experience is that this is one of the best ways to promote out-of-class effort.

C. Feelings and Phrases (Text, p. 49) and Stating Emotions Effectively, 4.3 in *Student Activities Manual*)

Objective

To help students develop ways of expressing feelings clearly.

Note: In a group activity, have members evaluate the effectiveness of different forms of expressing emotions (or of not expressing the feeling). Encourage group members to comment on the clarity of each expression and emotion.

Discussion Questions
1. How does the expression of feelings vary from situation to situation . . . from receiver to receiver?
2. What are some reasons for/for not expressing true feelings in each situation with each receiver?

D.   Talking to Yourself (Text, p. 153)

Objective

To help students better understand how their thoughts can shape their feelings.

E.   How Irrational Are You? (Text, p. 158)

Objective

To help students to identify debilitative feelings and check their biases. Do biases involve irrational thinking based on common fallacies?

F. Rational Thinking (Text, p. 162)

Objective

To assist students in replacing irrational thinking with rational thinking. This exercise affords students a chance to practice the procedure before a monitor.

Note: The instructor should probably go through the exercise with two others as a demonstration. The instructor should take the part of the "second party" (monitor).

G. Would You Share? Your Call—Emotions, 4.7 in *Student Activities Manual)*

Objective

To assist students in deciding what emotions to share with others.

Note: Use the case study in the *Student Activities Manual* to generate discussion about the appropriate sharing of emotions. Expand the discussion to other situations and challenge students to use the guidelines for expressing emotions to most effectively share the emotions they deem appropriate.

CHAPTER 5

LANGUAGE: BARRIER AND BRIDGE

OBJECTIVES

After studying the material in Chapter Five of *Looking Out/Looking In,* you should understand:

1. The symbolic nature of language.
2. That language is rule-governed.
3. That meanings are in people, not words.
4. Troublesome language that disrupts effective communication.
5. That language describes events at various levels of abstraction.
6. The problems that occur when overly abstract language is used.
7. How behavioral descriptions clarify thinking and communicating.
8. The manner in which a speaker's language can reflect responsibility.
9. The ways that sexist and racist language shape the attitudes of both speaker and person described.
10. How language and culture are related.

You should be able to:

1. Avoid using troublesome language by identifying the problematic terms you use, and compose alternatives.
2. Label inferences contained in your statements and separate them from the facts in your language.
3. Identify overly abstract statements you and others make and propose less abstract alternatives.
4. Identify ways in which your language and the language of others you know reflects degrees of responsibility.
5. Increase the clarity of your language by using
   a. behavioral descriptions.
   b. lower-level abstractions.
6. Identify the gender variables of language.
7. Identify the culture variables of language.

NOTES ON CLASS AND STUDENT ACTIVITIES

A. Your Linguistic Rules (Text, p. 178)

Objective

To give students awareness of their own and others' linguistic rules.

Note: Review with students semantic, syntactic and pragmatic definitions before attempting this exercise.

B. Down-to-Earth Language (Text, p. 175)

Objective

To give students practice using lower abstractions.

Note: This exercise can be a good precursor to coping with criticism in Chapter 9, as it may enable students to criticize specifically and constructively themselves before having to cope with the criticism of others later.

C. Responsible Language, 5.3 in the *Student Activities Manual*, and Practicing "I" Language (Text, p. 191, and 5.4 in the *Student Activities Manual*)

Objective

To give students practice speaking descriptively rather than evaluatively

Note: This exercise can be very difficult for students who are not used to describing behavior. It is best to give them many examples before they actually do this exercise (e.g., change "You're not telling me the truth!" to "I heard from Jane that you went out with the boys last night and you just told me you stayed home and watched a movie").

D. Conjugating Irregular Verbs (Text, p. 186)

Objective

To give the student some practice with using emotive words. To become sensitive to the practice we often have of using words that we think describe something or somebody but really announce to the receiver our attitude about it.

Note: This particular exercise seems to be one that the students like. It is, therefore, quite easy to get them to come up with their own "I am _____" and then pass it on to the next person in line for the "You are _____" and to a third person for the "He is _____" responses.

When you use this as a group exercise, it is important not to leave it as just a game; the discussion should be pursued to the point where students can identify instances in which they have unconsciously done the same.

E. The World of Abstraction

Objective

To give students practice in identifying high level abstractions.

Note: Bring in newspaper and magazine articles. Get a good variety so that you will have stories from writers, quotes from politicians and comments from movie stars. Have students identify the high level abstractions in each and discuss the effectiveness or ineffectiveness of each.

F. Words That Hurt and Heal

Objective

To help students identify words that have powerful effects on themselves and others.

Note: Make two columns on the board: Words that Hurt, and Words that Heal. For each column, have students brainstorm words that they or others respond to strongly. If the Hurt column seems longer than the Heal column (this is usually the case), challenge students to turn the Hurt column words into kinder terms. Remind them that they can still talk about things and behaviors that concern and bother them without using hurtful words.

CHAPTER 6

NONVERBAL COMMUNICATION:
MESSAGES BEYOND WORDS

OBJECTIVES

After studying the material in Chapter Six of *Looking Out/Looking In,* you should understand:
1. The importance of nonverbal communication.
2. The five characteristics of nonverbal communication.
3. The seven functions of nonverbal communication.
4. The differences between verbal and nonverbal communication.
5. The twelve types of nonverbal communication described in this chapter.

You should be able to:
1. Identify and describe
   a. your nonverbal behavior in a particular situation.
   b. examples of nonverbal behavior that repeats, substitutes for, complements, accents, regulates, or contradicts a verbal message.
   c. nonverbal behaviors of a variety of people in the same context.
   d. the emotions expressed in selected examples of your own nonverbal behavior.
2. Describe another's nonverbal behavior and use perception-checking statements to verify its meaning.
3. Describe the differences between verbal and nonverbal communication.
4. Explain why deception cues are not easy to detect.

NOTES ON CLASS AND STUDENT ACTIVITIES

A. Hello and Goodbye

Objective

To help students develop awareness of several dimensions of nonverbal communication.

Note: Assign students to visit airports, bus terminals, or anywhere that they are likely to be able to observe people greeting and leaving one another (they can even do this in groups to increase the fun). They should write down every nonverbal behavior they see (students usually record touching behaviors and facial expressions, but review the other types of nonverbal communication so that they will remember to record things like any paralanguage they overhear, the clothing people are wearing, and the actual spacing of people). They should then speculate on the relationship between the people, and bring their reports back to the class. This is a good exercise to use to reinforce reading material in the text.

B. Reading "Body Language" (Text, p. 220)

Objectives
1. To increase the participant's skill in observing nonverbal behavior.
2. To become more aware of some of the dangers inherent in interpreting nonverbal behavior.

Note: It is suggested that this exercise be done in pairs, but it can be done in larger groups.

C. Nonverbal Travels

Objective

To describe variations in nonverbal behaviors that students have encountered.

Note: Make use of student experiences and backgrounds to conduct a discussion on nonverbal differences across cultures (and co-cultures). Put columns on the board of the different types of nonverbal communication (e.g., proxemics, chronemics, facial expressions, gestures) and encourage students to describe the variations they have encountered in their travels (or perhaps in their culture of origin). The instructor should be careful not to generalize one student's experience to all situations. Compare and contrast these experiences to the descriptions in the text, and conduct a discussion about the importance of adjusting to nonverbal differences.

D. Paralanguage and Accent (Text, p. 234)

Objective

To help participants realize how much the words of a message are aided by the accompanying qualities of the voice; how much the meaning of a message can depend on the paralanguage: the tone of the voice, the pace, the punctuation (spacing of words), the emphasis, and so on.

Note: There are many variations of this particular activity. The partner doing the speaking can be given a list of things he or she is to attempt by means of paralanguage, with the listener responding as to what he or she is receiving. A single, short sentence can be used several times, putting the accent or emphasis on a different word each time.

E. The Rules of Touch (Text, p. 238)

Objective

To develop an awareness of appropriate touch and the ability to describe it within various relationships.

Note: This exercise can trigger strong feelings from students about their own instances of both appropriate and inappropriate touch. Guide students to use the language skills (e.g., "I" language) from Chapter 5 to voice their pleasure or displeasure to the person touching.

F. Distance Makes a Difference (Text, p. 238)

Objective

To let each student experience the difference distance can make to him or her when relating to another person.

Note: Often the room is not large enough to give the partners enough room so that they are not distracted by those lined up beside them. If this is the case, do the exercise in several groups so that there is at least an arm's length separating everyone.

CHAPTER 7

LISTENING: MORE THAN MEETS THE EAR

OBJECTIVES

After studying the material in Chapter Seven of *Looking Out/Looking In,* you should understand:
1. Seven types of ineffective listening.
2. The reasons why people listen poorly.
3. How effective questions can be used to improve listening.
4. Seven styles of listening to help others with problems, and the strengths and drawbacks of each.

You should be able to:
1. Identify your ineffective listening behavior, including
   a. the circumstances in which you listen ineffectively.
   b. the ineffective listening styles you use in each set of circumstances.
   c. the reasons why you listen ineffectively in each set of circumstances.
   d. the consequences of your ineffective listening behaviors.
2. Paraphrase another person by
   a. using appropriate nonverbal attending behaviors.
   b. fluently and concisely paraphrasing the speaker's thoughts.
   c. fluently and concisely paraphrasing the speaker's feelings.
   d. making open-ended requests for the speaker to verify the accuracy of your paraphrasing statements.
3. Demonstrate your ability to use the following response styles to help others with their problems:
   a. advising
   b. judging
   c. analyzing
   d. questioning
   e. supporting
   f. prompting
   g. paraphrasing

NOTES ON CLASS AND STUDENT ACTIVITIES

A. Listening Breakdowns (Text, p. 252)

Objective

To overcome common listening myths.

Note: If students have a difficult time coming up with examples of how they failed at listening, let them start with examples of how others have failed in listening to them. Then guide the students back into self-awareness.

B. Speaking and Listening with a "Talking Stick" (Text, p. 259)

Objective

To focus the student's attention on the benefits of talking less and listening more.

Notes:

1. Encourage students to talk about anything of interest to them. What happened to them this morning may seem as important as serious world events.
2. After the exercise, a valuable discussion can come from students discussing times they have not felt listened to, and in turn, not listened themselves.

C. Lecture Listening

Objective

To guide students to develop effective questions in listening in larger groups.

Note: Conduct a discussion of classroom listening and responding styles. Have students suggest questions they might ask during a lecture (have some of your "favorites" ready to get them started—e.g., "Professor Wiemann, don't you think paraphrasing sounds fake?"). Identify any counterfeit questions and suggest alternatives. Contrast this lecture listening to other types of listening.

D. Paraphrasing Practice
(Text, p. 267, and 7.3 in the *Student Activities Manual*)

Objective

To give the student practice in paraphrasing.

Note: Discussion questions are indicated in the text or use 7.3 in the *Student Activities Manual* as a stimulus.

E.   Listen to the Little Children

Objective

To give the student practice in paraphrasing.

Note: Assign students to visit with a child under the age of ten (a sibling or other relative, or perhaps a neighbor or volunteer at a nursery school). Tell them to ask questions about what the child is doing, interested in, or planning. Tell them to use a number of listening styles, but to particularly practice their paraphrasing skills. Little children are usually much more forgiving and less evaluative as students practice this very difficult skill. They can write a short report of what they learned or share this orally with the class.

F.   What Would You Do? (Text, p. 275-276)

Objective

To show students their typical style of responding to another's problem, and to demonstrate the frequent ineffectiveness of the typical response styles.

Note: In a variation of the exercise, assign one or two students each of the typical response styles, having them react to another student who role-plays the problems listed.

G. One-Way and Two-Way Communication

Objective

To demonstrate the advantages of checking back with the sender of a message.

Notes:

1. You can alert the observers (mentioned in step 3) to watch for certain behaviors: level of frustration, perceived confidence, and mistaken assumptions or misinterpretations. These observations will be helpful in the post-exercise discussion.
2. In the post-exercise discussion, make sure the students recognize all the characteristics of one-way and two-way communication.

ONE-WAY

Low sender frustration, High receiver frustration
Low accuracy
Short time necessary

TWO-WAY

High sender frustration, Low receiver frustration
High accuracy
Long time necessary

Instructions

1. Copy the following chart onto a chalkboard so that everyone can see it.

ONE-WAY		TWO-WAY	
TIME		TIME	
NUMBER CORRECT		**NUMBER CORRECT**	
ESTIMATE	ACTUAL	ESTIMATE	ACTUAL
	5		
	4		
	3		
	2		
	1		
	0		

2. Select one member of the group to act as a sender. The sender's job will be to describe two simple drawings to the rest of the group.

3. Select two observers, one to note the sender's behavior in the exercise, and the other to note the behavior of the group members.

4. Supply the group members with sheets of unlined 81/2-11- inch paper.

5. Make sure everyone hears and understands the following directions: "In a minute, the sender will describe a simple set of figures that the group members should draw as accurately as possible. The group members should ask no questions or respond in any way to the sender's directions. The idea is to create a one-way communication situation."

6. The sender now stands or sits so that he or she can be heard but not seen by the group. The instructor then gives the sender a copy of the first drawing found here. (Actually, any simple drawing will work in this exercise. A variation is to have the sender create his or her own drawing and describe it to the group. Remember, however, that the drawing should be quite simple. This exercise is hard enough this way!)

7. The sender should describe this drawing to the group as quickly and as accurately as possible. The instructor should make sure that the group members don't communicate with each other during this step. All should understand that a glance at another's drawing furnishes an additional source of information, thus destroying a one-way communication situation.

8. After the sender has finished, note the time that his or her description took and place it on the chart. Next, find out how many group members think they've drawn all five figures exactly, how many think they got four, three, and so on. Place the numbers in the appropriate spaces on the chart.

9. Now the sender should move so that he or she can see and be seen by the group. The instructor will give the sender the drawing he or she is to describe. This time, however, the group members should ask necessary questions to make sure they understand the drawing being described. This should be two-way communication. The only limitation on communication here is that the sender must use words only—no gestures—to describe the drawing to the group.

10. Remember, the goal is to have all group members reproduce the drawing perfectly, so everyone should feel free to ask plenty of questions.
11. Repeat step 8.
12. Now show the drawings one at a time to the group members so they can see how accurate their reactions are. The instructor should then record the accuracy of the group's drawings. For a figure to be correct, its size should be correct proportionately, and it should be positioned in the correct relationship to the preceding and following figures.
13. Now note the data the exercise has produced on your chart. After looking it over, what assumptions might you make about one-way and two-way communication? Which takes longer? Which is more accurate?
14. Which is more frustrating for the sender? For the receiver?
15. What parallels does this exercise have in your everyday life? Does the exercise tell you anything about the way you listen?
16. Consider the efficiency of one-way and two-way communication. Remember, efficiency takes into account time, cost, and so on. Are there situations in society where one-way communication is used? Consider the military, police and fire departments, and so on. What precaution is taken to ensure effective communicating situations where time is so important?

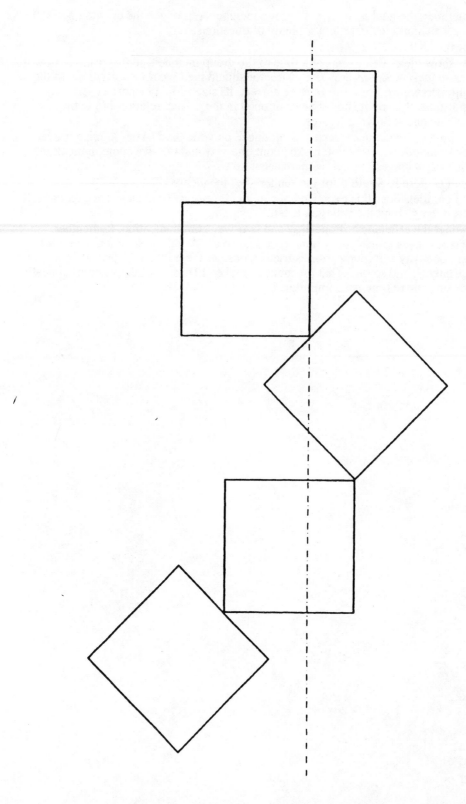

CHAPTER 8

COMMUNICATION AND RELATIONAL DYNAMICS

OBJECTIVES

After reading the material in Chapter Eight of Looking Out/Looking In,

You should understand:
1. The four dimensions of intimacy.
2. Five variables affecting interpersonal attraction.
3. The ten stages of interpersonal relationships.
4. How self-disclosure is defined.
5. How the Johari Window represents the relationship between self-disclosure and self-awareness and how it can describe self-disclosure in a dyadic relationship.
6. How the four types of self-disclosure affect breadth and depth in a relationship.
7. Seven guidelines for self-disclosure.
8. The alternatives to self-disclosure.

You should be able to:
1. Identify
    a. three reasons why we form relationships.
    b. three dialectical tensions at work in relationships.
    c. eight strategies for managing dialectical tensions.
    d. reasons why you self-disclose or fail to disclose.
    e. ten stages of development in interpersonal relationships.
2. Describe
    a. the breadth and depth of relationships that are important to you.
    b. the levels of self-disclosure you engage in and how they affect your relationships.
    c. behaviors reflecting stages in your relationships and your satisfaction with the relationship.
    d. the alternatives you have to self-disclosure and the ethics of evasion.

NOTES ON CLASS AND STUDENT ACTIVITIES

A. How Fast Should We Go?

Objective

To help students describe what leads them to be attracted to certain people, and to evaluate how they approach intimacy.

Notes

Ask students to describe what leads them to be attracted to certain people; compare this to the attraction variables in the text. Next, review the stages of coming together in the text; have students evaluate how quickly they should go through each increasing stage of intimacy.

Questions

1. To what extent are your strong, positive personal relationships based on the listed attraction variables?
2. Do you believe that knowing these attraction variables can influence the relationships you would like to make stronger?

To what extent do you "fit" the attraction variables for those people that you wish you were attractive to?

How fast is too fast when you are becoming intimate with someone?

How can you better evaluate how fast to proceed in relationships?

B.   Your IQ (Intimacy Quotient) (Text, p. 291)

Objective

To help students determine the levels of intimacy in their important relationships.

Note: Reinforce for students the many different types of intimacy (many think only of physical intimacy at first).

C.   Your Relational Stage (Text, p. 300) and Relational Stages, 8.2 in the *Student Activities Manual*)

Objective

To increase the students' awareness of stages of relational development.

Notes:

1. Some students have a tendency to describe romantic relationships of even a short duration as "bonded." Encourage them to see the value of behaviors at each stage in building the relationship over time. Remind them that one behavior does not make the stage, but a pattern and consistency of types of behavior.
2. Another problem some students have with relational stages is that they think "the higher the better." Help them to see that mutual understanding of and satisfaction with the stage is a far better guide.

D.   Your Dialectical Tensions (Text, p. 304),
and Discovering Dialectics, 8.1 in the *Student Activities Manual*)

Objective

To increase students' knowledge of the tensions at work in relationships.

NOTE: Have students make a column for each of the strategies for dealing with dialectical tensions. Record how frequently each is used and in which types of situations.

E.   Self-Disclosure Tales

Objective

To increase the students' awareness of the levels of self-disclosure others use with them, and how they use with self disclosure with others, and to evaluate the appropriate level of self-disclosure in relationships.

NOTE: Students should relate examples of times in which people self-disclosed too much or too little to them. If they are comfortable, they can also share times when they self-disclosed too much or too little. They should focus on different types of relationships (family, friends, romantic, work, etc.).

Discussion Questions

1.   How do you notice reciprocity of self-disclosure at work in your relationship?
     What level of self-disclosure is appropriate in this relationship versus others?
     What should we do when others are disclosing inappropriately to us?
     How can we better evaluate our own appropriate level of self-disclosure?

F.   Appropriate Self-Disclosure (Text, p. 316), and Disclosure Alternatives, 8.6 in the *Student Activities Manual*)

Objective

To examine the potential risks and benefits of self-disclosure.

Note: Have students compare the risks and benefits of disclosing in various situations. They can often reinforce for one another the guidelines for appropriate self-disclosure with their "war stories."

CHAPTER 9

IMPROVING COMMUNICATION CLIMATES

OBJECTIVES

After studying the material in Chapter Nine of *Looking Out/Looking In,* you should understand:

1. How confirming and disconfirming messages create positive and negative communication climates.
2. The relationship between a communicator's self-concept and his or her defensive reaction to a message.
3. How defense mechanisms operate when a communicator perceives attacking messages.
4. How and why Gibb's defensive and supportive behaviors can minimize or increase defensive responses to your message.
5. How seeking more information from a critic and agreeing with the criticism can minimize a communicator's defensive responses.

You should be able to:

1. Use feedback from a significant other to list the kinds of confirming and disconfirming messages you presently send.
2. Identify your unproductive defensive responses to perceived verbal attacks by listing
   a. the defense mechanisms you commonly use.
   b. the circumstances in which you use them.
   c. the parts of your presenting self-image you are attempting to defend.
   d. the consequences of your defensive behavior.
3. Send confirming messages by using Gibb's supportive behaviors:
   a. description
   b. problem-orientation
   c. empathy
   d. spontaneity
   e. equality
   f. Provisionalism
4. Use the clear messages to increase supportiveness that include
   a. behavior
   b. your interpretation(s)
   c. feelings
   d. consequences
   e. your intentions

5. Respond to the criticism of others nondefensively by
   a.   seeking additional information from your critic.
   b.   agreeing with your critic.

NOTES ON CLASS AND STUDENT ACTIVITIES

A. Evaluating Communication Climates (Text, p. 338-339)

Objective

To identify the communication climate in important relationships and to describe the confirming and disconfirming behaviors that help define this climate.

Note: One way to help the discussion along in this exercise is to allow some students to describe the negative behaviors, disconfirming ones, that their partners use (it is easier to criticize others) and again to describe the positive, confirming behaviors that their partners use (they don't have to brag about themselves in this instance). As this discussion progresses, lead the discussion into the spiral effect of behaviors in relationships (Gibb), and the effects of the students" own behaviors become more apparent.

B. Defense Mechanism Inventory (Text, p. 342), and Understanding Defensive Responses, 9.1 in the *Student Activities Manual*)

Objective

To encourage the student to reflect on the patterns of defensive behavior he or she may have and to encourage the student to create a plan for more satisfying behaviors.

Note: The Understanding Defensive Responses in the *Student Activities Manual* and Defense Mechanism Inventory are similar exercises. We believe they are both needed to help the student recognize his or her own defensive behaviors. It is better if some time elapses between the assignment of these exercises.

C. Defensiveness Feedback (Text, p. 349)

Objective

To provide the student with more information about the patterns of his or her defensive behaviors.

Note: The instructor may wish to use the statements in the concluding remarks (question 6) as the topics for discussion.

D. Name the Feeling (Text, p. 354)

Objective

To recognize the feelings the students would be likely to have in the listed circumstances and to evaluate the effect on the message based on expressing the feeling or not expressing the feeling.

Note: An interesting adaptation of this exercise is to have students come up with messages in which strong feelings existed but wouldn't, couldn't, or shouldn't be expressed. Compare and contrast these statements with the ones in the text. Sometimes class members will argue at this point that many more feelings should, could, or would be expressed if others only knew how to express them.

E. Putting Your Message Together (Text, p. 357), and Clear Messages, 9.3 in *Student Activities Manual*)

Objectives
1. To enable the student to practice expressing a satisfactory message.
2. To enable the student to gain confidence in communicating.
3. To enable the student to get feedback form his or her classmates.

Discussion Questions
1. What were some of the characteristics of satisfactory messages?
2. Were the messages difficult to clarify and express? Why or why not?
3. What were some useful bits of feedback you received?

Note: The instructor might wish to write these suggestions on the chalkboard or put them on a ditto, copies of which might be given to each student in the class.

F. Pushing My Buttons

Objective

To identify the words and behaviors that trigger defensiveness.

Note: In groups, have students create lists of words and behaviors that trigger their defensiveness. Lead them through a discussion about recognizing those triggers/buttons. Relate this back to chapter four's rational thinking, and help students dispute any irrational thoughts. This can be a good prelude to learning to cope with criticism.

G. "Yes, but . . ."

Objective

To identify common excuse-making that contributes to a defensive climate.

Note: In groups, have students think about the excuses that they and others give (for being late, out of money, unprepared, etc.). Describe the ways that we give excuses, and illustrate how this contributes to defensiveness (for example, saying "Yes, I was ten minutes late" has a different effect than saying, "Yes, I was late, but the traffic was terrible.") . Have students discuss alternate ways of simply admitting what is true without giving excuses. This is also a good prelude to learning to cope with criticism.

H. Coping with Criticism (Text, p. 366), Nondefensive Responses to Criticism, 9.4, and Coping with Criticism, 9.5 in the *Student Activities Manual*)

Objective

To practice responding nondefensively to criticism.

Note: Picking some students who are "good sports" to role-play some of these situations in front of the class is a good illustration to class members of "real" people responding in this manner. Encourage students to role-play situations that are real to them so that the practice is especially meaningful.

CHAPTER 10

MANAGING INTERPERSONAL CONFLICTS

OBJECTIVES

After studying the material in Chapter Ten of *Looking Out/Looking In,* you should understand:
1. That conflict is natural and inevitable.
2. Five personal styles of conflict:
    a. nonassertive
    b. direct aggression
    c. passive aggression
    d. indirect communication
    e. assertion
3. The characteristics of four types of conflict resolution:
    a. win-lose
    b. lose-lose
    c. compromise
    d. win-win

You should be able to:
1. Describe your personal conflict style by
    a. identifying the conflict style(s) you most commonly use.
    b. evaluating the appropriateness of the style(s).
    c. when necessary, choosing more productive alternatives.
2. Use the win-win problem-solving method by
    a. identifying your unmet needs.
    b. choosing the best time and place to resolve the conflict.
    c. describing your problem and unmet needs clearly and assertively.
    d. considering your partner's point of view.
    e. negotiating a win-win solution whenever possible.
    f. following up on the solution.

NOTES ON CLASS AND STUDENT ACTIVITIES

A. Your Conflict Style (Text, p. 383), and 10.3 in the *Student Activities Manual*

Objective

To discover some of the ways we deal with conflict in our lives.

Note: If your group is willing, this exercise can be more meaningful if the contents of the completed charts are discussed in small groups.

Perhaps it might help to stress that we can change nothing until we discover something we wish to change. In this context, this activity can be of great importance to the group members. However, care should be taken not to suggest that everyone needs to make changes. This decision needs to be made by the individual.

B. Understanding Conflict Styles (Text, p. 387), and 10.1 in the *Student Activities Manual*

Objectives
1. To illustrate how conflict styles differ.
2. To apply the concept of conflict style to conflict management.

C. Your Conflict Rituals (Text, p. 388)

Objective

To describe positive and negative conflict rituals.

Note: Because conflict rituals are unacknowledged patterns, they are often hard to recognize. Some students need help recognizing the role their behaviors play in the ritual (rather than just blaming the other person for the conflict).

D. Win-Win Solutions and You (Text, p. 404), and 10.4, 10.5 and 10.6 in the *Student Activities Manual*

Objective

To apply win-win problem-solving to real situations in which the students are involved.

Discussion Questions
1. Were there difficulties in getting the other people involved in your conflict to try win-win problem-solving?
2. Which of the win-win problem-solving steps seemed the easiest? The most difficult?
3. What kinds of brainstorming ideas were generated? Can you think of more ideas now that you are away form the other people? Can the class think of ideas not generated already?

4. What degree of satisfaction do you have with your first attempt at this method? How could you change that degree of satisfaction?
5. What adaptations may need to be made in different situations to make conflict resolution work for you?

E.   Play to Win

(This simulation exercise is not found in the text or the *Student Activities Manual*.)

Objective

To demonstrate through a simulation exercise the behaviors different people exhibit when they are in a situation they perceive as conflict or competition or win-lose.

1. Copy the following chart onto the chalkboard.

HOW TO SCORE POINTS

WHEN VOTE IS	GROUP'S SCORE
X X X X	Each group gets +50 pts.
X X X Y	Groups voting X get -100 pts.
	Groups voting Y get +300 pts.
X X Y Y	Groups voting X get -200 pts.
	Groups voting Y get +200 pts.
X Y Y Y	Groups voting X get -300 pts.
	Groups voting Y get +100 pts.
Y Y Y Y	Each group gets -50 pts.

How to Score

Each of the four groups will cast either an X or Y vote in each round. When the vote is tabulated, one of the preceding five combinations will result, and each group will score accordingly. (At this point, there's apt to be some confusion and questions such as "What are we voting on?" Don't get bogged down here. Everyone will understand the process as you move along.)

2. Divide your class into four equal groups.
3. Each group should now move to a corner of the room so that the members can talk together without interruption. There should be no communication—verbal or nonverbal—among groups except when instructions permit.
4. The group's first task is to decide on how it will make decisions: unanimous agreement, majority vote, decision of the leader, consensus, and so on.
5. Place this scoreboard where it can be easily seen.

ROUND	VOTE	GROUP I	GROUP II	GROUP III	GROUP IV
1					
2					
(N) 3					
4					
(N) 5	(2X)				
6					
(N) 7					
(N) 8					
9 (10X)					

The object of the game is for each group to score the greatest number of positive points possible.

6. Notice that there will be nine rounds of voting. In round 5 the scores will be doubled, and in round 9 they'll be multiplied by 10. The (N) that appears before rounds 3, 5, 7, and 8 means that the groups will be allowed to negotiate before voting in those rounds.

7. Take three minutes for each group to discuss how it will vote in round 1.

8. After the three minutes, the instructor will collect a ballot from each group. Tally the votes and score for round 1 on the scoreboard.

9. Repeat the same procedure for the remaining rounds. Before each N round, one negotiator from each team should come to the center of the room, and if they desire, negotiate the next vote or votes.

10. During negotiations, only negotiators can speak—group members must remain quiet so that they may hear negotiations. There will be time to discuss the vote in the groups after negotiations are completed.

11. After all rounds are completed, discuss the following questions:

   a. Who won the game?

   b. If two groups with the same goal finished with a tie score, did they both win? Did both lose?

   c. In this game, can there be more than one winner? Why?

   d. Did the groups cooperate during the game, helping the others reach their goals, or did they compete by trying to "beat" everyone?

   e. Did the simulation provide opportunities for the students to behave either cooperatively or competitively, or did the students add these as they went along?

   f. What did the students' behavior in this exercise tell them about how they handle conflict in their lives?

Note: This game usually illustrates some common ways people act when going after something they want. Most groups assume that to reach the goal they've chosen, they must keep others from reaching theirs, when, in fact, the surest way to succeed is to work together so all groups can score well. As one woman said when shown how all the groups could have reached their goal by cooperating, "But there can't be winners unless there are losers!"

PART
FOUR

TEST BANK

CHAPTER 1

A FIRST LOOK AT INTERPERSONAL RELATIONSHIPS

1. Chapter One indicates that effective interpersonal communication is strongly linked to social happiness and career success.
   Answer: T   **Type: T**   **Page: 8**   **Knowledge**

2. Communication is the only way we gain a sense of who we are.
   Answer: T   **Type: T**   **Page: 8**   **Knowledge**

3. A lack of social relationships may effect physical health and life span as dramatically as smoking or a lack of physical activity.
   Answer: T   **Type: T**   **Page: 6**   **Knowledge**

4. Immediacy isn't really possible when you dislike another person.
   Answer: T   **Type: T**   **Page: 28**   **Knowledge**

5. Competent communicators are nearly always described as "outgoing," "straightforward," and "humorous."
   Answer: F   **Type: T**   **Pages: 34–36**   **Analysis**

6. Shared understanding and clarity are the most important goals in achieving successful communication.
   Answer: F   **Type: T**   **Page: 18**   **Knowledge**

7. We learn who we are through communicating.
   Answer: T   **Type: T**   **Page: 7**   **Knowledge**

8. The major difference between impersonal communication and interpersonal communication is the number of people involved.
   Answer: F   **Type: T**   **Page: 20**   **Analysis**

9. You can fill even your instrumental goals through communication.
   Answer: T   **Type: T**   **Page: 9**   **Knowledge**

10. One element of the transactional communication model in the text is "needs."
    Answer: F   **Type: T**   **Pages: 11–14**   **Comprehension**

11. Communication competence is a trait that people either possess or lack.
    Answer: F   **Type: T**   **Page: 32**   **Knowledge**

12. Just as judges instruct juries to disregard some statements made in court, we can reverse or erase the effects of communication interactions in everyday life.
    Answer: F   **Type: T**   **Pages: 17–18**   **Comprehension**

13. There is no such thing as the "same" message; words and behavior are different each time they are spoken or performed.
    Answer: T   **Type: T**   **Page: 18**   **Knowledge**

14. It is impossible to repeat the same communication event.
     Answer: T   **Type: T**   **Pages: 17–18**   **Knowledge**

15. The transactional model of communication suggests that communicators usually send
     and receive messages simultaneously.
     Answer: T   **Type: T**   **Page: 11**   **Knowledge**

16. The transactional model represents communication as static – more like a gallery of
     still photographs than a motion picture film.
     Answer: F   **Type: T**   **Pages: 13**   **Knowledge**

17. The presence or absence of communication can affect both physical and
     psychological health.
     Answer: T   **Type: T**   **Page: 6**   **Comprehension**

18. Socially isolated people are much more likely to die prematurely than those with
     strong social ties.
     Answer: T   **Type: T**   **Page: 6**   **Knowledge**

19. Socially isolated people compensate effectively for lack of communication, so their
     longevity rates are about the same as those of people with strong social ties.
     Answer: F   **Type: T**   **Page: 6**   **Knowledge**

20. According to your text, impersonal communication is dehumanizing and should be
     avoided.
     Answer: F   **Type: T**   **Pages: 24–25**   **Comprehension**

21. According to your text, effective communicators are able to establish warm
     relationships with everyone they encounter.
     Answer: F   **Type: T**   **Pages: 24–25**   **Analysis**

22. Communicators who rely on standardized rules to guide their interactions are usually
     ineffective communicators.
     Answer: T   **Type: T**   **Page: 20**   **Analysis**

23. Your text argues that it is important to react in unique ways to every person we meet
     and respond to each as a unique individual.
     Answer: F   **Type: T**   **Page: 20**   **Synthesis**

24. Communication, as the term is used in your text, consists only of messages that a
     sender deliberately conveys.
     Answer: F   **Type: T**   **Page: 16**   **Comprehension**

25. It's impossible to stop communicating.
     Answer: T   **Type: T**   **Page: 17**   **Knowledge**

26. Impersonal communication follows standardized rules for behavior learned from
     parents, teachers, and other people with whom we interact.
     Answer: T   **Type: T**   **Page: 20**   **Comprehension**

27. Of the communication models described in your text, the linear model most
     accurately describes the interpersonal communication process.
     Answer: F   **Type: T**   **Pages: 10–14**   **Application**

28. We disclose more to people in interpersonal relationships than in impersonal ones.
     Answer: T   **Type: T**   **Page: 21**   **Knowledge**

29. Too much communication can be unproductive and damaging.
    Answer: T   **Type: T**   **Pages: 18–19**   **Knowledge**

30. All sexual encounters qualify as a form of interpersonal communication, as the term is used in your text.
    Answer: F   **Type: T**   **Pages: 19–20**   **Synthesis**

31. As the text points out, your goal should be to become a perfect communicator.
    Answer: F   **Type: T**   **Page: 32**   **Comprehension**

32. All you need to develop good communication skills is common sense.
    Answer: F   **Type: T**   **Pages: 33–34**   **Analysis**

33. According to your text, awareness of new ways of communicating is usually sufficient to enable people to communicate more effectively.
    Answer: F   **Type: T**   **Pages: 33–34**   **Analysis**

34. Dyadic communication is communication involving two people.
    Answer: T   **Type: T**   **Page: 19**   **Knowledge**

35. Communication is so important that its quantity and quality can affect blood pressure and coronary health.
    Answer: T   **Type: T**   **Page: 6**   **Comprehension**

36. When people communicate, they are often both senders and receivers of messages at the same time.
    Answer: T   **Type: T**   **Page: 11**   **Knowledge**

37. According to your text, the axiom "the more communication the better" is true.
    Answer: F   **Type: T**   **Pages: 18–19**   **Knowledge**

38. Your text promises that if you communicate skillfully enough, you should be able to solve every problem you encounter.
    Answer: F   **Type: T**   **Page: 18**   **Knowledge**

39. In impersonal communication we treat others as individuals.
    Answer: F   **Type: T**   **Page: 20**   **Knowledge**

40. Fortunately, just knowing about a communication skill makes us able to put it into practice.
    Answer: F   **Type: T**   **Page: 37**   **Comprehension**

41. The absence of communication can affect physical health in extremely negative ways.
    Answer: T   **Type: T**   **Page: 6**   **Knowledge**

42. Almost all verbal messages have a content dimension as well as convey relational information.
    Answer: T   **Type: T**   **Page: 27**   **Comprehension**

43. Your text argues that the physical setting in which communication takes place is not useful as a basis for categorizing whether the interaction is interpersonal or impersonal.
    Answer: T   **Type: T**   **Pages: 20–21**   **Knowledge**

44. The person who exercises the greatest amount of conversational control doesn't always make the decisions in interpersonal relationships.
   Answer: T   **Type: T**   **Page: 30**   **Comprehension**

45. Whenever we discuss our mutual relationship with the other person, we are meta–communicating.
   Answer: T   **Type: T**   **Page: 30**   **Synthesis**

46. According to Chapter One, interpersonal relationships are associations in which the parties meet each other's social needs to a greater or lesser degree.
   Answer: T   **Type: T**   **Pages: 8, 20**   **Knowledge**

47. Relational dimensions of messages make statements about how the parties feel toward one another.
   Answer: T   **Type: T**   **Page: 27**   **Knowledge**

48. A competent communicator strives for conversational control in all interpersonal encounters.
   Answer: F   **Type: T**   **Page: 30**   **Analysis**

49. Relational messages are frequently nonverbal.
   Answer: T   **Type: T**   **Pages: 24–26**   **Comprehension**

50. Metacommunication is a destructive substitute for real communication.
   Answer: F   **Type: T**   **Page: 27**   **Comprehension**

51. Lovers who argue constantly cease to have an interpersonal relationship.
   Answer: F   **Type: T**   **Page: 20**   **Analysis**

52. Affinity is defined as the degree to which two or more people like or appreciate one another.
   Answer: T   **Type: T**   **Page: 28**   **Knowledge**

53. There are two types of relational control: decision control and conversational control.
   Answer: T   **Type: T**   **Page: 30**   **Knowledge**

54. In the "Accidental Tourist" Communication Transcript in Chapter One, Macon and Muriel's discussion had problems because
   a. they couldn't agree about the importance of math skills.
   b. Macon didn't show enough immediacy cues like eye contact when talking.
   c. Macon stuck only to the content level of the conversational messages.
   d. Muriel and Macon communicated too much.
   e. Macon wanted relational control over Muriel.
   Answer: c   **Type: M**   **Page: 31**   **analysis**

55. In Chapter One Deborah Tannen claims that
   a. electronic mail can deepen the quality of relationships.
   b. electronic mail makes interpersonal communication more impersonal.
   c. everyone prefers face to face communication rather than electronic mail.
   d. relationships cannot be maintained using electronic mail.
   e. all of the above are claimed by Tannen.
   Answer: a   **Type: M**   **Page: 24**   **Knowledge**

56. In the Looking at Diversity reading in Chapter One, Daria Muse says that a big part of communicating well is
    a. speaking more than one language.
    b. staying true to your own communication style.
    c. understanding communication models.
    d. adjusting to different communication climates.
    e. having experiences in more than one culture.
    Answer: d   Type: M   Page: 35   Comprehension

57. Psychologist Abraham Maslow suggests that the most basic human needs
    a. are invented by other psychologists.
    b. must be satisfied before we concern ourselves with other ones.
    c. are proof that animals ascended from lower animal forms.
    d. prove the existence of a superior being.
    e. are generated by others in interpersonal interaction.
    Answer: b   Type: M   Page: 9   Knowledge

58. All of the following elements are included in the transactional communication model introduced in Chapter One except
    a. message.
    b. environment.
    c. channel.
    d. sender.
    e. noise.
    Answer: d   Type: M   Pages: 11–12   Knowledge

59. All of the following are involved in learning to perform effective communication skills effectively except
    a. awareness.
    b. prowess.
    c. awkwardness.
    d. skillfulness.
    e. integration.
    Answer: b   Type: M   Page: 37   Knowledge

60. The environments that communicators occupy are
    a. fields of experience that help them understand others' behavior.
    b. gaps that make common understanding impossible.
    c. the places where they stand or sit when they communicate.
    d. the attitudes they have about nature.
    e. the space that they require to communicate effectively.
    Answer: a   Type: M   Page: 12   Knowledge

61. "Decoding" is the process whereby
    a. we put our thoughts into words.
    b. we make sense out of the messages sent by others.
    c. we engage others in conversation.
    d. we choose the appropriate way to send messages.
    e. we create new ways of teaching reading and communication to children.
    Answer: b   **Type: M**   **Page: 10**   **Knowledge**

62. When Jeb decides that his grandson didn't mean to insult him by using slang, Jeb has
    a. encoded.
    b. integrated.
    c. related.
    d. decoded.
    e. metacommunicated.
    Answer: d   **Type: M**   **Page: 10**   **Analysis**

63. Almost all messages have
    a. a content dimension.
    b. a relational dimension.
    c. both content and relational dimensions.
    d. no dimensions unless the communicators intend them to.
    Answer: c   **Type: M**   **Page: 27**   **Comprehension**

64. The three types of noise that can block communication are
    a. loud, moderate, and soft.
    b. mass communicational, personal, and transactional.
    c. external, physiological, and psychological.
    d. sociological, psychological, and communicational.
    e. linear, interactional, and transactional.
    Answer: c   **Type: M**   **Page: 13**   **Knowledge**

65. Skillful, integrated communicators are characterized by
    a. a conscious focus on communicating effectively.
    b. a greater degree of sociability.
    c. communicating competently without needing to think constantly about how to behave.
    d. exposure to a wide range of communication styles.
    e. others helping them out.
    Answer: c   **Type: M**   **Page: 38**   **Comprehension**

66. Research has shown that competent communicators achieve effectiveness by
    a. using the same types of behavior in a wide variety of situations.
    b. developing large vocabularies.
    c. apologizing when they offend others.
    d. giving lots of feedback.
    e. adjusting their behaviors to the person and situation.
    Answer: e   **Type: M**   **Pages: 34–36**   **Synthesis**

67. According to your text, messages are
    a. vastly overrated as a communication tool.
    b. both verbal and nonverbal.
    c. not present in impersonal communication.
    d. only possible when communicators speak the same language.
    e. all of the above.
    Answer: b   **Type: M**   **Page: 11–12**   **Analysis**

68. When you carefully plan the words you use to avoid offending someone, you are
    a. decoding.
    b. encoding.
    c. self–actualizing.
    d. communicating impersonally.
    e. all of the above.
    Answer: b   **Type: M**   **Page: 10**   **Comprehension**

69. A family arguing about whether to spend the weekend together or apart might be trying to satisfy what social need?
    a. companionship
    b. affection
    c. control
    d. all of the above
    e. none of the above
    Answer: d   **Type: M**   **Page: 8**   **Application**

70. You want to let a close friend know how much she/he means to you in a way that is sincere and doesn't embarrass either of you. Following the advice on communication competence in your text, you would
    a. follow the approach that you saw another friend use successfully, assuming it would work for you.
    b. avoid sending any message until you were sure it would be well received.
    c. try to follow exactly the approach you used successfully with others in the past.
    d. react in the way that first occurred to you.
    e. consider a variety of alternatives, choosing the one that you think will be most successful under these circumstances.
    Answer: e   **Type: M**   **Pages: 34–36**   **Evaluation**

71. Maslow's hierarchy of needs is important to the study of interpersonal communication because
    a. we all have needs.
    b. we can't understand our needs without communication.
    c. communication can help us meet each of the needs.
    d. communication was Maslow's greatest need.
    e. the need for communication is the sixth "hidden" need.
    Answer: c   **Type: M**   **Page: 9**   **Comprehension**

72. Noise in the communication process is
     a. more than one communicator talking at a time.
     b. the nonverbal behaviors that accompany communication.
     c. the process of maintaining direct eye contact or not.
     d. the process of translating thoughts into words.
     e. any force that interferes with effective communication.
     Answer: e   **Type: M**   **Page: 13**   **Knowledge**

73. Which of the following is most clearly an example of interpersonal communication?
     a. Gaudet buys a sweater from the clerk.
     b. Rich invites the team to a party.
     c. Royce asks Jane about her sick child.
     d. Trent pleads for the class to vote.
     Answer: c   **Type: M**   **Pages: 19–20**   **Analysis**

74. In order for communication to take place, the sender and receiver need to be
     a. experiencing identical environments.
     b. alone together.
     c. looking at each other so that eye contact can be made.
     d. in the absence of all "noise."
     e. sending and receiving any type of message.
     Answer: e   **Type: M**   **Page: 11**   **Analysis**

75. Some of the social needs we strive to fulfill by communicating are
     a. encoding and decoding.
     b. control and affection.
     c. empathy and sympathy.
     d. talking and listening.
     e. communicating both verbally and nonverbally.
     Answer: b   **Type: M**   **Page: 8**   **Comprehension**

76. Some of the characteristics that make relationships more interpersonal than
     impersonal are
     a. higher levels of self–disclosure and intimacy.
     b. intrinsic rewards and proximity.
     c. scarcity, disclosure and intimacy.
     d. uniqueness, irreplaceability, and interdependence.
     Answer: d   **Type: M**   **Pages: 19–20**   **Comprehension**

77. Integrated communicators express themselves in skillful ways because
     a. their communication is a self-conscious act.
     b. they have had more experience.
     c. they have internalized effective behavior.
     d. skills are basic to communication.
     e. others help them out.
     Answer: c   **Type: M**   **Page: 38**   **Comprehension**

78. Effective communicators have been found to
    a. have a consistent set of five behaviors they can call up at will.
    b. have a wide range of behaviors from which to choose.
    c. exhibit behaviors that are predictable by their partners.
    d. exhibit unique behaviors more often than less effective communicators.
    e. frequently rehearse about 20 behaviors until they get them right for any interaction.
    Answer: b   **Type: M**   **Page: 34**   **Comprehension**

79. When you pay attention to your behavior in relationships, you are
    a. unlikely to pay attention to others.
    b. too uptight.
    c. probably ego–driven.
    d. self–monitoring.
    e. intrinsic.
    Answer: d   **Type: M**   **Page: 38**   **Knowledge**

80. Identity and communication are related in that we
    a. gain an idea of who we are from the way others communicate with us.
    b. are drawn to communicators who test and challenge our identity.
    c. find others' identities become our own through communication.
    d. control communication with our identity.
    Answer: a   **Type: M**   **Pages: 7–8**   **Comprehension**

81. Which is an example of "noise" as the term is defined in your text?
    a. someone tapping a pencil while you're trying to talk
    b. a headache that interferes with your listening
    c. feelings of anger directed toward a partner
    d. preoccupation with another topic during a lecture
    e. all of the above
    Answer: e   **Type: M**   **Page: 13**   **Application**

82. Which is an example of "psychological noise" as defined in your text?
    a. the sound of a lawn mower just outside your window
    b. the smell of smoke drifting into the room you are in
    c. feeling embarrassed about a mistake you made
    d. a light flickering on and off during a lecture
    Answer: c   **Type: M**   **Page: 13**   **Application**

83. Decoding is the same as
    a. a self–fulfilling prophecy.
    b. an irrational belief.
    c. interpreting.
    d. encoding.
    e. communication environment.
    Answer: c   **Type: M**   **Page: 10**   **Comprehension**

84. Two friends communicating would most likely be
    a. taking turns sending and receiving messages.
    b. primarily sending messages.
    c. primarily receiving messages.
    d. sending and receiving messages at the same time.
    e. neither sending nor receiving messages.
    Answer: d   **Type: M**   **Page: 11**   **Application**

85. Research on the effects of computer–mediated communication (CMC) indicates that
    a. time online has lessened time spent with family members.
    b. the quality and quantity of interpersonal communication has increased.
    c. communication by CMC is more complex than personal contact.
    d. CMC is reducing interpersonal communication competencies.
    e. all of the above.
    Answer: b   **Type: M**   **Page: 21**   **Analysis**

86. A cognitively complex communicator
    a. considers an issue from several angles.
    b. feels and experiences another's situation.
    c. usually has a high IQ.
    d. observes behavior with detachment.
    e. thinks and reacts quickly.
    Answer: a   **Type: M**   **Page: 38**   **Knowledge**

87. When you call three of your friends in one night to avoid studying, you are communicating to fulfill the social need of
    a. escape.
    b. control.
    c. affection.
    d. companionship.
    e. pleasure.
    Answer: a   **Type: M**   **Page: 8**   **Application**

88. When Susan realizes during an office meeting that she's interrupted a co–worker twice, she demonstrates the skill of
    a. empathy.
    b. self–monitoring.
    c. cognitive complexity
    d. affinity
    e. metacommunication
    Answer: b   **Type: M**   **Page: 38**   **Application**

89. Which of the following is a channel for communication?
    a. touching
    b. writing
    c. gesturing
    d. talking
    e. all of the above
    Answer: e   **Type: M**   **Page: 10**   **Comprehension**

90. Which of the following is a channel for communication?
a. escape
b. control
c. inclusion
d. esteem
e. touch
Answer: e   **Type: M**   **Pages: 10**   **Comprehension**

91. Maslow's hierarchy of human needs lists self–actualization as the highest need. What need is the most fundamental, or the lowest, in Maslow's hierarchy?
a. safety
b. psychological
c. social
d. esteem
e. physical
Answer: e   **Type: M**   **Page: 9**   **Comprehension**

92. Interpersonal relationships
a. develop unique qualities.
b. are mostly alike.
c. follow the same basic rules about how control is distributed between communicators.
d. have more relational talk than content talk.
e. are none of the above.
Answer: a   **Type: M**   **Pages: 19–20**   **Comprehension**

93. Relational dimensions of a message
a. deal with one or more social needs.
b. make statements about how the parties feel toward one another.
c. are usually expressed nonverbally.
d. all of the above
e. none of the above
Answer: d   **Type: M**   **Page: 27**   **Comprehension**

94. Relational dimensions of messages
a. must deal with individual problems and needs.
b. must make statements about facts and thoughts.
c. are usually expressed verbally.
d. all of the above
e. none of the above
Answer: e   **Type: M**   **Page: 27**   **Comprehension**

95. When you are unsure of the relational dimension of a message, it is best to
    a. go with the verbal interpretation.
    b. go with the nonverbal interpretation.
    c. metacommunicate.
    d. listen for all the possible messages.
    e. go back to the content dimension of the message for meaning.
    Answer: c   **Type: M**   **Page: 30**   **Comprehension**

96. Your roommate says, "It's your turn to take out the trash" in a demanding tone of voice. If you want to find out the relational dimension of the message, you should
    a. remind your roommate nicely that you took it out last night.
    b. point out the tone of voice and ask if your roommate is upset with you.
    c. negotiate other ways of dealing with the trash problem.
    d. ask your roommate's friends to explain the real problem.
    e. point out how defensive your roommate sounds.
    Answer: b   **Type: M**   **Page: 30**   **Application**

97. According to Chapter One, the two dimensions of most messages are
    a. content and relational.
    b. verbal and contextual.
    c. semantic and syntactic.
    d. defensive and supportive.
    e. controlling and affecting.
    Answer: a   **Type: M**   **Page: 27**   **Knowledge**

98. In any relationship, the power to determine what will happen in the relationship is a type of relational control called
    a. decision control.
    b. conversational control.
    c. distributional control.
    d. powerful control.
    e. context control.
    Answer: a   **Type: M**   **Page: 30**   **Knowledge**

99. Talking the most, interrupting the other person, and changing the topic most often are all common indicators of
    a. conversational control.
    b. decision control.
    c. powerful control.
    d. context control.
    e. distributional control.
    Answer: a   **Type: M**   **Page: 30**   **Knowledge**

100. Relational dimensions of messages
    a. deal with one or more social needs.
    b. make statements about how the parties feel toward one another.
    c. are usually expressed nonverbally.
    d. all of the above
    e. none of the above
    Answer: d   **Type: M**   **Page: 27**   **Comprehension**

101. Relational dimensions of messages
    a. deal with individual problems and needs.
    b. make statements about facts and thoughts.
    c. are usually expressed verbally.
    d. are usually expressed nonverbally.
    e. tell us the content of the message.
    Answer: d   **Type: M**   **Page: 27**   **Comprehension**

102. Whenever we discuss a relationship with others, we are
    a. arguing.
    b. improving our relationship.
    c. self–disclosing.
    d. metacommunicating.
    e. receiving double messages.
    Answer: d   **Type: M**   **Page: 30**   **Knowledge**

103. The degree to which the partners in an interpersonal relationship like or appreciate one another is called
    a. appreciation.
    b. self–respect.
    c. the communication of honesty.
    d. affinity.
    e. the like–love phenomenon.
    Answer: d   **Type: M**   **Page: 28**   **Knowledge**

104. The ability to construct a variety of different frameworks for viewing an issue is termed
    a. feedback framework.
    b. cognitive complexity.
    c. communication competence.
    d. metacommunicating
    e. integration.
    Answer: b   **Type: M**   **Page: 38**   **Knowledge**

105. Which of the following is true about computer–mediated communication (CMC) as it relates to interpersonal communication?
    a. CMC distances us from one another.
    b. CMC can enhance the quantity and quality of interpersonal.
    c. CMC replaces interpersonal communication.
    d. CMC is an inferior form of communication to interpersonal.
    Answer: b   **Type: M**   **Page: 21**   **Comprehension**

INSTRUCTIONS for questions 106–110: Match each of the statements below with the element of the communication model it illustrates most clearly.

    a.   external noise
    b.   environment
    c.   channel
    d.   decoding
    e.   psychological noise

106. You decide to write your friend a note instead of calling her.
    Answer: c   **Type: Matching**   **Page: 10**   **Application**

107. Alex decides what Dana meant by that scowl.
    Answer: d   **Type: Matching**   **Page: 10**   **Application**

108. Your friend's religion is different from yours, but you went to the same high school and college.
    Answer: b   **Type: Matching**   **Page: 12**   **Evaluation**

109. You are worried about how you'll get home today while your boss is giving the quarterly report.
    Answer: e   **Type: Matching**   **Page: 13**   **Application**

110. A person behind you in the theater fiddles with a crackling cellophane candy wrapper.
    Answer: a   **Type: Matching**   **Page: 13**   **Application**

111. Describe an interpersonal communication incident from your experience, identifying at least five elements of the transactional model of communication shown in *Looking Out/ Looking In.*
    Answer   **Type: E**   **Pages: 11–14**   **Synthesis**

112. Using the characteristics of "Communication Competence: What makes an effective communicator?" Evaluate your communication competence in the context of one interpersonal relationship in which you are involved. Discuss the range of behaviors in which you engage, your ability to choose the most appropriate behavior, your skill in performing certain behaviors, and your commitment to the relationship. Be sure to discuss this relationally, involving the behaviors of the other person, and how you adapt or fail to adapt to them.
    Answer   **Type: E**   **Pages: 32–39**   **Synthesis**

113. Using your own experiences as examples, explain the difference between interpersonal communication and impersonal communication.
    Answer   **Type: E**   **Pages: 19–20**   **Application**

114. Describe how you have filled each of the social needs listed in Chapter One through interpersonal communication.
    Answer   **Type: E**   **Page: 8**   **Application**

115. Explain the concept of "noise." First, define it according to its role in the transactional model of communication in Chapter One. Next, imagine you are being interviewed for a job. Name and give examples of each of the three types of noise described by your text that might be present during this interview experience.
    Answer   **Type: E**   **Page: 13**   **Evaluation**

116. Define the four types of relational messages presented in Chapter One and illustrate each of them with examples from your life.

Answer   **Type: E**   **Pages: 28–29**   **Application**

117. Describe an interpersonal relationship that you are in that involves at least some degree of computer–mediated communication (CMC). List the limitations of CMC in maintaining this relationship. Lastly, describe the ways in which CMC enhances the quantity and/or quality of this relationship.

Answer   **Type: E**   **Pages: 21–23**   **Application**

CHAPTER 2

COMMUNICATION AND IDENTITY:
THE SELF AND MESSAGES

1. Impression management occurs only in face–to–face interactions
   Answer: F   **Type: T**   **Page: 84**   **Knowledge**

2. Research indicates that computer–mediated communication (CMC) offers advantages for impression management.
   Answer: T   **Type: T**   **Page: 84**   **Knowledge**

3. The influence of significant others becomes less powerful as we grow older.
   Answer: T   **Type: T**   **Page: 52**   **Comprehension**

4. The self–concept is extremely resistant to change.
   Answer: T   **Type: T**   **Page: 59**   **Comprehension**

5. People who are confident that others support their presenting selves prefer CMC over face–to–face interaction.
   Answer: F   **Type: T**   **Pages: 72, 85**   **Synthesis**

6. Once formed, a self–concept rarely, if ever, changes.
   Answer: F   **Type: T**   **Page: 59**   **Comprehension**

7. In many cases a self–concept is based on data which may have been true at one time, but are now obsolete.
   Answer: T   **Type: T**   **Page: 59**   **Knowledge**

8. The influence of significant others becomes less powerful as people grow older.
   Answer: T   **Type: T**   **Page: 52**   **Knowledge**

9. The self–concept is extremely subjective, being almost totally a product of interaction with others.
   Answer: T   **Type: T**   **Page: 57**   **Comprehension**

10. You are unlikely to reveal all of the perceived self to another person.
    Answer: T   **Type: T**   **Page: 72**   **Knowledge**

11. People with high self–esteem tend to disapprove of others more than people with low self–esteem.
    Answer: F   **Type: T**   **Page: 58**   **Comprehension**

12. People who think highly of themselves are likely to think highly of others too.
    Answer: T   **Type: T**   **Page: 58**   **Knowledge**

13. Our concept of self is shaped by the culture in which we have been reared.
    Answer: T   **Type: T**   **Page: 61**   **Synthesis**

14. The self–concept is a relatively stable set of perceptions you hold of yourself.
    Answer: T   **Type: T**   **Page: 46**   **Knowledge**

15. The self–concept is a constantly changing set of perceptions that others have of you.
    Answer: F   **Type: T**   **Page: 46**   **Knowledge**

16. Both verbal and nonverbal messages contribute to a developing self–concept.
    Answer: T   **Type: T**   **Page: 54**   **Synthesis**

17. Personality traits are largely a result of genetics rather than of socialization.
    Answer: T   **Type: T**   **Page: 48**   **Knowledge**

18. People who don't like themselves are likely to believe that others don't like them either.
    Answer: T   **Type: T**   **Page: 58**   **Knowledge**

19. We tend to resist revising our own self–concept even if the new self image is more positive.
    Answer: T   **Type: T**   **Page: 60**   **Comprehension**

20. All inaccurate self–concepts are overly negative.
    Answer: F   **Type: T**   **Page: 57**   **Knowledge**

21. It is possible to have a more favorable image of yourself than the objective facts or the opinions of others warrant.
    Answer: T   **Type: T**   **Page: 57**   **Knowledge**

22. The person you believe yourself to be in moments of honesty is called the presenting self.
    Answer: F   **Type: T**   **Page: 72**   **Knowledge**

23. The face you try to show to others is called the perceived self.
    Answer: F   **Type: T**   **Page: 72**   **Knowledge**

24. The text advises that we shouldn't acknowledge our strengths because we will develop overly positive, distorted self–concepts.
    Answer: F   **Type: T**   **Page: 59**   **Comprehension**

25. Most Western cultures have what is called a collective identity.
    Answer: F   **Type: T**   **Page: 61**   **Knowledge**

26. The influence of significant others is more powerful as a person becomes an adult.
    Answer: F   **Type: T**   **Page: 52**   **Knowledge**

27. People commonly seek interaction with others who reinforce their view of themselves, even if that view is negative.
    Answer: F   **Type: T**   **Page: 59**   **Comprehension**

28. Nonverbal behaviors play a big role in managing impressions.
    Answer: T   **Type: T**   **Page: 82**   **Knowledge**

29. The process of impression management can result in dishonest behavior.
    Answer: T   **Type: T**   **Page: 85**   **Knowledge**

30. Most researchers agree that we are born with many of our personality traits.
    Answer: T   **Type: T**   **Page: 48–49**   **Knowledge**

31. According to your text, the self–concept influences much of our communication behavior.
    Answer: T   **Type: T**   **Page: 64**   **Knowledge**

32. According to your text, the self–concept is shaped by communication.
    Answer: T   **Type: T**   **Page: 51–56**   **Knowledge**

33. According to your text, the self–concept is influenced by significant others from both the past and present.
    Answer: T   **Type: T**   **Page: 52**   **Comprehension**

34. Luckily, communication from others does not affect our self–concept.
    Answer: F   **Type: T**   **Pages: 51–56**   **Comprehension**

35. You shouldn't listen to the "boosters" and "busters" others give you since your self–concept is only your view of yourself.
    Answer: F   **Type: T**   **Pages: 51**   **Comprehension**

36. All communication behavior is aimed at making impressions.
    Answer: F   **Type: T**   **Page: 76**   **Comprehension**

37. Research described in your text about CMC (computer–mediated communication) suggests that
    a. it may be an advantage for creating a desired impression.
    b. it permits a responder to ignore a message rather than be unpleasant.
    c. it lacks the "richness" of many nonverbal channels.
    d. all of the above are supported by research.
    e. none of the above are supported by research.
    Answer: d   **Type: M**   **Pages: 84–85**   **Knowledge**

38. In the example of schoolchildren taken from the book Pygmalion in the Classroom
    a. the less intelligent children performed better than expected.
    b. the more intelligent children performed better than expected.
    c. the children teachers predicted would do better, did so.
    d. all the children performed the same because they had similar self–concepts.
    e. teachers improved their self–concepts by working with good children.
    Answer: c   **Type: M**   **Page: 65**   **Recall**

39. Self–fulfilling prophecies are
    a. negative predictions of our behavior, imposed by others.
    b. negative predictions of our behavior, imposed by ourselves.
    c. positive or negative predictions of our behavior, imposed by others and/or ourselves.
    d. almost always negative predictions, imposed by ourselves and/or others.
    e. none of the above.
    Answer: c   **Type: M**   **Pages: 80–81**   **Knowledge**

40. People try to manage their identities in front of others to
     a. maintain a front to follow social rules.
     b. accomplish personal goals.
     c. to gain respect or a sense of belonging.
     d. establish relational control.
     e. all of the above.
     Answer: c   **Type: M**   **Page: 78, 81**   **Comprehension**

41. "Cipher in the Snow" is included in your text to illustrate
     a. the importance of honest self–appraisal.
     b. the impact of dishonest identity management.
     c. the way people construct multiple identities.
     d. the impact of significant others on self–concept
     e. all of the above.
     Answer: d   **Type: M**   **Pages: 55–56**   **Comprehension**

42. Which of the following is definitely not an example of a self–fulfilling prophecy?
     a. A child fails a test after hearing her teacher tell her mother that she is an underachiever.
     b. A student who previously complained of stage fright loses his place during a class speech and can't go on.
     c. A husband reluctantly agrees, with reservations, to his wife's request that they spend the holiday visiting Disneyland. He has a terrible time.
     d. Both b and c above qualify as examples of self–fulfilling prophecies.
     e. All of the above qualify as examples of self–fulfilling prophecies.
     Answer: e   **Type: M**   **Pages: 64–66**   **Analysis**

43. All of the following are methods you could use to make your self–concept more realistic except :
     a. Share your perception of yourself with a friend.
     b. Try to engage in more accurate self–talk.
     c. Make an effort to recognize more "ego buster" messages.
     d. Pay less attention to your past and more attention to your present behavior.
     Answer: c   **Type: M**   **Page: 68–69**   **Analysis**

44. All of the following are true of the self–concept except that
     a. it is objective.
     b. it is changing.
     c. it is, in part, a product of interaction with others.
     d. it is, in part, a product of our early childhood experience.
     e. it can be changed.
     Answer: a   **Type: M**   **Page: 57**   **Comprehension**

45. The term "self–concept" refers to
    a. the sum of one's physiological, social, and psychological attributes as perceived by an impartial observer.
    b. the way an individual believes others perceive her/him.
    c. the total of an individual's beliefs about his/her physical characteristics, intelligence, aptitudes, and social skills.
    d. the sum of one's psychological, social, and physical attributes as perceived by a significant other.
    e. none of the above.
    Answer: c   **Type: M**   **Page: 46**   **Comprehension**

46. A "significant other" is best defined as
    a. a powerful adult.
    b. a person who has affected one's self–concept.
    c. a totally supportive person.
    d. an extremely negative influence.
    e. all of the above.
    Answer: b   **Type: M**   **Page: 52**   **Comprehension**

47. According to your text, "ego–boosters and busters" are
    a. examples of how people ruin their self–concepts by taking drugs.
    b. people or words that influence the self–concept positively or negatively.
    c. the two essential elements of self–concept development.
    d. ways to predict how children will become good or bad readers.
    e. intentionally vague labels we give to mask true self–concepts.
    Answer: b   **Type: M**   **Pages: 50–51**   **Knowledge**

48. The higher levels of anxiety about speaking out in countries such as China, Korea, and Japan indicate that
    a. shyness is a problem in some cultures.
    b. reticence is valued in these cultures.
    c. assertiveness has not been taught correctly.
    d. the individualistic identity is better than the collective one.
    e. children are not taught public speaking in these countries.
    Answer: b   **Type: M**   **Page: 61**   **Comprehension**

49. People who are high self–monitors
    a. are much more aware of their impression management behavior than others.
    b. express what they are feeling without paying much attention to the impression their behavior creates.
    c. are usually bad actors.
    d. are not usually good "people readers."
    e. are easier to "read" than low self–monitors.
    Answer: a   **Type: M**   **Pages: 77**   **Comprehension**

50. The relatively stable set of perceptions you hold of yourself is called your
    a. self–concept.
    b. interpersonal self.
    c. perceptual bias.
    d. self–feedback.
    e. self–orientation.
    Answer: a   **Type: M**   **Page: 46**   **Knowledge**

51. A self–fulfilling prophecy is
    a. an accurate prediction about another's behavior, based on background
        knowledge.
    b. a prediction about one's own behavior, based on past experience.
    c. a prediction which affects the outcome of one's own or another's behavior.
    d. a mistaken prediction which fails to occur.
    e. none of the above.
    Answer: c   **Type: M**   **Page: 64**   **Comprehension**

52. In individualistic cultures, a view of self would involve all of the following except
    a. self–sufficiency.
    b. high value on tradition.
    c. high value on equality.
    d. high value on change.
    e. personal credit or blame.
    Answer: b   **Type: M**   **Page: 61**   **Comprehension**

53. A self–fulfilling prophecy is, in part,
    a. a way to discover how to act in the future.
    b. a test one can take to gauge one's self–concept.
    c. a way to discover the "real you."
    d. a prediction which affects behavior.
    e. a process to help you feel more satisfied with relationships.
    Answer: d   **Type: M**   **Page: 64**   **Comprehension**

54. Someone who is a "significant other" is
    a. "socially" conscious.
    b. a person whose opinion we especially value.
    c. always a supportive person.
    d. a person with significant goals.
    Answer: b   **Type: M**   **Page: 52**   **Knowledge**

55. A person whose opinions of you matter deeply is called a(n)
    a. all–knowing adult.
    b. superior.
    c. nonverbal influence.
    d. significant other.
    e. dyad.
    Answer: d   **Type: M**   **Page: 52**   **Comprehension**

56. The self–concept
    a. causes all of our communication behavior.
    b. prevents low self–esteem.
    c. is partially shaped by significant others from our past.
    d. is the way significant others will view us in the future.
    Answer: c   **Type: M**   **Pages: 46**   **Synthesis**

57. If you want to change your self–concept, you should
    a. have realistic expectations and perceptions.
    b. ask others to send you only positive messages.
    c. take yourself less seriously.
    d. It is not possible to change the self–concept.
    Answer: a   **Type: M**   **Pages: 67–69**   **Comprehension**

58. People who have low self–esteem
    a. are likely to approve of others.
    b. perform well when being watched.
    c. work harder for critical people.
    d. expect to be rejected by others.
    e. had traumatic childhoods.
    Answer: d   **Type: M**   **Page: 58**   **Comprehension**

59. People who have high self–esteem
    a. expect to be accepted by others.
    b. have less of a need to work hard for people who demand high standards.
    c. are unable to defend themselves against negative comments.
    d. don't perform well when being watched.
    Answer: a   **Type: M**   **Page: 58**   **Comprehension**

60. The process of judging ourselves by how we think others evaluate or judge us is called
    a. the "sell–out" self.
    b. self–matching.
    c. reflected appraisal.
    d. totality viewing.
    e. the feedback self.
    Answer: c   **Type: M**   **Page: 51**   **Knowledge**

61. The kind of person you believe yourself to be is called the
    a. perceived self.
    b. desired self.
    c. presenting self.
    d. myth of self.
    e. transient self.
    Answer: a   **Type: M**   **Page: 72**   **Knowledge**

62. All of the following are examples of social comparison <u>except</u>
    a. being judged for a test based on other student's grades.
    b. thinking over how you have added muscle mass in the last four months.
    c. being offered a job after several competitive interviews.
    d. judging your fitness level in contrast to others in the gym.
    e. all of the above are examples of social comparison.
    Answer: b   **Type: M**   **Page: 72**   **Application**

63. The most significant part of one person's self–concept is
    a. social roles.
    b. appearance.
    c. health.
    d. accomplishments.
    e. dependent on the individual.
    Answer: e   **Type: M**   **Page: 46–50**   **Analysis**

64. During childhood, the self–concept is affected by what type(s) of behavior of others?
    a. verbal
    b. nonverbal
    c. verbal and nonverbal
    d. only positive behavior
    e. only negative behavior
    Answer: c   **Type: M**   **Page: 51–54**   **Application**

65. "Reference groups" are
    a. people whose self–concepts we have influenced.
    b. individuals whose self–esteem has been diminished.
    c. groups against which a person compares him/herself.
    d. groups formed to improve shaky self–esteem.
    e. people who hang around the library.
    Answer: c   **Type: M**   **Page: 54**   **Knowledge**

66. According to your text, the word "can't" often serves to
    a. let others share control in the relationship.
    b. help us accept our limitations.
    c. create a self–fulfilling prophecy.
    d. express equality through our humanity.
    Answer: c   **Type: M**   **Page: 69**   **Analysis**

67. Jane did better than Barbara on the math test. Jane can't do math as well as Barbara normally, but her teacher kept telling her how smart she was, and how her hard work would help her do better on the test. The fact that Jane did do better because of her own expectations is an example of
    a. distorted feedback.
    b. a good math teacher.
    c. clear message format.
    d. defensiveness.
    e. a self–fulfilling prophecy.
    Answer: e   **Type: M**   **Page: 64**   **Application**

68. When trying to change one's self–concept, it is important to remember all of the following except that
    a. one should set realistic goals.
    b. one should have a real desire to change.
    c. one should expect rapid change.
    d. one should possess the skills to change.
    e. all of the above
    Answer: c   **Type: M**   **Pages: 68–69**   **Comprehension**

69. Which of the following would definitely <u>not</u> contribute to the formation of a self–concept?
    a. promotion to a more responsible job
    b. a conversational partner who blames you for fights
    c. having one's birthday or anniversary forgotten
    d. having one's child win a scholarship
    e. All of the above might contribute.
    Answer: e   **Type: M**   **Pages: 51–54**   **Application**

70. Negative self–fulfilling prophecies you impose upon yourself are a form of
    a. psychological noise.
    b. inclusion need.
    c. reflected appraisal.
    d. the presenting self.
    e. none of the above.
    Answer: a   **Type: M**   **Pages: 13, 65**   **Synthesis**

71. If you want to feel more self–confident when meeting new people, your text advised you to
    a. subscribe to the myth of perfection.
    b. compare yourself to reference groups above you.
    c. quit thinking you can change.
    d. disregard obsolete or inaccurate feedback.
    Answer: d   **Type: M**   **Pages: 56**   **Analysis**

72. All of the following are examples of social comparison except
    a. being graded for a test on a class curve.
    b. judging your attractiveness while working out at Nautilus gym.
    c. reflecting on how you've changed in the last year.
    d. being offered a job after competitive interviews.
    e. All of the above are examples of social comparison.
    Answer: c   **Type: M**   **Page: 52**   **Application**

73. Nonverbal messages we receive from significant others about our competence are always a kind of
    a. self–fulfilling prophecy.
    b. feedback.
    c. positive influence.
    d. defensiveness.
    e. competitive symmetry
    Answer: b   **Type: M**   **Page: 10, 51**   **Synthesis**

74. A self–fulfilling prophecy is
    a. a way to discover how to act in the future.
    b. a test one can take to analyze one's self–concept.
    c. a way to discover the "real you."
    d. an expectation that affects behavior.
    e. a psychological form of extrasensory perception
    Answer: d   **Type: M**   **Page: 64**   **Comprehension**

75. The tendency to seek and attend to information that conforms to an existing self–concept has been labeled
    a. reflected appraisal.
    b. significance posturing.
    c. the stability hypothesis.
    d. cognitive conservatism.
    e. the weak spine phenomenon.
    Answer: d   **Type: M**   **Page: 59**   **Knowledge**

76. The tendency to look for people who confirm our existing self–concept is termed
    a. behavioral conservatism.
    b. self–verification.
    c. cognitive monitoring.
    d. self–fulfillment.
    e. relational prophecy.
    Answer: b   **Type: M**   **Page: 56**   **Knowledge**

77. The communication strategies people use to influence how others view them is the process of
    a. ego–video.
    b. reflected appraisal.
    c. manipulation.
    d. social ethics.
    e. identity management.
    Answer: e   **Type: M**   **Page: 71**   **Knowledge**

78. People try to shape the opinion others have of them in order to
    a. get feedback.
    b. manipulate cognitive complexity.
    c. get affiliation or respect.
    d. establish effective listening patterns.
    Answer: c   **Type: M**   **Page: 78–81**   **Comprehension**

INSTRUCTIONS for questions 79–83: Match each description below with the most accurate term.

    a. reflected appraisal
    b. significant other
    c. self–fulfilling prophecy
    d. presenting self
    e. perceived self

79. The private self you honestly believe you are
    Answer: e   **Type: Matching**   **Page: 72**   **Knowledge**

80. A prediction that affects behavior
    Answer: c   **Type: Matching**   **Page: 64**   **Knowledge**

81. A person whose opinion we especially value
    Answer: b   **Type: Matching**   **Page: 52**   **Knowledge**

82. Process of judging ourselves by the evaluations of others
    Answer: a   **Type: Matching**   **Page: 51**   **Knowledge**

83. The "face" you show to others
    Answer: d   **Type: Matching**   **Page: 73**   **Knowledge**

84. Pick the three most important communication–related "cant's" (using the exercise on page 69 in your text or exercise 2.4 in your activities manual). Next, explain whether each item is really a "can't," a "won't," or a "don't know how." Next, describe how that item affects your relationship with the person in question. Finally, explain how happy or unhappy you are with each item and what, if anything, you could do to change it.
    Answer   **Type: E**   **Page: 69**   **Evaluation**

85. Barry Stevens's piece in the text entitled "Will the Real Me Please Stand Up?" talks about a split between the basic spirit and that which is learned through experience—the social self. From your own background, explain the nature of this split, the struggle between different aspects of the self, and talk about its effect on your self–concept.
    Answer   **Type: E**   **Pages: 79–80**   **Synthesis**

86. Explain two recent changes that took place in your self–concept. Indicate how communication influenced the change.
    Answer   **Type: E**   **Pages: 67–69**   **Analysis**

87. Describe two people for whom you are a significant other. Describe your communication behavior with each of them, giving examples of how (a) you deliver "booster" and "buster" messages to each of them; (b) you create self–fulfilling prophecies that work for and against each of them; and (c) they allow your communication with them to affect their behavior.
    Answer   **Type: E**   **Pages: 50–69**   **Synthesis**

88. Describe a recent self–fulfilling prophecy which you have imposed upon yourself that affects your communication. In what cases have you imposed it? What have the results been? How realistic was the prophecy? Does answering these questions change how you'll talk to yourself in the future? How? Next, describe a self–fulfilling prophecy you have imposed upon another person. How did you communicate it (i.e., what messages did you send, and what channels did you use)? What effect did your prophecy have upon your partner? Does answering this question affect how you'll communicate with the other person in the future? How?

Answer   **Type: E**   **Pages: 64–67**   **Evaluation**

89. We have certain expectations which are products of our prejudices. How do you think these expectations have affected certain groups of people (e.g., blacks, Chicanos, women, college students, the elderly)? Select two groups of people you think have been affected by prejudice, and explain how reflected appraisal influences identity.

Answer   **Type: E**   **Pages: 51–5**   **Evaluation**

90. Explain how you managed impressions with others in a recent important event in your life. Cite the reasons why you managed impressions and then evaluate the way you presented yourself.

Answer   **Type: E**   **Pages: 82–84**   **Analysis**

91. Describe how you have managed your manner, appearance, and setting to create desired impressions in two different specific instances.

Answer   **Type: E**   **Pages: 82–84**   **Application**

CHAPTER 3

PERCEPTION:
WHAT YOU SEE IS WHAT YOU GET

1. While culture has a great deal to do with our perception, it is understood that self–esteem and moods of a person do not.
   Answer: F   **Type: T**   **Page: 103–4. 112**   **Knowledge**

2. It is human nature to assume other people are essentially the same as ourselves.
   Answer: F   **Type: T**   **Page: 114**   **Knowledge**

3. Perception checking is a type of metacommunication.
   Answer: T   **Type: T**   **Page: 115–116, 30**   **Synthesis**

4. The text argues that an ailment may have a strong impact on how you relate to others.
   Answer: T   **Type: T**   **Page: 102**   **Knowledge**

5. Total empathy is impossible to achieve.
   Answer: T   **Type: T**   **Page: 121**   **Knowledge**

6. Practicing empathy tends to make people more tolerant of others.
   Answer: T   **Type: T**   **Page: 119**   **Comprehension**

7. It's hardest to empathize with people who are radically different from us.
   Answer: T   **Type: T**   **Page: 119**   **Comprehension**

8. In order to understand another's thinking on an issue empathetically, you must accept it as being valid or true.
   Answer: F   **Type: T**   **Page: 119**   **Comprehension**

9. It is necessary to feel sympathy in order to truly empathize with another person.
   Answer: F   **Type: T**   **Page: 119**   **Knowledge**

10. Identical foods can actually taste different to various individuals.
    Answer: T   **Type: T**   **Page: 102**   **Knowledge**

11. Sensory data can be different to different people.
    Answer: T   **Type: T**   **Page: 102**   **Knowledge**

12. Periodic changes (hormonal, emotional) in men and women are all in their minds, but they try to blame them on physical factors.
    Answer: F   **Type: T**   **Pages: 103**   **Comprehension**

13. We can change our emotional cycles by refusing to let biology interfere with our lives.
    Answer: F   **Type: T**   **Page: 103**   **Comprehension**

14. Since older people have a greater number of experiences from which to draw, their perceptions are more accurate than those of younger people.
    Answer: F   **Type: T**   **Page: 102**   **Comprehension**

15. We are influenced more by subtle stimuli rather than obvious ones.
    Answer: F   **Type: T**   **Page: 93**   **Knowledge**

16. In our perceptions, we cling more strongly to first impressions, even when they are wrong.
    Answer: T   **Type: T**   **Page: 114**   **Knowledge**

17. In our perceptions, we tend to assume that others are similar to us.
    Answer: T   **Type: T**   **Page: 114**   **Knowledge**

18. Your text points out that people with high self–esteem are quicker to assume the worst possible motives on the part of others.
    Answer: F   **Type: T**   **Page: 112**   **Knowledge**

19. In perceiving others, we usually blame their problems on their personal qualities rather than on factors outside them.
    Answer: T   **Type: T**   **Page: 112**   **Knowledge**

20. Since we are the ones who experience reality, we have a complete idea of what that reality is.
    Answer: F   **Type: T**   **Page: 93**   **Comprehension**

21. Luckily, we've been gifted with our senses, which usually make us aware of all that is going on around us.
    Answer: F   **Type: T**   **Pages: 101–102**   **Comprehension**

22. It's simply impossible to be aware of everything, no matter how attentive we may be.
    Answer: T   **Type: T**   **Pages: 93**   **Analysis**

23. Since stimuli that are intense often attract our attention, we're more likely to remember extremely talkative people than those who are quiet.
    Answer: T   **Type: T**   **Page: 93**   **Knowledge**

24. Most of the time, people to whom we're repetitiously exposed become noticeable.
    Answer: T   **Type: T**   **Page: 94**   **Comprehension**

25. Unchanging people or things become less noticeable, and thus occupy less of our attention than those that change.
    Answer: T   **Type: T**   **Page: 94**   **Comprehension**

26. Selection is an objective process.
    Answer: F   **Type: T**   **Page: 93–94**   **Comprehension**

27. No two people perceive a given set of sense data identically.
    Answer: T   **Type: T**   **Page: 93–94**   **Comprehension**

28. The sensory data we receive are the same for all of us; perceptual differences occur only after we begin to process those data.
    Answer: F   **Type: T**   **Page: 93–94**   **Comprehension**

29. After using the "Pillow Method" you should typically conclude that the issue being considered is not important enough to worry about.
    Answer: F   **Type: T**   **Page: 121–123**   **Comprehension**

30. Effective interpersonal communication between two persons would tend to narrow their perceptual differences.
    Answer: T   **Type: T**   **Pages: 118–119**   **Analysis**

The "halo effect" is a perceptual tendency which causes us to be more generous in our judgment of ourselves over others.
    Answer: F   **Type: T**   **Page: 114**   **Knowledge**

32. People's occupations have little bearing on their perception of the world.
    Answer: F   **Type: T**   **Page: 109**   **Knowledge**

33. Only women are affected by changes in mood.
    Answer: F   **Type: T**   **Page: 103**   **Comprehension**

34. The self–serving bias illustrates our tendency to judge others more charitably than ourselves.
    Answer: F   **Type: T**   **Page: 112**   **Knowledge**

35. An individual's idea of reality is incomplete.
    Answer: T   **Type: T**   **Page: 93**   **Synthesis**

36. True empathy involves agreeing with the other person's point of view.
    Answer: F   **Type: T**   **Page: 119**   **Comprehension**

37. Your text claims that there is nothing wrong with the generalizations we make, using our organization constructs, as long as they are accurate.
    Answer: T   **Type: T**   **Page: 95–96**   **Knowledge**

38. Punctuation is the process of organizing a series of events to determine causes and effects.
    Answer: T   **Type: T**   **Page: 97**   **Knowledge**

39. According to your text, each of us experiences a different reality.
    Answer: T   **Type: T**   **Page: 93**   **Knowledge**

40. Silence is valued over talk in most Asian cultures.
    Answer: T   **Type: T**   **Page: 105**   **Knowledge**

41. The three phases of perception—selection, organization, and interpretation—can occur in differing sequences.
    Answer: T   **Type: T**   **Page: 100**   **Knowledge**

42. Whites are more likely than blacks to use eye contact as a measure of how closely the other person is listening.
    Answer: T   **Type: T**   **Page: 107**   **Knowledge**

43. According to your text, unhappy spouses are more likely than happy ones to make negative interpretations of their mates' behavior.
Answer: T   **Type: T**   **Page: 100**   **Knowledge**

44. In Philip Zimbardo's mock prison experiment, described in Chapter Three, illustrated the perceptual influence of _____ in the behavior changes noticed.
a. hunger and fatigue
b. biological cycles
c. gender
d. occupational roles
e. culture
Answer: d   **Type: M**   **Pages: 110**   **Comprehension**

45. The Pillow Method is designed to
a. persuade someone to accept your viewpoint.
b. settle a dispute.
c. minimize an issue.
d. gain insight into another's viewpoint.
e. punctuate the cause and effect of an argument.
Answer: d   **Type: M**   **Page: 100**   **Comprehension**

46. The story in your text about six men from Indostan illustrates
a. the phenomenon called "culture shock."
b. the way people tend to punctuate a series of events differently.
c. the "Pillow Method" applied to resolve a problem.
d. different interpretations depending on point of view.
e. self–serving bias.
Answer: d   **Type: M**   **Page: 122**   **Comprehension**

47. In a perception reading in Chapter Three, a police officer temporarily assumed the role of a derelict and
a. was shot by another officer.
b. was recognized by a fellow officer.
c. was beaten up by a street gang.
d. panicked and identified himself to other officers.
e. prevented a robbery while in disguise.
Answer: d   **Type: M**   **Pages: 111**   **Recall**

48. All of the following would be included in a good definition of empathy except:
a. It helps rid communication of an indifferent quality.
b. It minimizes threat to self–concept.
c. It includes nonverbal behavior.
d. It is likely to reduce defensiveness.
e. It involves agreeing with the other's position.
Answer: e   **Type: M**   **Page: 118–119**   **Synthesis**

49.   A perception check includes
    a.   a description of the behavior you have noticed.
    b.   two possible interpretations of the behavior.
    c.   a request for clarification about how to interpret the behavior correctly.
    d.   all of the above
    e.   none of the above

Answer: d   **Type: M**   **Page: 115–116**   **Knowledge**

50.   What's missing from this perception check? "When you didn't do the grocery shopping today like you usually do, I figured you weren't feeling good or were mad at me."
    a.   It doesn't describe behavior.
    b.   It has only one interpretation.
    c.   It doesn't request clarification.
    d.   It is too specific.
    e.   Nothing is missing from this perception check.

Answer: c   **Type: M**   **Page: 115–116**   **Application**

51.   What's missing from this perception check? "I figure you're either upset with me or worried about your test. Is it something like that?"
    a.   It doesn't describe behavior.
    b.   It has only one interpretation.
    c.   It doesn't request clarification.
    d.   It is too wordy.
    e.   Nothing is missing from this perception check.

Answer: a   **Type: M**   **Page: 115–116**   **Application**

52.   What's missing from this perception check? "When I saw you having lunch with Emily, I figured you liked her more than me. What's going on?"
    a.   It doesn't describe behavior.
    b.   It has only one interpretation.
    c.   It doesn't request clarification.
    d.   It is too wordy.
    e.   Nothing is missing from this perception check.

Answer: b   **Type: M**   **Page: 115–116**   **Application**

53.   What's missing from this perception check? "When you bought that pink shirt, I figured you did it just to please me or really liked how you looked in it. Why did you buy it?"
    a.   It doesn't describe behavior.
    b.   It has only one interpretation.
    c.   It doesn't request clarification.
    d.   It is too wordy.
    e.   Nothing is missing from this perception check.

Answer: e   **Type: M**   **Page: 115–116**   **Application**

54. How could you improve this perception–checking statement? "When you gave me an F on my essay, I figured you hated me. Right?"
    a. Describe behavior.
    b. Give another interpretation.
    c. Request clarification.
    d. Say less.
    e. It is great as a perception–checking statement just the way it is.
    Answer: b   Type: M   Page: 115–116   Analysis

55. Communicating to a friend how sorry you are about the breakup of his or her romance is an example of
    a. sympathy.
    b. role–taking.
    c. perception–checking.
    d. assumption.
    Answer: a   Type: M   Page: 119   Application

56. All of the following are physiological factors shaping perception except:
    a. the senses.
    b. age and health.
    c. fatigue.
    d. ethnicity.
    e. hunger.
    Answer: d   Type: M   Pages: 101–102   Knowledge

57. The recognition of a "figure" as standing out from a "ground" of other stimuli takes place during what phase of the perception process?
    a. ideation
    b. stimulation
    c. verification
    d. organization
    e. sensation
    Answer: d   Type: M   Page: 94   Knowledge

58. All of the following perceptual factors influence the way we interpret behavior except:
    a. relational satisfaction
    b. assumptions about human behavior
    c. androgynous style
    d. past experience
    e. expectations
    Answer: c   Type: M   Pages: 99–100   Comprehension

59. All of the following are terms to describe the ability to put ourselves into another person's shoes (to view an experience from his or her perspective) except:
    a. sympathy.
    b. empathy.
    c. role–taking.
    d. perspective–taking.
    Answer: a   **Type: M**   **Page: 119**   **Analysis**

60. Talk is viewed as desirable and useful for both task and social purposes in
    a. Western culture.
    b. Asian culture.
    c. upper– and middle–class groups.
    d. older people.
    e. all of the above.
    Answer: a   **Type: M**   **Page: 105**   **Knowledge**

61. Which of the following statements is not true?
    a. People agree about what smells good or bad.
    b. People's sensitivity to temperature varies significantly.
    c. Odors that please some people repel others.
    d. Men have mood cycles of ups and downs.
    e. All of the above are true.
    Answer: a   **Type: M**   **Pages: 101–103**   **Analysis**

62. We notice some stimuli over others in our environment because they are
    a. mild.
    b. singular.
    c. contrasting or changing.
    d. related to modular communication.
    Answer: c   **Type: M**   **Pages: 94**   **Knowledge**

63. The three stages in the perception process are
    a. initial, intermediate, final.
    b. assumption, experience, expectation.
    c. physical, psychological, experimental.
    d. selection, organization, interpretation.
    e. response, action, interaction.
    Answer: d   **Type: M**   **Pages: 93–100**   **Comprehension**

64. Over lunch Susan and James discuss the committee meeting they just left. She asks James if he thought that the other members of the group seemed preoccupied and anxious. James thinks back and says, *"I hadn't noticed it then, but now you mention it, I do think several people looked worried about something."* James' interpretation of the meeting was influenced by
    a. self–serving bias.
    b. narrative.
    c. punctuation.
    d. social roles.
    Answer: b   **Type: M**   **Pages: 100**   **Application**

65. In order to understand another person's perception of a problem, it is necessary to
    a. assume that person's social role.
    b. spend time in that person's culture or subculture.
    c. experience that person's physiological differences.
    d. all of the above
    e. none of the above
    Answer: e   **Type: M**   **Page: 119**   **Synthesis**

66. Empathy is related to perception in that
    a. the more perceptive you are, the less empathetic you need be.
    b. the more perceptive you are, the easier it is to forget to be empathetic.
    c. empathy is facilitated by trying to perceive things from the other person's point of view.
    d. empathy and perception are both a result of self–fulfilling prophecies.
    Answer: c   **Type: M**   **Page: 119**   **Analysis**

67. Curt made a poor first impression on Carol as he first arrived, so throughout their evening date, despite his pleasant behavior, Carol continued to see him in an unfavorable light due to
    a. her feelings of empathy.
    b. the halo effect.
    c. her punctuation of the events of the evening.
    d. the narrative of the date.
    e. physiological factors influencing Carol's perception.
    Answer: b   **Type: M**   **Page: 114**   **Application**

68. All of the following are causes of inaccurate perception except
    a. We cling to first impressions.
    b. We're influenced by what is most obvious.
    c. We assume others are similar to us.
    d. We rate ourselves more negatively than others see us.
    e. We judge ourselves more charitably than others.
    Answer: d   **Type: M**   **Pages: 112–114**   **Comprehension**

69. When you can't find any reasons to accept the behavior of another person, it can be helpful to
    a. use perception checking.
    b. examine your own self–concept.
    c. use a different communication channel.
    d. use the Pillow Method.
    e. reduce the level of feedback.
    Answer: d   **Type: M**   **Page: 121**   **Evaluation**

70. Being able to pick out your sister's statements from a babble of voices at a party illustrates the organizational principle of
     a. figure–ground organization.
     b. alternative patterning.
     c. perceptual freezing.
     d. selection of empathetic other.
     e. attention to the irritating.
     Answer: a   **Type: M**   **Page: 94**   **Application**

71. Classifying people according to age, sex, and physical attractiveness, rather than education or occupation, illustrates the cognitive framework called
     a. figure–ground organization.
     b. perceptual schema.
     c. perceptual freezing.
     d. selection.
     e. selective attention.
     Answer: b   **Type: M**   **Page: 94**   **Application**

72. Five–year–old Johnny picks out his friend Matt because he is also five and he likes Legos. Johnny never even realizes that Matt's skin is a different color from his own or that his family goes to a different church. This illustrates the organizing framework called
     a. organizational clusters.
     b. perceptual schema.
     c. perceptual freezing.
     d. evolutional selection.
     e. trivial attention.
     Answer: b   **Type: M**   **Page: 94**   **Application**

73. Two people organize a series of events in different ways; the man says that he goes out drinking with the guys because she always fusses at him when he gets home; she says she fusses at him when he gets home because he always goes out drinking after work. This process of organizing events in different ways is called
     a. selection.
     b. interpretation.
     c. omission.
     d. punctuation.
     e. blocking.
     Answer: d   **Type: M**   **Page: 97**   **Comprehension**

74. Perception checking focuses on what part of the perception process?
     a. selection
     b. organization
     c. interpretation
     d. all of the above
     e. none of the above
     Answer: d   **Type: M**   **Pages: 115–116**   **Synthesis**

75. Shannon says that she works out in the evenings instead of the afternoons because Roger is always late coming home from work. Roger says he doesn't bother to rush home from work because Shannon is always working out. This process of organizing the series of events in different ways is called
    a. punctuation.
    b. interpretation.
    c. perceptuation.
    d. conjugation.
    e. intrepidation.
    Answer: a   **Type: M**   **Page: 97**   **Application**

76. The term that refers to men and women possessing a mixture of traits that have previously been considered exclusively masculine or feminine is
    a. chauvinistic.
    b. adaptable.
    c. rhetorically sensitive.
    d. androgynous.
    e. analogous.
    Answer: d   **Type: M**   **Page: 109**   **Knowledge**

77. What's missing from this perception check? "I'm not sure you bought me that present as a genuine thank you, or if you were hoping I'd be less angry about what you said last night. I'd like to know what your reason was."
    a. It doesn't describe behavior.
    b. It has only one interpretation.
    c. It doesn't request clarification.
    d. It is too wordy.
    e. Nothing is missing from this perception check.
    Answer: e   **Type: M**   **Page: 115–116**   **Application**

78. Using the skill of perception checking will help prevent
    a. negative self–fulfilling prophecies.
    b. physiological noise.
    c. inaccurate decoding of messages.
    d. excessive feedback.
    e. none of the above.
    Answer: c   **Type: M**   **Page: 115–116**   **Synthesis**

79. Exaggerated beliefs associated with a perceptual categorizing system are
    a. role constructs.
    b. self–judgments.
    c. white lies.
    d. subcultural translations.
    e. stereotypes.
    Answer: e   **Type: M**   **Page: 96**   **Knowledge**

INSTRUCTIONS for questions 80–84: Match each of the descriptions below with the term it best describes.

    a.   punctuation
    b.   interpretation
    c.   empathy
    d.   attribution
    e.   androgynous behavior

80.   You communicate your understanding of a friend's housing problem to that friend.
    Answer: c   **Type: Matching**   **Page: 118**   **Application**

81.   You exhibit both sensitivity and strength when faced with a difficult decision.
    Answer: e   **Type: Matching**   **Page: 109**   **Application**

82.   You say you're late because your partner is never ready on time; your partner says she takes her time getting ready because you're always late.
    Answer: a   **Type: Matching**   **Page: 97**   **Application**

83.   You think all children are hyperactive.
    Answer: d   **Type: Matching**   **Page: 112**   **Application**

84.   You figure your friend's smile means she's happy.
    Answer: b   **Type: Matching**   **Page: 99–100**   **Application**

INSTRUCTIONS for questions 85–89: Match each of the descriptions below with the term it best describes.

    a.   self–serving bias
    b.   organization
    c.   sympathy
    d.   narrative
    e.   selection

85.   You hear the laugh of your boss in a crowded, noisy room.
    Answer: b   **Type: Matching**   **Page: 94**   **Application**

86.   You notice car advertisements more when you need a new car.
    Answer: e   **Type: Matching**   **Page: 93–94**   **Application**

87.   You show you're sorry that your friend was robbed.
    Answer: c   **Type: Matching**   **Page: 119**   **Application**

88.   You claim your roommates are lazy when they don't clean up, but when you fail to clean, it's because of your many commitments.
    Answer: a   **Type: Matching**   **Page: 112**   **Application**

89.   Your interaction with your coworkers creates a shared perspective of your boss.
    Answer: d   **Type: Matching**   **Page: 100**   **Application**

INSTRUCTIONS for questions 90–97: Match each of the perceptual schema examples below with constructs that describe it.

    a. appearance
    b. social roles
    c. interaction style
    d. psychological trait
    e. membership

90. Jeri thinks Alicia is a typical lawyer.
    Answer: b   **Type: Matching**   **Pages: 94–95**   **Application**

91. Bertha did not want to associate with the girl wearing a ring in her nose.
    Answer: a   **Type: Matching**   **Pages: 94–95**   **Application**

92. " Hi, Janina's mother," the new playgroup member said.
    Answer: b   **Type: Matching**   **Pages: 94–95**   **Application**

93. Darin decided LuAnn was insecure when he heard her ask for help twice.
    Answer: d   **Type: Matching**   **Pages: 94–95**   **Application**

94. "Chad's the organizer in our group," Linda said.
    Answer: c   **Type: Matching**   **Pages: 94–95**   **Application**

95. "That's just what a Democrat would say," Mario thought.
    Answer: e   **Type: Matching**   **Pages: 94–95**   **Application**

96. The bartender decided to ask the woman for identification to prove she was 21.
    Answer: a   **Type: Matching**   **Pages: 94–95**   **Application**

97. Alexandria thought John was friendly from the first time they met.
    Answer: c   **Type: Matching**   **Pages: 94–95**   **Application**

INSTRUCTIONS for questions 98–102: Match each of the descriptions below with the term it best describes.

    a. punctuation
    b. interpretation
    c. empathy
    d. organization
    e. selection

98. Your friend comes into the room and slams the door, so you assume he is angry with you.
    Answer: b   **Type: Matching**   **Pages: 99–100**   **Application**

99. As you listen to a classmate give a speech you notice her saying "you know" and "um" many times.
    Answer: e   **Type: Matching**   **Pages: 93–94**   **Application**

100. She says she's forced to tell him over and over to pick up his things because he never listens to her. He says he has to "tune her out" because she is always complaining about something.
    Answer: a   **Type: Matching**   **Pages: 97**   **Application**

101. You tell your friend that you understand why he was confused by an instructor's reaction.
Answer: c   **Type: Matching**   **Pages: 118**   **Application**

102. Explain the differences between understanding someone and agreeing with him/her. Use a specific interpersonal example from your own life.
Answer   **Type: E**   **Pages: 122–123**   **Analysis**

103. Identify a situation from your recent experience in which you disagree with another person due to differing physiological environments. Show how these different environments led to the disagreement.
Answer   **Type: E**   **Pages: 103–104**   **Synthesis**

104. Describe the four perceptual accuracies/inaccuracies identified by researchers in Chapter Three. What role has each played/not played in the formation of your perceptions of three people important to you?
Answer   **Type: E**   **Pages: 116–119**   **Application**

105. Apply the Pillow Method to an interpersonal issue which has recently affected you. Describe your thoughts and feelings at each position on the pillow.
Answer   **Type: E**   **Pages: 125–128**   **Synthesis**

106. Describe two people with whom you live, work, or study. For each person, (a) record at least five of your perceptions of the person, and (b) describe the perceptual influence factors (listed on pages 103–115 in your text) that contribute to each of your perceptions.
Answer   **Type: E**   **Pages: 103–115**   **Application**

107. Your text identified a variety of influences on perception. Name two of these categories of influence and apply them to the situation described below in terms of their effect on your interpretation of the event.
The situation: Imagine you've been walking down the street with another friend. You both are aware that three individuals have been walking behind you for some time. As you turn into a restaurant and sit down, the other three enter and take a booth directly behind you and your friend.
Answer   **Type: E**   **Pages: 101–112**   **Application**

(NOTE: The following essay questions work best as "take–home" exams because of the time necessary to effectively complete them.)

108. Imagine yourself a member of the opposite sex. Describe all the events of a particular day from the vantage point of your "new" sex. What clothes would you want to wear? How would you greet your friends? How would you eat? How would you play? How would your perceptions of the world change? Be very specific and use concrete examples as well as vocabulary items from this chapter.
Answer   **Type: E**   **Page: 110**   **Evaluation**

109. Describe a subculture to which you belong. Give examples and explain several misunderstandings you have had with members of another subculture. What do these misunderstandings indicate about the way in which you view the world? Use terms and theory from text.
Answer   **Type: E**   **Pages: 105–108**   **Evaluation**

CHAPTER 4

EMOTIONS: THINKING, FEELING, AND COMMUNICATING

1. People who act out their anger generally feel better than those who express anger without physically lashing out.
   Answer: F   **Type: T**   **Page: 148**   **Knowledge**

2. Generally speaking, people are more likely to share negative emotions rather than positive emotions.
   Answer: F   **Type: T**   **Pages: 142**   **Knowledge**

3. Historically, people were discouraged from expressing the level of anger that is currently tolerated by contemporary society.
   Answer: F   **Type: T**   **Page: 142**   **Knowledge**

4. Social rules discourage too much expression of negative emotion, but there are really no social limits to expressing positive emotions.
   Answer: F   **Type: T**   **Page: 142**   **Knowledge**

5. Men are more likely than women are to reveal their strengths and positive emotions.
   Answer: T   **Type: T**   **Page: 147**   **Comprehension**

6. Research indicates that people from warmer climates are more emotionally expressive than people from cooler climates.
   Answer: T   **Type: T**   **Page: 139**   **Knowledge**

7. People all over the world tend to express sadness, anger, and joy the same way facially.
   Answer: T   **Type: T**   **Page: 139**   **Knowledge**

8. Chapter Four argued that the complete and open expression of emotions is one key to positive relationships.
   Answer: F   **Type: T**   **Page: 144**   **Comprehension**

9. Over-expression of emotion may create physiological ailments as much as under-expression of emotion.
   Answer: T   **Type: T**   **Page: 144**   **Knowledge**

10. By thinking rationally, you will be able to eliminate debilitative emotions from your life.
    Answer: F   **Type: T**   **Page: 151**   **Knowledge**

11. When sharing your feelings, it's not necessary to accept responsibility for them because so often others cause them.
    Answer: F   **Type: T**   **Page: 148**   **Knowledge**

12. Fortunately, for people who want to hide their emotions, all the physical changes that accompany emotions are internal.
    Answer: F   **Type: T**   **Page: 133**   **Knowledge**

13. Some people fail to communicate their emotions clearly because they understate or downplay them.
    Answer: T   **Type: T**   **Page: 147**   **Knowledge**

14. Since collectivist cultures pay more attention to nonverbal behaviors, they are better at expressing both positive and negative emotions.
    Answer: F   **Type: T**   **Page: 139**   **Knowledge**

15. The physiological changes that accompany many strong emotions are similar.
    Answer: T   **Type: T**   **Page: 133**   **Comprehension**

16. An event that generates facilitative self-talk for one person might stimulate debilitative thinking for someone else.
    Answer: T   **Type: T**   **Page: 156**   **Comprehension**

17. Emotional states are connected to physical behavior.
    Answer: T   **Type: T**   **Page: 133**   **Comprehension**

18. While there is a link between physical behavior and emotional states, mental behavior plays no role in determining how we feel.
    Answer: F   **Type: T**   **Page: 133**   **Comprehension**

19. The approach to handling emotions described in your text involves talking yourself out of feeling unnecessarily bad.
    Answer: T   **Type: T**   **Page: 161**   **Knowledge**

20. The chapter on emotions argues that we can stop others from doing things that make us feel bad.
    Answer: F   **Type: T**   **Page: 133**   **Analysis**

21. It is important to express all your emotions to all the important people in your life as soon as you experience those emotions.
    Answer: F   **Type: T**   **Page: 149**   **Knowledge**

22. Your text advises that when you feel a certain way, you should act on that feeling immediately.
    Answer: F   **Type: T**   **Page: 149**   **Knowledge**

23. All emotions are caused by self-talk.
    Answer: F   **Type: T**   **Page: 151**   **Comprehension**

24. People will respect and like you more if you go out of your way to please them.
    Answer: F   **Type: T**   **Page: 154**   **Comprehension**

25. One of the primary reasons we don't express emotions is that we don't recognize when they occur.
    Answer: T   **Type: T**   **Page: 145**   **Comprehension**

26. The text explains that you should always share your positive feelings (love, affection, etc.).
    Answer: F   **Type: T**   **Page: 149**   **Knowledge**

27. By avoiding the fallacy of approval, you will become unconcerned about what other people think of you.
    Answer: F   **Type: T**   **Page: 154**   **Knowledge**

28. Anger can be either a facilitative or debilitative emotion.
    Answer: T   **Type: T**   **Page: 150**   **Comprehension**

29. One way to reduce your anxiety about communicating is to stop talking to yourself.
    Answer: F   **Type: T**   **Page: 151**   **Analysis**

30. All of our emotions are a direct result of self-talk.
    Answer: F   **Type: T**   **Page: 150–151**   **Comprehension**

31. The "amygdale" refers to
    a. the threat alarm system in the brain.
    b. a type of emotional contagion.
    c. a reservoir of emotional memories
    d. nonverbal reactions expressed on the face.
    e. none of the above.
    Answer: a   **Type: M**   **Page: 151**   **Knowledge**

32. The "Looking at Diversity" reading about the ways Zuni and Anglo cultures deal with emotion expression indicates that
    a. Anglos don't show love as much as Zunis.
    b. Zunis emphasize listening over talking.
    c. Zunis encourage their children to freely express intense emotions.
    d. Zunis feel emotions less intensely than Anglos.
    e. All of the above were mentioned by the reading.
    Answer: b   **Type: M**   **Pages: 141**   **Comprehension**

33. Social scientists generally agree that there are four components to the phenomena we label as "feelings." They are:
    a. physiological changes, nonverbal reactions, cognitive interpretations, and verbal expression.
    b. physical changes, mental recognition, and verbal description.
    c. sensing, organizing, interpreting, and encoding.
    d. verbal and nonverbal manifestations, physical depression, and catharsis.
    e. stimulus, proprioception, emotional contagion and response.
    Answer: a   **Type: M**   **Pages: 132–134**   **Comprehension**

34. Emotions that we experience are a result of
    a. our own temperaments.
    b. beliefs we hold.
    c. self-talk.
    d. emotional memories.
    e. all of the above.
    Answer: b   **Type: M**   **Page: 152**   **Comprehension**

35. Proprioceptive stimuli refer to
    a. deep-seated fears of emotional breakdown.
    b. emotional memories locked in our brains.
    c. sensations that are activated by movement of internal tissues.
    d. debilitative self-talk.
    e. types of emotional contagion.
    Answer: c   **Type: M**   **Page: 133**   **Knowledge**

36. Your text tells you that you should
    a. express all your emotions to your friends.
    b. try to recognize your emotions.
    c. be glad you have debilitative emotions.
    d. express only positive emotions.
    e. stop being so emotional.
    Answer: b   **Type: M**   **Pages: 145**   **Comprehension**

37. Your book categorizes emotions in all of the following ways except
    a. primary and mixed.
    b. intense and mild.
    c. facilitative and debilitative.
    d. internal and external.
    Answer: d   **Type: M**   **Pages: 135–136, 149 Synthesis**

38. According to Chapter Four, one reason people don't express feelings is
    a. they aren't aware of having them.
    b. it's a waste of time.
    c. interpretations are easier to understand.
    d. they are rarely asked to do so.
    e. many people rarely have feelings.
    Answer: a   **Type: M**   **Page: 145**   **Comprehension**

39. Robert Plutchik's "emotion wheel" illustrates
    a. proprioceptive stimuli.
    b. rational emotive therapy.
    c. primary and mixed emotions.
    d. cognitive interpretations.
    e. facilitative and debilitative emotions.
    Answer: c   **Type: M**   **Page: 135**   **Comprehension**

40. Research described in this chapter found that when subjects were coached to move their facial muscles in ways so that they appeared afraid, angry, disgusted, amused, sad, etc., others responded
    a. as if they themselves were having these feelings.
    b. by showing the opposite feeling.
    c. by showing more intense feelings than the volunteers.
    d. with no emotion at all.
    e. with pity for the volunteers.
    Answer: a   **Type: M**   **Pages: 133**   **Comprehension**

41. Many of our debilitative feelings come from

a. the way others treat us.

b. an overly flexible self-concept.

c. the anxiety we experience when positive expectations are placed on us.

d. accepting irrational beliefs which lead to illogical conclusions.

e. experiencing activating events.

Answer: d   **Type: M**   **Page: 151–152**   **Knowledge**

42. Which of the following is true of debilitative feelings?

    a. They often last a long time.

    b. They keep you from functioning effectively.

    c. They are intense.

    d. They are a product of your beliefs.

    e. All of the above are true of debilitative feelings.

    Answer: e   **Type: M**   **Pages: 150–152**   **Comprehension**

43. People who subscribe to the fallacy of perfection believe

    a. everyone is perfect except them.

    b. there's no point in striving for perfection since it is unattainable.

    c. a worthwhile communicator should be able to handle any situation with confidence and skill.

    d. perfection requires much practice.

    e. only professors are perfect.

    Answer: c   **Type: M**   **Page: 153**   **Knowledge**

44. Which of the following is an example of falling for the fallacy of causation?

    a. "People at parties make me nervous."

    b. "If I ask her/him for a date the answer will probably be no."

    c. "I'm no good at anything!"

    d. "Everybody is against me."

    e. "I should be a better person."

    Answer: a   **Type: M**   **Pages: 156**   **Application**

45. Which of the following does the text offer as a guideline for expressing emotions?

    a. The sooner a feeling is shared, the better.

    b. Try to avoid sharing negative feelings whenever possible.

    c. Share mixed feelings when appropriate.

    d. Let others know that they have caused you to feel a certain way.

    e. Try to avoid getting too emotional.

    Answer: c   **Type: M**   **Pages: 148**   **Application**

46. Which of the following is the best statement to describe a feeling clearly?

    a. "I get embarrassed when you tease me about the shape of my nose."

    b. "I get a little confused when you tease me about being Polish."

    c. "You're driving me crazy with that teasing."

    d. "I get angry when you tease me."

    e. "Stop teasing me or I'll leave you."

    Answer: a   **Type: M**   **Pages: 146–149**   **Application**

47. All of the following are parts of the procedure for dealing with debilitative feelings except:
    a. Pay attention to your self-talk.
    b. Become more aware of your emotional reactions.
    c. Dispute irrational beliefs.
    d. Identify the activating event.
    e. Analyze your motives.
    Answer: e   **Type: M**   **Pages: 158–160**   **Comprehension**

48. "Men are so egotistical; I'm never getting involved with a man again" is an example of subscribing to the fallacy of
    a. overgeneralization.
    b. perfection.
    c. shoulds.
    d. causation.
    e. helplessness.
    Answer: a   **Type: M**   **Page: 155–156**   **Application**

49. Stan felt angry when Sue, a woman he'd gone out with twice, went out with Steve. Stan's anger is a direct result of
    a. Sue going out with Steve.
    b. Steve betraying Stan.
    c. Stan believing Sue should go out only with him.
    d. Stan's childishness.
    e. Sue's and Steve's thoughtlessness.
    Answer: c   **Type: M**   **Pages: 152**   **Analysis**

50. John felt discouraged when he got a "C" on his speech. John's discouragement was a direct result of
    a. giving an average speech.
    b. his parents' expectations.
    c. an unfair teacher.
    d. John's friend getting a "B" for the same speech.
    e. John thinking he should get an "A."
    Answer: e   **Type: M**   **Pages: 152**   **Analysis**

51. "My roommate ought to be more understanding." This quote is an example of the fallacy of
    a. shoulds.
    b. causation.
    c. approval.
    d. perfection.
    e. helplessness.
    Answer: a   **Type: M**   **Pages: 155**   **Application**

52. Which of the following is the best advice for sharing feelings?
   a. Accept responsibility for your own feelings.
   b. Express your feelings as soon as they occur.
   c. Recognize that feeling and acting out the feeling are the same.
   d. Express only primary feelings.
   e. Tell yourself you shouldn't feel bad.

   Answer: a   **Type: M**   **Pages: 148**   **Evaluation**

53. According to your text, women are more likely than men to express all of the following emotions except their own
   a. vulnerability.
   b. loneliness.
   c. strength.
   d. fear.
   e. sadness.

   Answer: c   **Type: M**   **Page: 140**   **Comprehension**

54. When you believe that a worthwhile communicator should be able to handle every situation with complete confidence and skill, you are falling for the fallacy of
   a. perfection.
   b. causation.
   c. approval.
   d. shoulds.
   e. overgeneralization.

   Answer: a   **Type: M**   **Page: 153**   **Knowledge**

55. When you think it is not just desirable but vital to get the acceptance of virtually every person, you are falling for the fallacy of
   a. perfection.
   b. causation.
   c. approval.
   d. shoulds.
   e. overgeneralization.

   Answer: c   **Type: M**   **Page: 153**   **Knowledge**

56. When you believe that others cause your emotions rather than your own self-talk, you are falling for the fallacy of
   a. perfection.
   b. causation.
   c. approval.
   d. shoulds.
   e. overgeneralization.

   Answer: b   **Type: M**   **Pages: 156**   **Knowledge**

57. When you believe that satisfaction in life is determined by forces beyond your control, you are falling for the fallacy of
    a. causation.
    b. helplessness.
    c. catastrophic expectations.
    d. approval.
    e. shoulds.
    Answer: b   **Type: M**   **Pages: 157**   **Knowledge**

58. According to your text, the first step in minimizing your debilitative emotions is to
    a. monitor your emotional reactions.
    b. note the activating event.
    c. record your self-talk.
    d. dispute your irrational beliefs.
    e. confront the person who caused them.
    Answer: a   **Type: M**   **Page: 158**   **Knowledge**

59. Which of the following is an example of self-talk?
    a. Jim shouldn't drink three beers.
    b. Jim's always drinking.
    c. He'll have an accident.
    d. Jim makes me feel insecure.
    e. All of the above might be examples of self-talk.
    Answer: e   **Type: M**   **Page: 153–158**   **Application**

60. Which of the following is an example of self-talk?
    a. I shouldn't have pushed so hard.
    b. I'll make her neurotic.
    c. I'll never be able to make her see my side.
    d. I can't get anyone to listen to me.
    e. All of the above might be examples of self-talk.
    Answer: e   **Type: M**   **Page: 153–158**   **Application**

61. Frowning, sweating, and a sudden change in vocal pitch are all emotional changes classified as
    a. proprioceptive stimuli.
    b. nonverbal reactions.
    c. cognitive interpretations.
    d. physio-emotional changes.
    e. all of the above.
    Answer: b   **Type: M**   **Pages: 133**   **Knowledge**

62. An empty feeling in the pit of your stomach, tense muscles, and headaches are examples of the emotional component labeled
    a. nonverbal reactions.
    b. cognitive interpretations.
    c. physiological changes.
    d. rational-emotive therapy.
    e. environment.

    Answer: c   **Type: M**   **Page: 132**   **Comprehension**

63. Your text says we don't express our emotions very well or very frequently because
    a. of social rules and roles.
    b. others put us down.
    c. we recognize so many emotions.
    d. self-disclosure is already high enough.
    e. of inadequate self-concepts.

    Answer: a   **Type: M**   **Pages: 143**   **Comprehension**

64. Which of the following improves the expression of emotion in the statement: "You're making me nervous"?
    a. Say "I feel nervous when you drive over the speed limit."
    b. Say "Your fast driving is not making me feel very safe."
    c. Say "I feel like taking the keys."
    d. All of the above could improve the statement.
    e. No improvement is needed.

    Answer: a   **Type: M**   **Pages: 146**   **Evaluation**

65. Which of the following best improves the emotional statement, "I'm a little upset and wonder where you get off acting like that"?
    a. "You're driving me crazy."
    b. "I can't figure out what to do when you won' tell me what's wrong."
    c. "Your emotions are getting the best of you right now."
    d. "I'm upset that our food budget for the month is spent."
    e. The original statement is the best expression of emotion.

    Answer: d   **Type: M**   **Pages: 146–147**   **Evaluation**

66. Facilitative feelings
    a. are emotional counterfeits.
    b. happen only when you feel good.
    c. keep us from communicating effectively.
    d. contribute to effective functioning.
    e. are more common in other cultures.

    Answer: d   **Type: M**   **Page: 149**   **Comprehension**

67. Debilitative emotions
    a. are emotional counterfeits.
    b. happen only when you feel bad.
    c. keep you from feeling and communicating effectively.
    d. contribute to effective functioning.
    e. none of the above
    Answer: c   **Type: M**   **Page: 149**   **Comprehension**

68. Two things that distinguish facilitative feelings from debilitative ones are
    a. emotions and behavior.
    b. interpretation and intention.
    c. longevity and interpretation.
    d. intention and intensity.
    e. intensity and duration.
    Answer: e   **Type: M**   **Page: 150**   **Knowledge**

69. Sensations activated by the movement of internal tissue are called
    a. emotional senses.
    b. internal emotions.
    c. sensational stimulation.
    d. proprioceptive stimuli.
    e. practical defenses.
    Answer: d   **Type: M**   **Page: 133**   **Knowledge**

70. The element of the communication model that is most closely involved with causing an emotion is
    a. channel.
    b. decoding.
    c. noise.
    d. environment.
    e. encoding
    Answer: b   **Type: M**   **Pages: 10, 133–134 Synthesis**

71. The relationship between thinking and feeling described in your text involved which dimensions of the perception process?
    a. selection
    b. organization
    c. interpretation
    d. all of the above
    e. none of the above
    Answer: d   **Type: M**   **Page: 133–134**   **Synthesis**

72. Which of the following is an example of the fallacy of causation?
    a. "My boss makes me so nervous that I can't do a good job."
    b. "I hurt Laura's feelings yesterday when I asked her to stop being so critical."
    c. "Bruce is driving me crazy with his excuses."
    d. both a and b above
    e. a, b, and c above
    Answer: e   **Type: M**   **Page: 156**   **Application**

73. You're fed up with a close friend's habit of offering unsolicited advice about how to live your life. Which of the following is a useful guideline for expressing your feelings?
    a. Play it cool at first; don't let your friend know how much the advice irritates you.
    b. Demonstrate the strength of your feelings by refusing to talk with your friend for a while.
    c. Avoid bringing up this difficult subject until you can't tolerate it any longer.
    d. Don't dilute the strength of your message by sharing positive feelings about your friendship along with your irritation.
    e. Say you're annoyed by one specific piece of advice because you'd prefer to make your own decision on that matter.
    Answer: e   **Type: M**   **Pages: 146–149**   **Evaluation**

74. Self-talk can be
    a. facilitative or debilitative.
    b. a form of psychological noise.
    c. influenced by selective perception.
    d. part of a self-fulfilling prophecy.
    e. all of the above.
    Answer: e   **Type: M**   **Pages: Ch 1–3, p. 149**   **Synthesis**

75. You are fed up with the way certain family members insist on knowing the details of your personal life. According to your text, what causes your feelings?
    a. the way your family phrases their questions
    b. expecting your family to respect your privacy
    c. self-fulfilling prophecies your family imposes on you
    d. lack of feedback
    e. the fallacy of perfection
    Answer: b   **Type: M**   **Page: 152**   **Analysis**

76. The statement "Bob never has a good word to say about anyone" is an example of the fallacy of
    a. shoulds.
    b. approval.
    c. overgeneralization.
    d. causation.
    e. all of the above
    Answer: c   **Type: M**   **Page: 155–156**   **Application**

77. Subscribing to the fallacy of catastrophic expectations can lead to
    a. self-fulfilling prophecies.
    b. erroneous perception checking.
    c. reflected appraisals.
    d. physiological noise.
    e. both c and d above.
    Answer: a   **Type: M**   **Pages: 64, 157**   **Synthesis**

78. "I feel like quitting school" is an example of
     a. a feeling statement.
     b. an emotionally counterfeit statement.
     c. an emotional intention.
     d. a contextual emotion.
     e. a self-fulfilling prophecy.
     Answer: b   **Type: M**   **Page: 146**   **Application**

79. Your brother asks about the money you got from your parents and then hangs up the
     telephone when you tell him. If you want to truly express your emotion, what is one
     good way to restate, "I feel you've been unfair"?
     a. "I think you tricked me, and I feel that's unfair."
     b. "I feel duped."
     c. "I'm disappointed you didn't ask me to explain."
     d. "You're making me mad by not letting me explain."
     e. The original statement is a good-feeling statement.
     Answer: c   **Type: M**   **Pages: 146–149**   **Synthesis**

80. What's ineffective about this feeling statement: "I feel you are lazy"?
     a. It doesn't accept responsibility for a feeling.
     b. It doesn't describe the speaker's feeling.
     c. It interprets another's behavior.
     d. All of the above describe what's ineffective about the statement.
     e. There is nothing ineffective about the original statement.
     Answer: d   **Type: M**   **Pages: 146–149**   **Synthesis**

81. Revealing multiple feelings means
     a. mixing up all the feelings you have.
     b. expressing more than one feeling.
     c. sharing what you feel and what your partner feels, too.
     d. all of the above.
     e. none of the above.
     Answer: b   **Type: M**   **Page: 148**   **Comprehension**

INSTRUCTIONS for questions 82–91: Match each of the statements below with the fallacy it most clearly
represents.
     a. fallacy of causation
     b. fallacy of shoulds
     c. fallacy of overgeneralization
     d. fallacy of perfection
     e. fallacy of catastrophic expectations

82. "Those interviewers made me so nervous."
     Answer: a   **Type: Matching**   **Page: 156**   **Application**

83. "You ought to keep in touch more."
     Answer: b   **Type: Matching**   **Page: 155**   **Application**

84. "I know he'll be crushed if I don't go out with him."
     Answer: a   **Type: Matching**   **Page: 156**   **Application**

85. "You never tell me how you feel."
    Answer: c   **Type: Matching**   **Page: 155**   **Application**

86. "I lost my temper with Mac last night. I've had interpersonal communication; I know better."
    Answer: d   **Type: Matching**   **Pages: 153**   **Application**

87. "All you do is criticize me!"
    Answer: c   **Type: Matching**   **Page: 155**   **Application**

88. "You're driving me crazy."
    Answer: a   **Type: Matching**   **Page: 156**   **Application**

89. "You should be more patient."
    Answer: b   **Type: Matching**   **Page: 155**   **Application**

90. "You're always finishing my sentences for me."
    Answer: c   **Type: Matching**   **Page: 155**   **Application**

91. "I know I'll make a complete idiot of myself if I tell him how I feel."
    Answer: e   **Type: Matching**   **Page: 157**   **Application**

92. "There is nothing good or bad but thinking makes it so." Apply this Shakespeare quote to communication in one of your relationships. Give specific examples and describe details.
    Answer   **Type: E**   **Pages: 133–134, 150–151 Application**

93. Give examples of cultural, gender, and social influences on emotional expression from your own life.
    Answer   **Type: E**   **Pages: 139–140   Application**

94. "When emotions begin to be shared, a relationship begins to deepen." How does this come about? Give two examples from your own experience that support this statement.
    Answer   **Type: E**   **Pages: 134–135   Analysis**

95. Report on three situations from your life that illustrate the primary and mixed emotions illustrated by Robert Plutchik's "emotion wheel."
    Answer   **Type: E**   **Page: 135   Application**

\96. Identify at least three irrational fallacies in the text you most commonly accept. Explain each fallacy and explain the potential harm each may cause if you fail to dispute it.
    Answer   **Type: E**   **Pages: 153–157   Analysis**

97. Explain the relationship between interpersonal perception as described in Chapter Three and the rational-emotive approach to emotions in Chapter Four.
    Answer   **Type: E**   **Page: Ch 3 and 152 Synthesis**

(NOTE: The following essay question works best as a " take-home" exam because of the time necessary to effectively complete it.)

98. What are the guidelines suggested in your text for expressing feelings? Describe how you can apply these guidelines to your life. Give specific examples.
    Answer   **Type: E**   **Pages: 146–149   Application**

CHAPTER 5

LANGUAGE: BARRIER AND BRIDGE

1. To be effective, an "I" statement must include all four elements, in the order described in your textbook.
   Answer: F   **Type: T**   **Page: 189**   **Knowledge**

2. "It's A Girl Thing For Women," suggests that the word "girl" is most often viewed by women as a derogatory term.
   Answer: F   **Type: T**   **Page: 179**   **Comprehension**

3. A group of synonyms such as one finds in a dictionary can completely define an object.
   Answer: F   **Type: T**   **Page: 170**   **Comprehension**

4. "The Many Meanings of 'I Love You'" in this chapter points out how several different interpretations of the phrase 'I love you' may be misinterpreted due to semantic rules.
   Answer: T   **Type: T**   **Page: 171**   **Comprehension**

5. Because meanings rest more in people than in words, labels are unimportant.
   Answer: F   **Type: T**   **Pages: 180**   **Comprehension**

6. Equivocal words are words that can be interpreted in more than one way.
   Answer: T   **Type: T**   **Pages: 172**   **Knowledge**

7. Emotive words are words that sound as if they're describing something, but are really announcing the speaker's attitude toward it.
   Answer: T   **Type: T**   **Page: 185**   **Knowledge**

8. Linguistic relativism is a notion that holds that our language exerts a strong influence on our perceptions.
   Answer: T   **Type: T**   **Page: 201**   **Knowledge**

9. "I'm rather upset" is more powerful language than "I'm upset."
   Answer: F   **Type: T**   **Page: 183**   **Comprehension**

10. A perfectly worded "I" statement delivered with total sincerity will ensure that the other person will not get defensive.
    Answer: F   **Type: T**   **Page: 188**   **Knowledge**

11. American Sign Language is a system of symbols rather than natural signs.
    Answer: T   **Type: T**   **Page: 169**   **Knowledge**

12. Syntactic rules govern the grammatical aspects of a language.
    Answer: T   **Type: T**   **Page: 176**   **Knowledge**

13. Relative words gain their meaning from comparison.
     Answer: T   **Type: T**   **Page: 172**   **Knowledge**

14. The U.S. is a high-context language culture.
     Answer: F   **Type: T**   **Page: 199**   **Comprehension**

15. High-level abstractions can be useful as verbal shorthand between two people who
     know each other well.
     Answer: T   **Type: T**   **Page: 174**   **Knowledge**

16. The best way to move down the abstraction ladder when someone confronts you with
     vague language is to look up the confusing words in a dictionary.
     Answer: F   **Type: T**   **Pages: 173–174**   **Application**

17. Gender is by far the most influential factor influencing conversational style.
     Answer: F   **Type: T**   **Page: 196**   **Analysis**

18. All human languages are symbolic in nature.
     Answer: T   **Type: T**   **Page: 169**   **Knowledge**

19. Much of the awkwardness that comes with first using "I" language is due to its
     unfamiliarity.
     Answer: T   **Type: T**   **Pages: 191**   **Knowledge**

20. Emotive words sound like statements of fact, but they're typically opinions.
     Answer: T   **Type: T**   **Page: 185**   **Knowledge**

21. Inferential statements are interpretations of behavior.
     Answer: T   **Type: T**   **Page: 185**   **Comprehension**

22. Meanings are best found by studying the words people use, not by observing how
     people use them.
     Answer: F   **Type: T**   **Pages: 172**   **Comprehension**

23. A formal language culture will have different vocabularies for different sexes, levels
     of social status, or degrees of intimacy.
     Answer: T   **Type: T**   **Page: 200**   **Comprehension**

24. "I" language statements may contain the word "I" more than once.
     Answer: T   **Type: T**   **Page: 189**   **Evaluation**

25. "No" is so clear and short that it is one of the few words that is never misinterpreted.
     Answer: F   **Type: T**   **Page: 200**   **Analysis**

26. Asking questions may be a linguistic way to avoid making a declaration.
     Answer: T   **Type: T**   **Page: 188**   **Comprehension**

27. Statements that contain the word "is" ("Kyle is an active guy") may lead to the
     assumption that people are unchanging.
     Answer: T   **Type: T**   **Page: 173**   **Knowledge**

28. Studies have found that females use as much cursing or profanity as males.
     Answer: T   **Type: T**   **Page: 196**   **Knowledge**

29. Women use more indirect and elaborate ways of talking than men do.
     Answer: T   **Type: T**   **Page: 195**   **Knowledge**

30. Research shows that linguistic differences are more often a function of sex roles than they are of biological sex.
    Answer: T   **Type: T**   **Page: 197**   **Comprehension**

31. Men discuss with other men the same conversation topics that women discuss with other women.
    Answer: F   **Type: T**   **Page: 193**   **Knowledge**

32. Your text confirms the stereotype that women are more likely to talk about feelings and relationships than men are.
    Answer: T   **Type: T**   **Pages: 193–194**   **Knowledge**

33. Men talk more about sports figures and current events than women do.
    Answer: T   **Type: T**   **Page: 193**   **Knowledge**

34. Men and women report using language for different purposes.
    Answer: T   **Type: T**   **Page: 194**   **Knowledge**

35. The process of static evaluation implies that people or things are unchanging.
    Answer: T   **Type: T**   **Page: 173**   **Knowledge**

36. "The Challenging the 'S Word'" reading in Chapter Five describes how the word _____ is emotive for many people.
    a.   superior
    b.   saint
    c.   slow
    d.   squaw
    e.   sex
    Answer: d   **Type: M**   **Pages: 181, 185**   **Knowledge**

37. In the "Looking At Diversity" reading in Chapter Five, a woman points out that some Spanish words
    a.   are not tied to culture.
    b.   have caused international war.
    c.   are English derivatives.
    d.   describe English culture better than English does.
    e.   express family relationships better than English.
    Answer: e   **Type: M**   **Page: 197**   **Knowledge**

38. In the "Looking At Diversity" reading in Chapter Five, Alma Villasenor Green describes
    a.   the way English is more formal than Spanish.
    b.   the reasons why learning English was difficult for her.
    c.   the benefits speaking two languages offers interpersonal expression.
    d.   the difficulties that arise in marriage when two languages are spoken.
    e.   her family's resistance to her speaking English at home.
    Answer: c   **Type: M**   **Page: 197**   **Knowledge**

39. When a speaker uses powerful speech patterns he/she
    a. tends to be received more positively in cultures like Mexico.
    b. stesses relational goals over content goals.
    c. may undermine relational goals to accomplish content goals.
    d. will use very polite phrases and intensifiers.
    e. will be successful in all communication encounters.
    Answer: c   **Type: M**   **Page: 184**   **Knowledge**

40. "We" language
    a. may accomplish the goals of "I" language and sound less egotistical.
    b. should be avoided when expressing personal feelings and thoughts.
    c. can signal closeness and cohesiveness with others.
    d. can offend another person in some circumstances.
    e. all of the above
    Answer: e   **Type: M**   **Pages: 192–193**   **Knowledge**

41. "It's a 'girl' thing for women" in Chapter Five illustrates
    a. that who uses the term "girl" determined the reaction to it.
    b. the use of "girl" is a sexist term.
    c. that "no" is more clear to women than to girls.
    d. how inexpressive the term "girl" is.
    e. how feminists have overreacted and banned the use of the term "girl."
    Answer: a   **Type: M**   **Page: 179**   **Comprehension**

42. According to the text, one semantic problem is that much language is too
    a. wordy.
    b. sentimental.
    c. unfeeling.
    d. abstract.
    e. specific.
    Answer: d   **Type: M**   **Page: 173**   **Comprehension**

43. A behavioral description should include
    a. "you" language.
    b. high context speech.
    c. static evaluation.
    d. all of the above.
    e. none of the above.
    Answer: e   **Type: M**   **Pages: 173**   **Analysis**

44. The Sapir-Whorf hypothesis postulates that
    a. all languages share the same pragmatic rules.
    b. language operates as a perceptual schema.
    c. language patterns reflect and shape an individual's power.
    d. men and women use language for different purposes.
    e. the majority of the world's languages are low context.
    Answer: b   **Type: M**   **Pages: 94, 202–203**   **Synthesis**

45. In a low-context language culture, you will notice
    a. indirect expression of opinions.
    b. use of silence admired.
    c. less reliance on explicit verbal messages.
    d. self-expression valued.
    e. ambiguity admired.
    Answer: d   **Type: M**   **Page: 199**   **Comprehension**

46. Succinctness in language is most extreme in cultures where
    a. silence is valued.
    b. the language system is limited.
    c. more than one language is spoken.
    d. verbal fluency is admired.
    e. the use of equivocation is high.
    Answer: a   **Type: M**   **Page: 200**   **Knowledge**

47. All of the following statements about language are true except:
    a. Men's speech is more direct and task-oriented.
    b. Women's speech is more indirect and elaborate.
    c. Men are more likely to talk about themselves with women.
    d. Men accommodate more to topics women raise.
    e. In some cases there is no difference in male and female language.
    Answer: d   **Type: M**   **Pages: 193–195**   **Synthesis**

49. On the strength of a recommendation from one of your friends, you took a class from
    an instructor that your friend had described as "witty, bright, and a fair grader." You
    fell asleep in the class and received a "D" in the course, although you thought you
    deserved a "B." You were a victim of misunderstanding because of
    a. emotive language.
    b. irregular words.
    c. euphemistic language.
    d. divergence.
    e. linguistics.
    Answer: a   **Type: M**   **Page: 185**   **Application**

50. Which of the following is the highest-level abstraction?
    a. complaining
    b. complaining about chores
    c. complaining about my housekeeping
    d. reminding me to wash the dishes
    e. reminding me about chores I haven't done
    Answer: a   **Type: M**   **Pages: 174**   **Application**

51. Which of the following is the lowest-level abstraction?
     a. paying attention to me every day
     b. letting me know you appreciate me
     c. saying "thanks" when I help with your work
     d. paying attention to me
     e. giving me more time
     Answer: c   **Type: M**   **Page: 174**   **Evaluation**

52. Which of the following is the best example of highly abstract language?
     a. "Turn to page 116 and do the exercise at the bottom of the page."
     b. "My car wouldn't start this morning; I wish I had never bought it."
     c. "John is a patriotic person."
     d. "Can you play tennis?"
     e. "My favorite course is Interpersonal Communication."
     Answer: c   **Type: M**   **Pages: 174**   **Application**

53. When we study semantics, we learn that
     a. words mean a lot in and of themselves.
     b. the labels we attach to our experiences can shape the attitudes we hold.
     c. words typically can be interpreted in only one way.
     d. meanings rest more in words than in the people who use them.
     Answer: b   **Type: M**   **Page: 170**   **Comprehension**

54. In cultures that stress formality in language,
     a. using correct grammar is most important.
     b. language use defines social position.
     c. the people talk less.
     d. there are fewer real friendships.
     e. the people are too stiff to really communicate.
     Answer: b   **Type: M**   **Page: 200**   **Comprehension**

55. Equivocal words
     a. have more than one commonly accepted definition.
     b. are low-level abstractions.
     c. mean the same to all people and are thus redundant.
     d. have meanings one person can guess at but another can't.
     e. have no known nonverbal signals to accompany them.
     Answer: a   **Type: M**   **Page: 172**   **Knowledge**

56. When I refer to my math classmates and say they're a "bunch of good guys," I may
     have caused a misunderstanding in that I used
     a. equivocal words.
     b. emotive words.
     c. semantic words.
     d. behavioral interpretations.
     e. a euphemism.
     Answer: b   **Type: M**   **Page: 185**   **Knowledge**

57. Which of the following is the least abstract definition of a successful college experience?
   a. a better understanding of Western civilization
   b. completion of the requirements listed on page 24 of the college catalog with a grade-point average of 2.0 or higher
   c. the ability to express oneself clearly, understand principles of the arts and sciences, and have some expertise in a chosen field of study
   d. both intellectual and social adjustment
   e. the ability to contribute to society
   Answer: b   **Type: M**   **Pages: 174**   **Analysis**

58. One of the problems we run into when we use abstract language is that we
   a. tend to avoid finding the generalizations we need for understanding.
   b. may clarify things for others instead of ourselves.
   c. may send too clear a message
   d. may tend to think in general terms.
   Answer: d   **Type: M**   **Pages: 174**   **Comprehension**

59. Using high-level abstractions may be helpful when the abstractions
   a. let us talk about the similarities between several objects or events.
   b. act as a verbal shorthand.
   c. avoid confrontation with others.
   d. all of the above
   e. High-level abstractions are never helpful.
   Answer: d   **Type: M**   **Page: 174**   **Comprehension**

60. A speaker's willingness to take responsibility for his/her thoughts or feelings can be indicated by the use of
   a. singular terms.
   b. "I" language.
   c. "you" language.
   d. consequence terms.
   e. euphemisms.
   Answer: b   **Type: M**   **Page: 188**   **Analysis**

61. "People from the East Coast are rude." Which of the following abstraction problems is illustrated by this statement?
   a. stereotyping
   b. confusing others
   c. confusing yourself
   d. being too frank
   e. bicoastalism
   Answer: a   **Type: M**   **Pages: 173–174**   **Application**

62. Which of the following statements avoids high abstractions?
   a. "You're the best friend I've ever had."
   b. "I think you've just been terrific."
   c. "I appreciated you loaning us that pan on Monday."
   d. "You are so thoughtful."

e.   "I love the way you always come through for me."
Answer: c   **Type: M**   **Page: 174**   **Application**

63. Which of the following is a way to avoid the abstraction in the statement "I've got to be a better student"?
a.   "I'm going to spend two hours a day studying."
b.   "I'm going to try harder."
c.   "I'm going to get some help from some places on campus."
d.   "My mother and father will be happier if I'm a better student."
e.   "Instructors like students who try hard."
Answer: a   **Type: M**   **Page: 174**   **Evaluation**

64. A behavioral description should include
a.   who is involved.
b.   in what circumstances the behavior occurs.
c.   what behaviors are involved.
d.   all of the above.
e.   none of the above.
Answer: d   **Type: M**   **Page: 175**   **Comprehension**

65. Which of the following is the least abstract statement?
a.   "I love dinner parties."
b.   "I love eating out in all the cities of the United States."
c.   "I like to have eight people over for a six-course French meal including a chocolate mousse dessert."
d.   "The eight friends had forty-eight dollars between them to eat a healthy dinner last night."
e.   "The chocolate cake at Piero's is an ultimate delight."
Answer: c   **Type: M**   **Page: 174**   **Evaluation**

66. If I say "here the drink bring," I have violated a(n) _____ rule of our language.
a.   initial
b.   syntactic
c.   median
d.   semantic
e.   final
Answer: b   **Type: M**   **Page: 176**   **Knowledge**

67. Syntactic rules of language govern
a.   the ways in which symbols can be arranged.
b.   the ways in which speakers respond to symbols.
c.   the words that become slang.
d.   the creation of new tactics.
e.   the way that semanticists create meaning.
Answer: a   **Type: M**   **Page: 176**   **Knowledge**

68. Linguistic relativism is a concept that signifies that
    a. language exerts a strong influence on perceptions.
    b. language is relatively formal in European countries.
    c. language determines culture.
    d. truth is a relative cultural experience.
    e. everything is relative.
    Answer: a   **Type: M**   **Page: 201**   **Knowledge**

69. Making an inference is a reasonable thing to do relationally as long as
    a. you make a number of them.
    b. you wait for the other to infer also.
    c. the other person understands you.
    d. you identify the inference to the other person.
    e. you first describe the fact that led to the inference.
    Answer: e   **Type: M**   **Page: 185**   **Synthesis**

70. Which of the following statements is a fact?
    a. "It's clear you shouldn't have said that."
    b. "Fact number one: you said a dumb thing."
    c. "It's a fact that playing mind games always backfires."
    d. "I heard you say you weren't interested."
    e. "You should have thought about the result of saying you weren't interested before you opened your mouth."
    Answer: d   **Type: M**   **Page: 185**   **Knowledge**

71. Which of the following is the highest-level abstraction?
    a. Jake Adams
    b. human being
    c. man
    d. farmer
    e. wheat farmer
    Answer: b   **Type: M**   **Pages: 174**   **Evaluation**

72. Which of the following is the lowest-level abstraction?
    a. car
    b. Chevy
    c. 1986 Chevy Nova
    d. blue Chevy
    e. reliable car
    Answer: c   **Type: M**   **Pages: 174**   **Evaluation**

73. "Californians love to surf." Which of the following abstraction problems is illustrated by this statement?
    a. stereotyping
    b. confusing others
    c. confusing yourself
    d. static evaluation
    e. none of the above
    Answer: a   **Type: M**   **Page: 174**   **Analysis**

74. Words that have more than one dictionary definition are called
    a. emotive language.
    b. relative words.
    c. equivocal words.
    d. fiction terms.
    e. semantic distracters.
    Answer: c   **Type: M**   **Page: 172**   **Knowledge**

75. If you take an "easy" class your friend recommended and find it "hard," you have had semantic problems due to
    a. euphemistic language.
    b. relative words.
    c. equivocal words.
    d. fiction terms.
    e. semantic distracters.
    Answer: b   **Type: M**   **Pages: 172–173**   **Knowledge**

76. Convergent speech patterns
    a. demonstrate superiority over others.
    b. express power and a sense of formality.
    c. are used by people who wish to fit in.
    d. always utilize "I" statements instead of "you" statements.
    e. none of the above.
    Answer: c   **Type: M**   **Page: 182**   **Knowledge**

77. You promise to return your friend's tape "soon" and your friend gets mad when you don't return it that day. You originally meant "soon" to be the end of the week. You and your friend experienced a semantic problem due to
    a. emotive language.
    b. relative words.
    c. equivocal words.
    d. euphemisms.
    e. semantic distracters.
    Answer: b   **Type: M**   **Page: 172**   **Application**

78. A culture is unavoidably shaped and reflected by the language its members speak. This concept is
    a. high-context culture.
    b. low-context culture.
    c. cultural anthropology.
    d. cognitive determinism.
    e. linguistic determinism.
    Answer: e   **Type: M**   **Page: 201**   **Comprehension**

79. "You can't trust a woman." Which of the following errors is illustrated in this statement?
    a. stereotyping
    b. confusing denotation and connotation
    c. the fallacy of causation
    d. static evaluation
    e. semantic distraction
    Answer: a   **Type: M**   **Page: 174**   **Application**

80. Using language that incorrectly represents people as unchanging (e.g., " Frank is selfish") can lead to
    a. psychological noise.
    b. the fallacy of overgeneralization.
    c. self-fulfilling prophecies.
    d. static evaluation.
    e. all of the above.
    Answer: e   **Type: M**   **Page: 173**   **Synthesis**

81. You think Erin is "arrogant." Your friend thinks she has a lot of "self-confidence." An argument over who is right would revolve around
    a. syntactic rules.
    b. relative terms.
    c. emotive language.
    d. sequential placement.
    e. linguistic determinism.
    Answer: c   **Type: M**   **Page: 185**   **Evaluation**

82. Misunderstandings that revolve around emotive, equivocal, and relative language can all be clarified by
    a. clearer punctuation of perceptual events.
    b. more interpersonal and less impersonal communication.
    c. replacing abstract terms with concrete ones.
    d. static definitions.
    e. sequential placement.
    Answer: c   **Type: M**   **Pages: 174–175**   **Synthesis**

83. You tell a friend "I wish you'd be direct instead of hinting around," but your friend responds by denying that she/he hints. One way to help resolve the issue is to
     a. describe the hinting according to the dictionary.
     b. give a behavioral description of your mother's hinting so they get the idea.
     c. specifically describe the friend's hinting when it occurs.
     d. describe all at once the many times that the troublesome behavior occurs.
     Answer: c   **Type: M**   **Pages: 173–175**   **Evaluation**

84. Which of the following is the clearest behavioral description?
     a. "I wish you were as friendly as you used to be to people we meet at parties."
     b. "I'd like you to invite the Molitors over this weekend."
     c. "You always look so glum these days - cheer up."
     d. "I wish you'd warm up around my friends."
     e. "You've changed."
     Answer: b   **Type: M**   **Page: 175**   **Evaluation**

85. Semantic misunderstandings often arise because of
     a. differing psychological environments.
     b. sloppy encoding by the sender.
     c. distorted perceptions of the receiver.
     d. failure to use perception checking.
     e. all of the above.
     Answer: e   **Type: M**   **Page: 170**   **Analysis**

86. How could you increase the power of the statement "I, uh, think I'd be a little happier if you could make it on time. Okay?"?
     a. Revise the sequential placement.
     b. Use perception checking.
     c. Use more disclaimers.
     d. Add a tag question.
     e. None of the above increases the power of the statement.
     Answer: e   **Type: M**   **Page: 183**   **Evaluation**

87. Which of the following illustrates stereotyping?
     a. Women comprise less than 10 percept of that population.
     b. Old people get senile.
     c. Disabled workers claim over $1 million per year in benefits.
     d. Forty percent of the wealthiest people in the U.S. give 20 percent of their income to charity.
     Answer: b   **Type: M**   **Page: 182**   **Application**

88. Which element of an "I" statement does this phrase represent? "I am having a really hard time concentrating when the TV volume is so loud."
     a. a description of the other person's behavior.
     b. a description of the speaker's feelings.
     c. the consequences of the other person's behavior.
     d. the speaker's interpretation of the other's behavior.
     e. none of the above, this is a "You" statement.
     Answer: c   **Type: M**   **Page: 188**   **Application**

89. Which element is not included in this "I" language statement? "When you hung up without saying where we'd meet, I felt confused and so I went to the wrong place."
    a. It doesn't describe the other person's behavior.
    b. It doesn't describe the speaker's feelings.
    c. It doesn't describe the consequences the other's behavior has for the speaker.
    d. It doesn't describe the speaker's interpretation of the behavior.
    e. This "I" language statement is fine just the way it is.
    Answer: d   **Type: M**   **Page: 188**   **Analysis**

INSTRUCTIONS for questions 90–99: Identify each of the following statements as fact or inference.

    a. inference
    b. fact

90. You are trying to hurt me.
    Answer: a   **Type: Matching**   **Pages: 185**   **Evaluation**

91. You told Jimmy that I didn't want to go out with him.
    Answer: b   **Type: Matching**   **Pages: 185**   **Evaluation**

92. Jim is so cute and helpful.
    Answer: a   **Type: Matching**   **Pages: 185**   **Evaluation**

93. Jim wrote me a letter to help me get that job.
    Answer: b   **Type: Matching**   **Pages: 185**   **Evaluation**

94. Your children are disruptive.
    Answer: a   **Type: Matching**   **Pages: 185**   **Evaluation**

95. Your children interrupted me when I spoke.
    Answer: b   **Type: Matching**   **Pages: 185**   **Evaluation**

96. The school board president was arrested for drunken driving.
    Answer: b   **Type: Matching**   **Pages: 185**   **Evaluation**

97. Their new apartment is more comfortable than the old one.
    Answer: a   **Type: Matching**   **Pages: 185**   **Evaluation**

98. Liz's outfit has many colors in it.
    Answer: b   **Type: Matching**   **Pages: 185**   **Evaluation**

INSTRUCTIONS for questions 99-102: Read the following statements and identify what type of language is being used in the underlined words or phrases. You will use some letters more than once.

    a. emotive language
    b. relative language
    c. equivocal language

99. I'm not sure what to think. First, he said he would let me know <u>soon</u> about whether or not I get a second interview, but that was a week ago.
    Answer: b   **Type: Matching**   **Pages: 172**   **Evaluation**

100. No one seemed to want to talk about the person who had the job before this. They just kept referring to the "previous situation."
    Answer: c   **Type: Matching**   **Pages: 172**   **Evaluation**

101. It's a pretty good job and he told me that the pay was average.
    Answer: c   **Type: Matching**   **Pages: 172**   **Evaluation**

102. The building where we had the interview wasn't much. I don't want to call it a shack. Let's just say it was an economical structure.
    Answer: c   **Type: Matching**   **Pages: 185**   **Evaluation**

103. "Language is power." Discuss this statement, using (a) an explanation of the types of powerful/powerless language given in your text, and (b) examples of these types of language in your own life.
    Answer   **Type: E**   **Pages: 183**   **Analysis**

104. Using "I" language patterns from the text, create five "I" language statements you could actually deliver to people important in your life. Identify the three parts of each of your complete "I" statements.
    Answer   **Type: E**   **Page: 188**   **Synthesis**

105. Compare and contrast your use of language with that of someone else you know, pointing out the similarities or differences in: 1) verbal communication style (direct/indirect, elaborate/succinct, formal/informal) and 2) worldview. Cite specific examples.
    Answer   **Type: E**   **Pages: 198–201**   **Synthesis**

106. Using low–level abstractions, describe two ways in which you presently communicate successfully or two ways in which you would like to communicate better in interpersonal situations. For each goal, be sure to describe the people involved, the circumstances in which the communication takes place, and the current or desired behaviors.
    Answer   **Type: E**   **Pages: 173–175**   **Synthesis**

107. Describe what abstract language is and how you use unnecessarily abstract language that causes communication problems. Give at least five examples. Tell how you could lower the level of abstraction in each of the examples you have given or provide reasons why the higher-level abstraction is justified and relationally beneficial.
    Answer   **Type: E**   **Page: 173–175**   **Synthesis**

108. In your own words, explain the statement "meanings rest more in people than in words." Cite examples from your own experience.
    Answer   **Type: E**   **Page: 170–201**   **Application**

(NOTE: The following essay questions work best as " take-home" exams because of the time necessary to effectively complete them.)

109. Tape-record two separate 10- to 15-minute conversations you have with a man and a woman who are important in your life. Describe these conversations briefly in terms of content and style. Compare the conversations and comment on any variables involved, using terms and research from your text that address the issue of gender and language.
    Answer   **Type: E**   **Pages: 193–195**   **Synthesis**

110. The text describes some ways in which men and women use language both differently and similarly. Cite a major research finding in each of the following areas and cite examples from your life that reflect these findings or contradict them: a) content, b) reasons for communicating, c) conversational style, and d) non-gender variables.

Answer   **Type: E**   **Pages: 193–196**   **Synthesis**

CHAPTER 6

NONVERBAL COMMUNICATION:
MESSAGES BEYOND WORDS

1. In the Chapter Six reading, "The Way You Talk Can Hurt You?" the author asserts that contemporary young women use paralanguage in a way which creates the impression that they are timid and weak.
   Answer: T   **Type:** T   **Page:** 233   **Knowledge**

2. "The Way You Talk Can Hurt You?" reading in Chapter Six insists that it would be beneficial for men to change their vocal patterns to sound more cooperative and friendly in everyday interactions.
   Answer: F   **Type:** T   **Page:** 233   **Knowledge**

3. In the Sherlock Holmes story in Chapter Six, Holmes cautions Watson against making hasty deductions based on facial expression and posture of a suspect.
   Answer: F   **Type:** T   **Page:** 210   **Knowledge**

4. One study, reported in the nonverbal communication chapter, revealed that rapists sometimes use the postural clues of potential victims to choose those they believe are easy to intimidate.
   Answer: T   **Type:** T   **Page:** 228   **Recall**

5. In "The Look of a Victim" story in Chapter Six, prisoners convicted of assault revealed how many times they had mugged men based on their clothing.
   Answer: F   **Type:** T   **Page:** 228   **Knowledge**

6. Results of the "ugly room" experiment, described in the environment section of the nonverbal chapter, showed that subjects showed a greater desire to work in the ugly room because they didn't have any other distractions.
   Answer: F   **Type:** T   **Page:** 241   **Knowledge**

7. Nonverbal messages cannot convey information in the past or future tenses.
   Answer: T   **Type:** T   **Page:** 213   **Recall**

8. According to the text, you can not avoid communicating.
   Answer: T   **Type:** T   **Page:** 212   **Comprehension**

9. Nonverbal communication is usually specific and clear.
   Answer: F   **Type:** T   **Page:** 218   **Comprehension**

10. Nonverbal communication is not as effective at conveying thoughts or ideas as it is at conveying relational messages.
    Answer: T   **Type:** T   **Page:** 212   **Comprehension**

11. Once you increase your awareness of nonverbal messages, you can "read" another person's nonverbal behavior accurately in most situations.
    Answer: F   **Type: T**   **Page: 218**   **Comprehension**

12. According to your text's definition of nonverbal communication, it follows that the way a person styles his/her hair is a nonverbal message.
    Answer: T   **Type: T**   **Pages: 211**   **Analysis**

13. Nonverbal and verbal behaviors operate together to create messages.
    Answer: T   **Type: T**   **Page: 214**   **Comprehension**

14. In social transactions, the higher status person is generally the more rigid, tense-appearing one, whereas the one with lower status is usually more relaxed.
    Answer: F   **Type: T**   **Page: 229**   **Knowledge**

15. Information about the status of two individuals in conversation can be communicated by not only their posture, but also eye contact and touch.
    Answer: T   **Type: T**   **Pages: 229, 231, 235 Synthesis**

16. In laboratory settings, subjects are better judges of positive facial expressions than they are of negative ones.
    Answer: T   **Type: T**   **Page: 219**   **Comprehension**

17. Gestures can be intentional or unintentional.
    Answer: T   **Type: T**   **Page: 229-230**   **Synthesis**

18. Research reveals that increased use of manipulators is often a sign of discomfort.
    Answer: T   **Type: T**   **Page: 230**   **Knowledge**

19. In many instances, the use of touch increases liking and boosts compliance.
    Answer: T   **Type: T**   **Page: 235**   **Knowledge**

20. Nonverbal messages convey relational information such as respect and affinity.
    Answer: T   **Type: T**   **Pages: 212**   **Knowledge**

21. Generally, facing someone directly signals your interest in that person.
    Answer: T   **Type: T**   **Page: 226**   **Knowledge**

22. Research shows that people who question deceptive communicators get no better at detecting their lies.
    Answer: T   **Type: T**   **Page: 219**   **Knowledge**

23. Most communication scholars don't define American Sign Language as nonverbal communication.
    Answer: T   **Type: T**   **Page: 211**   **Knowledge**

24. Nonverbal communication can be very revealing, but it can have so many possible meanings that it's foolish to think your interpretation will always be correct.
    Answer: T   **Type: T**   **Page: 218**   **Comprehension**

25. Some people are more skillful than others at accurately decoding nonverbal behavior.
    Answer: T   **Type: T**   **Page: 220**   **Knowledge**

26. Your text defines nonverbal communication as any type of communication that isn't expressed by speech.
    Answer: F   **Type: T**   **Page: 211**   **Comprehension**

27. Different emotions show most clearly in various parts of the face.
    Answer: T   **Type: T**   **Page: 230**   **Knowledge**

28. According to your text, some researchers claim that over 90 percent of the emotional impact of a message comes from nonverbal sources.
    Answer: T   **Type: T**   **Page: 211**   **Knowledge**

29. According to your text, research has demonstrated that over 60 percent of the emotional impact of a message comes from the words themselves rather than nonverbal cues.
    Answer: F   **Type: T**   **Page: 211**   **Comprehension**

30. When we are interested in something or someone, the pupils of our eyes usually get smaller.
    Answer: F   **Type: T**   **Page: 231**   **Knowledge**

31. Women's advantage over men in sensitivity to nonverbal cues likely has more to do with social status than with biological gender.
    Answer: T   **Type: T**   **Page: 222**   **Knowledge**

32. Stammering and saying "uh" are actually nonverbal behaviors termed disfluencies.
    Answer: T   **Type: T**   **Page: 232**   **Knowledge**

33. "Learning To Grin and Bear It" is an article about encouraging Japanese employees to smile more to boost sales.
    Answer: T   **Type: T**   **Page: 225**   **Comprehension**

34. Paralinguistic elements always accompany the spoken word.
    Answer: T   **Type: T**   **Page: 231**   **Comprehension**

35. Nonverbal behavior can initiate interaction or serve as feedback to prior messages.
    Answer: T   **Type: T**   **Pages: 212–218**   **Synthesis**

36. Many nonverbal behaviors are governed by cultural rules.
    Answer: T   **Type: T**   **Page: 223**   **Knowledge**

37. Silence or pauses count as nonverbal communication.
    Answer: T   **Type: T**   **Page: 232**   **Comprehension**

38. Patterns of eye contact are fairly consistent across cultures.
    Answer: F   **Type: T**   **Page: 224**   **Comprehension**

39. Emblems are nonverbal behaviors that have the same meaning to all members of a particular culture or co-culture.
    Answer: T   **Type: T**   **Page: 229**   **Knowledge**

40. It is possible to recognize paralinguistic messages, even if you don't understand the language being spoken.
    Answer: T   **Type: T**   **Page: 232**   **Comprehension**

41. According to research cited in your text, touch and health are not related.
    Answer: F   **Type: T**   **Page: 235**   **Knowledge**

42. One way to signal a desire to avoid involvement when forced into intimate distance with another is to position yourself in an indirect body orientation.
    Answer: T   **Type: T**   **Page: 226**   **Comprehension**

43. Researchers have found that the face and eyes are capable of only five basic expressions.
    Answer: F   **Type: T**   **Page: 230**   **Knowledge**

44. Pupil dilation can be a sign of interest.
    Answer: T   **Type: T**   **Page: 231**   **Knowledge**

45. Disfluencies are one type of paralanguage.
    Answer: T   **Type: T**   **Page: 232**   **Comprehension**

46. According to your text, people usually get more social meaning from what others do than from what they say.
    Answer: T   **Type: T**   **Pages: 2212–213**   **Comprehension**

47. If you get within one foot of someone else in U.S. culture, you've invaded their intimate zone, according to researcher Edward Hall.
    Answer: T   **Type: T**   **Page: 239**   **Evaluation**

48. Messages about status can be conveyed through clothing and chronemics.
    Answer: T   **Type: T**   **Pages: 237, 242**   **Knowledge**

49. By making another person wait, you are sending messages about status, whether you intend to or not.
    Answer: T   **Type: T**   **Page: 242**   **Analysis**

50. Research indicates that there is virtually no difference between men and women concerning ability to decode nonverbal messages.
    Answer: F   **Type: T**   **Page: 218**   **Knowledge**

51. Verbal messages are more intentional than nonverbal messages.
    Answer: T   **Type: T**   **Page: 212**   **Analysis**

52. Nonverbal cues are especially likely to carry weight when they contradict a speaker's words.
    Answer: T   **Type: T**   **Page: 216**   **Knowledge**

53. At the poker table, Bill watched Abigail, noting that she was fiddling with her ring more than usual, which he interpreted as her having a strong betting hand. Her fiddling behavior would be an example of a "leakage cue."
    Answer: T   **Type: T**   **Page: 216**   **Application**

54. Deception studies have found that deceivers are more likely to be found out when they feel don't feel very strongly about the information being hidden.
    Answer: F   **Type: T**   **Page: 218**   **Knowledge**

55. If deceivers feel confident and not guilty, their deception is more likely to be found out.
    Answer: F   **Type: T**   **Page: 236**   **Knowledge**

56. Disfluencies could be leakage cues.
    Answer: T   **Type: T**   **Pages: 216, 232**   **Analysis**

57. In the excerpt from the Sherlock Holmes story in Chapter Six, Holmes points out that Watson
    a. listens but fails to see.
    b. sees but does not observe.
    c. can't observe well because he doesn't communicate.
    d. fails to solve cases because he pays too much attention to nonverbal messages.
    e. watches but fails to listen.
    Answer: b   **Type: M**   **Page: 210**   **Knowledge**

58. The Looking at Diversity reading in Chapter Six ("Nonverbal Stereotyping") features a black man who says he is frequently
    a. given more traffic tickets than white men in his age group.
    b. is viewed as arrogant because of his posture and stride.
    c. asked to speak to black groups because he knows how to behave nonverbally.
    d. assumed to be a potential shoplifter.
    e. suspected of violence because of his race.
    Answer: e   **Type: M**   **Page: 221**   **Knowledge**

59. In the Sherlock Holmes story in this chapter, Holmes deduces facts about Watson due to Watson's
    a. disfluency.
    b. early arrival.
    c. nervous fingering of his beard.
    d. all of the above
    e. none of the above
    Answer: d   **Type: M**   **Page: 210**   **Knowledge**

60. "The Look of a Victim" story in this chapter points out that victims of assault may set themselves up as easy targets because of
    a. their friendly facial expressions.
    b. the way they walk.
    c. their hairstyles.
    d. eye contact with the attacker.
    e. all of the above
    Answer: b   **Type: M**   **Page: 228**   **Knowledge**

61. Status can be conveyed nonverbally through
    a. chronemics.
    b. touch.
    c. clothing.
    d. posture.
    e. all of the above
    Answer: e   **Type: M**   **Pages: 229–242**   **Synthesis**

62. When Martha entered the room she noticed that three women, who were talking together, saw her then immediately drew closer together and angled themselves away from her, which indicated that they didn't want her to feel welcome to join them. The women used _____ to avoid Martha.
    a. kinesics and eye contact.
    b. territoriality and chronemics.
    c. proxemics and touch.
    d. paralanguage.
    e. all of the above
    Answer: a   **Type: M**   **Page: 226, 231**   **Application**

63. Amanda wants to make a sale. According to the nonverbal information in presented in Chapter 6, to get compliance from a customer she might try
    a. speaking in a rate much faster than her customer's
    b. lightly touching her customer.
    c. avoiding direct eye contact with her customer.
    d. keeping her facial expression as neutral as possible.
    e. none of the above are advisable to gain compliance.
    Answer: b   **Type: M**   **Page: 235**   **Application**

64. Studies of nonverbal communication across cultures reveal that
    a. smiles and laughter are a universal signal of positive emotions.
    b. sour expressions convey displeasure in some cultures and pleasure in others.
    c. the expression of feelings is discouraged in most cultures.
    d. all facial expressions are inborn.
    Answer: a   **Type: M**   **Page: 226**   **Synthesis**

65. The design and environment of rooms
    a. communicate information about the owner's personality.
    b. shape the interaction that takes place there.
    c. communicate information about the interests of the owner.
    d. b and c above
    e. all of the above
    Answer: e   **Type: M**   **Page: 241**   **Synthesis**

66. Kinesics is the study of
    a. personal distances.
    b. verbal and nonverbal behavior.
    c. body position and motion.
    d. environmental stress.
    e. clothing and color.
    Answer: c   **Type: M**   **Page: 226**   **Knowledge**

67. Proxemics is the study of
    a. the way people and animals use space.
    b. the way people use words to transmit messages.
    c. the way people use facial expressions.
    d. the way people use silence.
    e. the way people use vocal cues.
    Answer: a   **Type: M**   **Page: 238**   **Knowledge**

68. The many ways the voice communicates - including tone, speed, pitch, number and length of pauses, volume, etc. - are called
    a. paralanguage.
    b. vocalics.
    c. noncommunicators.
    d. nonvocals.
    e. proxemics.
    Answer: a   **Type: M**   **Page: 231**   **Knowledge**

69. The nonverbal researchers cited in your text claim that, when we consider the actual meaning involved in communication situations, verbal messages
    a. carry less meaning than nonverbal ones.
    b. carry more meaning than nonverbal ones.
    c. aren't really listened to.
    d. are too full of nonverbal signals.
    e. define the communication situation.
    Answer: a   **Type: M**   **Page: 211**   **Comprehension**

70. The main reason we miss many nonverbal clues contained in posture messages is that
    a. people don't stand up straight.
    b. the clues don't stand on their own.
    c. they aren't very obvious.
    d. sitting and standing aren't important clues.
    e. the clues are so blatantly obvious that people ignore them.
    Answer: c   **Type: M**   **Page: 227**   **Knowledge**

71. The first of Edward T. Hall's proxemic zones, the closest distance is
    a. social distance.
    b. skin distance.
    c. intimate distance.
    d. touching distance.
    e. eye distance.
    Answer: c   **Type: M**   **Page: 238**   **Knowledge**

72. Nonverbally, women _____ more than men.
    a. make less eye contact
    b. smile less
    c. are less vocally expressive
    d. gesture more
    e. require more personal space
    Answer: d   **Type: M**   **Page: 222**   **Comprehension**

73. Interpretation of nonverbal messages (decoding ability) is more accurate
    a. with age and training.
    b. among introverts.
    c. among dogmatists.
    d. among men.
    e. all of the above
    Answer: a   **Type: M**   **Page: 218**   **Comprehension**

74. Studies of nonverbal posture behaviors have found that
    a. we are generally unaware of posture.
    b. different facial expressions help posture interpretation.
    c. we should use unambiguous postural cues.
    d. tension and relaxation of muscles can indicate status differences.
    e. posture is not important to body image.
    Answer: d   **Type: M**   **Page: 229**   **Comprehension**

75. All of the following statements are true except:
    a. The eyes can communicate positive and negative attitudes.
    b. Nonverbal messages of the face and eyes are the easiest to read.
    c. Even the pupils of the eyes can communicate messages.
    d. The eyes can indicate dominance and submission.
    e. The eyes send involvement messages.
    Answer: b   **Type: M**   **Page: 230–231**   **Knowledge**

76. All of the following are characteristics of nonverbal behavior except:
    a. Nonverbal communication is culture-bound.
    b. Nonverbal behavior is clear and unambiguous.
    c. Nonverbal communication is primarily relational.
    d. All nonverbal behavior has communicative value.
    e. Nonverbal communication serves many functions.
    Answer: b   **Type: M**   **Pages: 212–223**   **Knowledge**

77. All of the following are true about touch except:
    a. Touch can be of life-and-death importance to a child.
    b. Touch can signal a variety of relationships.
    c. Touch can be a way to communicate both negative and positive feelings.
    d. Touch can increase a child's mental functioning.
    e. Touch in any of its forms can have positive effects.
    Answer: e   **Type: M**   **Pages: 234–235**   **Synthesis**

78. People's nonverbal behavior generally expresses
    a. relational messages.
    b. what they think.
    c. no communication at all.
    d. indifference.
    e. more about what they think than they are able to say.
    Answer: a   **Type: M**   **Page: 212–213**   **Comprehension**

79. When you become aware of nonverbal messages in your everyday life, you should interpret them as
    a. reliable facts.
    b. clues that need to be checked out.
    c. ways of knowing what a person is thinking.
    d. ways to understand meanings.
    e. double meanings.
    Answer: b   **Type: M**   **Page: 218**   **Comprehension**

80. When our nonverbal behavior is unintentional,
    a. others disregard it.
    b. others attach more significance to it.
    c. others can't make interpretations based on it.
    d. others respond with their own unintentional behaviors.
    e. others recognize it and make interpretations based on it.
    Answer: e   **Type: M**   **Page: 212**   **Comprehension**

81. The study of the way people and animals use space is termed
    a. paralanguage.
    b. space technology.
    c. kinesics.
    d. proxemics.
    e. none of the above.
    Answer: d   **Type: M**   **Page: 238**   **Knowledge**

82. The nonverbal ways the voice communicates are termed
    a. paralanguage.
    b. nonverbal toners.
    c. prekinesics.
    d. pitches.
    e. chronemics.
    Answer: a   **Type: M**   **Page: 231**   **Knowledge**

83. Hall's Distance Zones are
    a. personal, impersonal, social, public.
    b. intimate, personal, social, public.
    c. intimate, non-intimate, social, public.
    d. open, blind, hidden, unknown.
    e. none of the above.
    Answer: b   **Type: M**   **Pages: 238–239**   **Knowledge**

84. Most adaptors (self-touching behaviors) are
    a. unconscious.
    b. signs of deception.
    c. excitement cues.
    d. attempts to attract others.
    e. signs of vulnerability.
    Answer: a   **Type: M**   **Pages: 229–230**   **Knowledge**

85. Nonverbal communication is related to perception in that
    a. people who perceive better exhibit more nonverbal behaviors.
    b. we can't perceive most nonverbal behaviors.
    c. we perceive only what our own nonverbal behaviors are.
    d. cultural factors influence how we interpret many nonverbal behaviors.
    e. cultural perception and nonverbal behavior are identical terms.
    Answer: d   **Type: M**   **Ch. 3 & Pages: 223–224**   **Synthesis**

86. Using stammering or "uh, um, er" in conversation is the nonverbal behavior called
    a. affect displays.
    b. microexpressions.
    c. illustrators.
    d. disfluencies.
    e. macroexpressions.
    Answer: d   **Type: M**   **Page: 232**   **Knowledge**

87. The eyes typically send messages of
    a. involvement and avoidance.
    b. primarily negative attitudes.
    c. deception.
    d. contradiction.
    Answer: a   **Type: M**   **Pages: 231**   **Knowledge**

88. The nonverbal term for brief flashes of emotion in the face is
    a. microexpressions.
    b. miniemotions.
    c. manipulators.
    d. disfluencies.
    e. multi–expressions.
    Answer: a   **Type: M**   **Page: 230**   **Knowledge**

89. If you see someone smiling, you could interpret this communication to mean
    a. the other is friendly.
    b. the other is happy.
    c. the other wants to communicate.
    d. the other is faking something.
    e. any of the above
    Answer: e   **Type: M**   **Page: 219**   **Application**

90. Facial expressions are
    a. the easiest nonverbal messages to decode accurately.
    b. often difficult to understand because of their rapid rate of change.
    c. rarely genuine and therefore impossible to decode.
    d. limited, relatively few emotions are shown in the face.
    e. usually more sincere if they last more than 10 seconds.
    Answer: b   **Type: M**   **Page: 230**   **Knowledge**

91. George is staring at Sally for an extended length of time. Research about eye contact indicates that
    a. George is attempting to dominate Sally.
    b. George is trying to avoid Sally.
    c. George is attracted to Sally.
    d. George is angry with Sally.
    e. We cannot accurately decode George's eye contact behavior.
    Answer: e   **Type: M**   **Page: 231**   **Analysis**

92. Your friend insists that she is interested in what you are saying, but she keeps looking out the window while you speak. She is most probably
    a. telling a lie.
    b. bored with the conversation.
    c. noticing something out the window.
    d. daydreaming.
    e. any of the above are equally possible.
    Answer: e   **Type: M**   **Pages: 219**   **Application**

93. Nonverbal communication serves the functions of
    a. repeating and substituting.
    b. complementing and accenting.
    c. regulating and contradicting.
    d. all of the above.
    e. none of the above.
    Answer: d   **Type: M**   **Pages: 214–216**   **Knowledge**

94. In our culture, nodding your head up and down is a deliberate nonverbal behavior with a very precise meaning of "yes." According to your text, this is termed a(n)
    a. facilitator.
    b. interlocutor.
    c. emblem.
    d. nonverbalator.
    e. encoder.
    Answer: c   **Type: M**   **Page: 229**   **Synthesis**

95. All of the following are true about nonverbal communication across cultures, except that
    a. distance patterns vary across cultures.
    b. patterns of eye contact vary around the world.
    c. emblems have precise and distinct meanings within cultural groups.
    d. interpretations of acceptable touch does not vary across cultures.
    e. smiles, laughter, and sour expressions are universal signals of positive or negative emotion.
    Answer: d   **Type: M**   **Pages: 226**   **Synthesis**

96. The nonverbal function equivalent to using italics in print is called
    a. complementing.
    b. accenting.
    c. regulating.
    d. contradicting.
    e. substituting.
    Answer: b   **Type: M**   **Page: 215**   **Comprehension**

97. Which of the following is an example of what social scientists call an emblem?
    a. shaking your head side to side
    b. leaning back in your chair
    c. cracking your knuckles
    d. brushing your hair
    e. increasing your volume
    Answer: a   **Type: M**   **Page: 229**   **Application**

98. Research reveals that increased use of manipulators is often a sign of
    a. discomfort.
    b. power.
    c. shyness.
    d. dogmatism.
    e. inferiority.
    Answer: a   **Type: M**   **Page: 230**   **Comprehension**

99. Vocal intonation patterns, audible breaths, eye contact patterns, and pauses in a conversation are nonverbal behaviors that illustrate the nonverbal function of
   a. substituting.
   b. regulating.
   c. accenting.
   d. repeating.
   e. complementing.
   Answer: b   **Type: M**   **Page: 215–216**   **Application**

100. Apply the research cited in the nonverbal chapter to your life by indicating which effect the following message would have: Your friend says, "I'm really interested in you" while he or she is looking at TV.
   a. You believe the words.
   b. You believe that the speaker is nervous.
   c. You believe the speaker may not be too interested in you since she's/he's not looking at you.
   d. You believe that since there is a good TV program on, you should watch it.
   e. You believe that the speaker has just finished a book on nonverbal communication.
   Answer: c   **Type: M**   **Page: 216**   **Application**

101. All of the following are true about the voice and communication except:
   a. Communicators who speak loudly and without hesitations are viewed as more confident than those who pause and speak quietly.
   b. Younger-sounding communicators whose language is accent-free are rated as more competent than older-sounding communicators.
   c. Some vocal factors influence the way a speaker is perceived.
   d. Accents that identify a speaker's membership in a group lead to more positive evaluations of that person if the group is a prestigious one.
   e. People with more attractive voices are rated more highly than those whose speech sounds less attractive.
   Answer: b   **Type: M**   **Page: 234**   **Comprehension**

102. All of the following behaviors have communicative value except
   a. closed eyes.
   b. walking out of a room.
   c. sitting forward.
   d. an expressionless face.
   e. all of the above do have communicative value.
   Answer: e   **Type: M**   **Page: 212**   **Analysis**

103. The nonverbal behavior of smiling at a friend as you say "come on over here" is an example of the nonverbal function called
    a. substituting.
    b. regulating.
    c. complementing.
    d. contradicting.
    e. accenting.

Answer: c   **Type: M**   **Page: 216**   **Application**

104. If you don't want a friend to know you are unhappy with your relationship, the thing to do is
    a. avoid eye contact.
    b. say less than usual.
    c. stay away from the friend more than usual.
    d. keep your voice free of emotion.
    e. none of the above.

Answer: e   **Type: M**   **Pages: 216–217**   **Analysis**

105. Nonverbal regulators can signal
    a. turn-taking.
    b. the desire to end a conversation.
    c. an invitation to respond.
    d. all of the above.
    e. none of the above.

Answer: d   **Type: M**   **Page: 215–216**   **Knowledge**

106. Nonverbal evidence of lying is most likely to occur when the deceiver
    a. has no strong feelings about the deception.
    b. has not rehearsed the deception.
    c. does not feel anxious or guilty about the lies.
    d. has lack of emotional involvement with the deception.
    e. doesn't know people are watching.

Answer: b   **Type: M**   **Page: 216–217**   **Comprehension**

107. Adaptors are
    a. vocal cues indicating agreement.
    b. a type of unconscious gesture.
    c. facial expressions used to hide deception.
    d. ways to signal turn-taking in conversations.
    e. none of the above.

Answer: b   **Type: M**   **Page: 229**   **Knowledge**

108. In nonverbal communication, studies of leakage deal with
    a. innate behaviors.
    b. illness behaviors.
    c. environmental issues.
    d. deception signals.
    e. perceptions of illness.
    Answer: d   **Type: M**   **Page: 216**   **Application**

109. Someone biting his/her fingernails may be communicating
    a. nervousness.
    b. anticipation.
    c. shyness.
    d. thoughtfulness.
    e. any of the above.
    Answer: e   **Type: M**   **Page: 230**   **Analysis**

110. All of the following are true about nonverbal communication except:
    a. Nonverbal communication is universal for all cultures.
    b. Nonverbal communication may function to contradict verbal messages.
    c. Nonverbal communication is more ambiguous than verbal communication.
    d. Nonverbal signals are much more powerful than verbal messages when they are
        delivered at the same time.
    e. Nonverbal messages aren't as deliberate as verbal messages.
    Answer: a   **Type: M**   **Pages: 223–224**   **Comprehension**

INSTRUCTIONS for questions 111–116: Match each description below with the term it best describes.

    a. chronemics
    b. paralanguage
    c. touching
    d. proxemics
    e. kinesics

111. Study of use and structure of time
    Answer: a   **Type: Matching**   **Page: 242**   **Knowledge**

112. Waving, shaking head or finger
    Answer: d   **Type: Matching**   **Page: 223**   **Knowledge**

113. Arriving early for an appointment.
    Answer: a   **Type: Matching**   **Pages: 242**   **Knowledge**

114. A strong accent or husky voice.
    Answer: e   **Type: Matching**   **Page: 232**   **Knowledge**

115. Hitting, punching, patting, and pinching
    Answer: c   **Type: Matching**   **Pages: 226**   **Knowledge**

116. Stepping closer to indicate intimacy
    Answer: d   **Type: Matching**   **Pages: 238**   **Knowledge**

INSTRUCTIONS for questions 117–124: Match each nonverbal function with the description below it best describes. You will use some letters more than once.

    a. substituting
    b. contradicting
    c. regulating
    d. accenting
    e. repeating

117. Richard fell silent and looked expectantly at Doreen.
     Answer: c   **Type: Matching**   **Page: 216**   **Application**

118. Lois snapped her fingers and shouted, "Hurry up! Get a move on!"
     Answer: d   **Type: Matching**   **Page: 215**   **Application**

119. Nathan suppressed a yawn and slumped in his chair while saying, "Sure I'm interested in hearing about your trip. I'm all ears."
     Answer: b   **Type: Matching**   **Page: 216**   **Application**

120. When asked if she wanted a refill on her coffee, Maria covered the cup with her hand and shook her head.
     Answer: a   **Type: Matching**   **Page: 215**   **Application**

121. When he was asked how old he was, Davie held up four fingers and announced proudly, "I'm four!"
     Answer: e   **Type: Matching**   **Page: 215**   **Application**

122. George folded his arms, leaned nonchalantly against the wall and said sarcastically, "Oooo, yeah, I'm really scared now, I'm trembling."
     Answer: b   **Type: Matching**   **Page: 216**   **Application**

123. Noelle pinched her nose and waved her arms frantically in the air.
     Answer: a   **Type: Matching**   **Page: 215**   **Application**

124. He said quietly, "I'm Paul" and pointed to the name tag on his chest.
     Answer: f   **Type: Matching**   **Page: 215**   **Application**

125. Imagine that you have been commissioned to design a new campus center. What sort of communication should take place there? What kinds of furnishings and decorations would you suggest to increase the likelihood of this communication occurring? What messages would your choice of designs and decorations communicate?
     Answer   **Type: E**   **Pages: 241**   **Evaluation**

126. One characteristic of nonverbal communication is "all behavior has communicative value." Describe two incidents from your experience which illustrate both deliberate and unintentional meaning derived from nonverbal communication in these two incidents. Identify the nonverbal behaviors that occurred. Identify the meanings you did/did not intend to convey and the meanings that were conveyed from your perspective and that of your partner in each incident.
     Answer   **Type: E**   **Page: 212**   **Analysis**

127. Using at least two of the types of nonverbal communication described in your text, and referring to your own experience, describe an incident which illustrates how nonverbal behavior can be ambiguous. How could you or the other person involved reduce the ambiguity of that situation?

Answer   **Type: E**   **Page: 218**   **Application**

128. Describe two interpersonal situations from your experience in which nonverbal behavior accented or contradicted the message being expressed verbally. Be sure that your descriptions of both the verbal message and the nonverbal behaviors are specific. Avoid obvious situations (i.e., yelling reinforces words like "I'm angry").

Answer   **Type: E**   **Pages: 215–216**   **Application**

129. Nonverbal communication reveals attitudes about status. Using examples, describe how status might be communicated through five different types of nonverbal messages.

Answer   **Type: E**   **Pages: 226–242**   **Synthesis**

CHAPTER 7

LISTENING: MORE THAN MEETS THE EAR

1. When deciding how to respond as a listener, men and women alike are most likely to ask a question.
    Answer: F   **Type: T**   **Page: 256**   **Knowledge**

2. According to research, most listeners retain 70% of a message for several weeks.
    Answer: F   **Type: T**   **Page: 256**   **Knowledge**

3. There is no single "best" listening style to use in all situations.
    Answer: T   **Type: T**   **Page: 276**   **Comprehension**

4. A good listener will always state her own opinion so the other person knows where she stands on the issue.
    Answer: F   **Type: T**   **Page: 275**   **Comprehension**

5. You should do more paraphrasing than any other type of listening.
    Answer: F   **Type: T**   **Page: 269**   **Comprehension**

6. We spend more time listening than in any other type of communication.
    Answer: T   **Type: T**   **Page: 248**   **Knowledge**

7. It's impossible to listen effectively all of the time.
    Answer: T   **Type: T**   **Page: 254**   **Knowledge**

8. During careful listening, your heart rate will quicken and your body temperature will rise.
    Answer: T   **Type: T**   **Page: 256**   **Knowledge**

9. Speaking has more apparent advantages than listening does.
    Answer: T   **Type: T**   **Page: 257**   **Knowledge**

10. Like defensiveness, listening is often reciprocal.
    Answer: T   **Type: T**   **Pages: 262**   **Synthesis**

11. Questioning is one type of listening response used to help others.
    Answer: T   **Type: T**   **Page: 264**   **Knowledge**

12. One characteristic of effective paraphrasing is its tentative nature.
    Answer: T   **Type: T**   **Page: 267**   **Synthesis**

13. Your text recommends paraphrasing whenever someone wants your help.
    Answer: F   **Type: T**   **Page: 269**   **Comprehension**

14. Because of its lively, segmented bursts of information, contemporary mass media has helped develop a generation of better listeners.
    Answer: F   **Type: T**   **Page: 259**   **Knowledge**

15. Studies show that good listeners keep eye contact and react with appropriate facial expressions.
    Answer: T   **Type: T**   **Pages: 252**   **Knowledge**

16. According to the text, the most helpful way of responding to a problem is to offer good, specific advice.
    Answer: F   **Type: T**   **Page: 274**   **Comprehension**

17. Speaking is an active process; listening is a passive activity.
    Answer: F   **Type: T**   **Page: 256**   **Comprehension**

18. Paraphrasing is a valuable communication tool because it enables the people who practice it to share more about themselves with others.
    Answer: F   **Type: T**   **Page: 265**   **Comprehension**

19. Listening is an innate ability. Most people become good listeners as they mature.
    Answer: F   **Type: T**   **Page: 257**   **Comprehension**

20. If senders express themselves clearly, there is little need for listeners to respond.
    Answer: F   **Type: T**   **Page: 253**   **Comprehension**

21. Listening behaviors such as insulated listening, pseudolistening, and selective listening are often reasonable responses to a deluge of relatively worthless information.
    Answer: T   **Type: T**   **Page: 254**   **Comprehension**

22. Because prompting involves using silences, it is not classified as a listening response.
    Answer: F   **Type: T**   **Page: 263**   **Knowledge**

23. Prompting is a more passive listening style than advising.
    Answer: T   **Type: T**   **Page: 263**   **Evaluation**

24. Paraphrasing is a good listening style to use if you want to ease back mentally and be entertained.
    Answer: F   **Type: T**   **Pages: 265**   **Evaluation**

25. A questioning response is not really a form of feedback.
    Answer: F   **Type: T**   **Page: 264**   **Synthesis**

26. Even if you give accurate advice to a person, that advice may not be helpful.
    Answer: T   **Type: T**   **Page: 274**   **Knowledge**

27. Accurate analysis of a problem may arouse defensiveness.
    Answer: T   **Type: T**   **Page: 273**   **Knowledge**

28. Sometimes asking questions of a person with a problem only leads to a long digression that confuses matters.
    Answer: T   **Type: T**   **Page: 264**   **Evaluation**

29. When you use paraphrasing as a helping tool, your reflection should usually contain both thoughts and feelings.
    Answer: T   **Type: T**   **Page: 267**   **Knowledge**

30. Questioning and paraphrasing are both forms of feedback.
    Answer: T   **Type: T**   **Pages: 264–265**   **Synthesis**

31. Paraphrasing is recommended as a good listening style both for informational listening and listening to help.
   Answer: T   **Type: T**   **Pages: 266**   **Comprehension**

32. Counterfeit questions are aimed at understanding others.
   Answer: F   **Type: T**   **Pages: 264**   **Comprehension**

33. Analyzing can be one way to help a speaker consider alternative meanings.
   Answer: T   **Type: T**   **Page: 273**   **Knowledge**

34. Counterfeit questions could be a type of ambushing.
   Answer: T   **Type: T**   **Pages: 253, 264**   **Synthesis**

35. Advice given in a respectful, caring way, is always the best listening response to use when listening to help.
   Answer: F   **Type: T**   **Page: 278**   **Knowledge**

36. While paraphrasing responses can be helpful, they are useful only when they accurately reflect the other persons message.
   Answer: F   **Type: T**   **Page: 267**   **Synthesis**

37. Of the many different elements in the listening process, hearing is the physiological dimension.
   Answer: T   **Type: T**   **Page: 249**   **Comprehension**

38. According to your text, people usually try their best to listen but their effectiveness is limited primarily by biological factors.
   Answer: F   **Type: T**   **Pages: 256–258**   **Comprehension**

39. When you are paraphrasing, you need to repeat what the speaker has said word for word.
   Answer: F   **Type: T**   **Page: 267**   **Comprehension**

40. Informational paraphrasing focuses on the ideas a speaker has expressed.
   Answer: T   **Type: T**   **Pages: 266**   **Comprehension**

41. Prompting is a more passive approach to problem-solving than advising or judging.
   Answer: T   **Type: T**   **Page: 363**   **Comprehension**

42. It is possible to use a helping response style that is actually unhelpful.
   Answer: T   **Type: T**   **Pages: 276**   **Synthesis**

43. Since all listening judgments are negative, we should avoid them at all cost.
   Answer: F   **Type: T**   **Page: 275**   **Comprehension**

44. "Stage-hogging" is likely to encourage the pseudolistening response.
   Answer: T   **Type: T**   **Page: 253**   **Analysis**

45. You should rotate your styles of listening after one or two responses so that you don't become bored by any one style.
   Answer: F   **Type: T**   **Page: 276**   **Evaluation**

46. You should use the styles of listening that help the other person and not worry about whether these styles feel comfortable to you.
   Answer: F   **Type: T**   **Page: 279**   **Evaluation**

47. In Paraphrasing on the Job transcript in Chapter Seven, Mark listens to Jill's problems with her boss, most often responding with
   a.   advice and questions.
   b.   prompting and analyzing.
   c.   paraphrasing and questioning.
   d.   supporting and advising.
   e.   judgment

   Answer: c   **Type: M**   **Page: 268**   **Knowledge**

48. In the "Finding Common Ground through Listening" reading in Chapter Seven, pro-choice and pro-life groups overcome which common reasons for ineffective listening?
   a.   message overload
   b.   preoccupation
   c.   faulty assumptions
   d.   rapid thought
   e.   external noise

   Answer: c   **Type: M**   **Page: 262**   **Evaluation**

49. The listening program described in Chapter Seven, "They Learn to Aid Customers," cosmetologists were trained listening skills to
   a.   help customers clarify their thinking.
   b.   provide appropriate advice to their customers.
   c.   frame questions that help sell products.
   d.   constructively criticize customer's hair style choices.
   e.   all of the above

   Answer: a   **Type: M**   **Page: 277**   **Comprehension**

50. In the Looking at Diversity reading in this chapter, Bruce Anderson
   a.   proposes solving inner city problems through listening.
   b.   discusses the advantages to listening to classical music.
   c.   defends his choice to lip-read over learning American Sign Language.
   d.   eliminate overly loud music that leads to hearing problems.
   e.   explains his experience with hearing disability.

   Answer: e   **Type: M**   **Page: 250**   **Knowledge**

51. His supervisor asked Michael to generate a PowerPoint presentation for the Thursday team meeting. On Thursday, Michael showed up without the presentation. Which element of the listening process is where Michael's listening failed?
   a.   hearing
   b.   attending
   c.   understanding
   d.   remembering
   e.   any of above

   Answer: e   **Type: M**   **Pages: 249–252**   **Analysis**

52. According to a study of college students and their communication activities, about 30 percent of their communication time was spent
    a. writing.
    b. speaking.
    c. engaging in face-to-face listening.
    d. reading.
    e. engaging in listening to mass communication media.
    Answer: c   **Type: M**   **Page: 248**   **Recall**

53. All of the following are ineffective listening styles mentioned in the text except
    a. ambushing.
    b. insulated listening.
    c. stage hogging.
    d. pseudolistening.
    e. signal listening.
    Answer: e   **Type: M**   **Pages: 252–254**   **Knowledge**

54. Which best describes the relationship between our rate of hearing speech and the average rate of speaking?
    a. We speak at nearly the same rate we are able to listen.
    b. We can listen 4-6 times faster than an average person speaks.
    c. We are able to speak 2 times faster than an average person can listen.
    d. We are able to listen slightly faster than an average person speaks.
    e. We can listen twice as fast as an average person speaks.
    Answer: b   **Type: M**   **Page: 256**   **Knowledge**

55. The process of using questioning and paraphrasing messages is a type of
    a. linear communication.
    b. insensitive listening.
    c. selective perception.
    d. defensive behavior.
    e. perception checking.
    Answer: e   **Type: M**   **Pages: 115, 288**   **Synthesis**

56. Two kinds of listening to help are
    a. analyzing and supporting.
    b. informational and helpful.
    c. simple and complex.
    d. facilitative and debilitative.
    e. verbatim and restatement.
    Answer: a   **Type: M**   **Pages: 269, 273**   **Comprehension**

57. All of the following are reasons why it is difficult to listen all the time except:
    a. We hear so many verbal messages.
    b. We are often wrapped up in personal concerns.
    c. We comprehend words at a slower rate than people speak them.
    d. We have many physical distractions.
    e. We think speaking has more advantages than listening.
    Answer: c   **Type: M**   **Pages: 256–258**   **Comprehension**

58. Giving only the appearance of being attentive is termed
    a. pseudolistening.
    b. selective listening.
    c. defensive listening.
    d. insensitive listening.
    e. fake listening.
    Answer: a   **Type: M**   **Page: 253**   **Knowledge**

59. Which of the following are styles of listening to help?
    a. advising, judging, analyzing, questioning, and supporting
    b. erupting, advising, sharing, withholding, and evaluating
    c. nonlistening, pseudolistening, evaluating, questioning, and advising
    d. feedback, encoding, decoding, and channel selection
    e. informing, facilitating, sensitizing and sharing
    Answer: a   **Type: M**   **Pages: 263–275**   **Comprehension**

60. The advantage of paraphrasing to help is that
    a. you can clarify your partner's concerns.
    b. you can suggest the solution that's best for your partner.
    c. you can point out your partner's good ideas.
    d. you can share your own experiences and ideas.
    e. all of the above.
    Answer: a   **Type: M**   **Pages: 265–267**   **Comprehension**

61. According to your text, advice is
    a. only to be used when paraphrasing fails.
    b. helpful when it is correct or accurate.
    c. best when preceded by your analysis of a situation.
    d. not necessarily helpful to others just because it worked for you.
    e. less helpful than either supporting or judging response styles.
    Answer: d   **Type: M**   **Page: 274**   **Synthesis**

62. Which is the best helping paraphrase response to the following statement? "My boss
    keeps kidding me about how we should have an affair. I don't know what to do.
    Sometimes I think he's just joking, and sometimes I think it's a real proposition."
    a. "Either way it's sexual harassment, which is illegal. You shouldn't let him get
       away with it!"
    b. "So you can't figure out his motives . . . is that it?"
    c. "You sound upset by this."
    d. "You sound worried and confused because you're not sure if he's coming on to
       you or not?"
    e. "That's a common problem these days. I can see why you're upset, and I don't
       blame you."
    Answer: d   **Type: M**   **Page: 267**   **Analysis**

63. Imagine you've been listening for some time to a friend talk about whether or not to drop out of school. Which is the best helpful paraphrasing response?
   a. "You're confused because there are as many reasons to stay as there are to leave, huh?"
   b. "Which alternative sounds best to you?"
   c. "When you're this confused, it's best to go with your heart."
   d. "You do sound mixed up. Maybe you ought to hold off making a decision for a while."
   e. "Tell me more. I think we can get to the bottom of this if we talk it out. I'm listening."
   Answer: a   **Type: M**   **Pages: 267**   **Analysis**

64. You meet a friend at the supermarket who asks how you are doing. You say, "I'm simply at wits' end--too busy." Which of the following from your friend would qualify as an insensitive listening response?
   a. "Will you come help me study for my math test?"
   b. "So your wits are being tried?"
   c. "Sounds like you are really busy."
   d. "So you're feeling stressed because you've got too much to do?"
   Answer: a   **Type: M**   **Page: 254**   **Analysis**

65. You meet a friend at the supermarket and ask how he is doing. He replies, "I'm OK - just stressed with all these finals." Which of the following is the best helping paraphrasing response you can make?
   a. "Yeah, I know what you mean."
   b. "So, you're stressed, huh?"
   c. "You'll be fine; you always get good grades."
   d. "Bet you're wishing you hadn't taken 18 units, huh?"
   e. "So, you're managing most things just fine, but will be relieved when finals are over?"
   Answer: e   **Type: M**   **Pages: 267**   **Analysis**

66. When you try to reflect the underlying message in a statement, you are engaging in
   a. judging.
   b. questioning.
   c. paraphrasing.
   d. prompting.
   e. pseudolistening.
   Answer: c   **Type: M**   **Page: 267**   **Comprehension**

67. Which of the following bodily changes occurs during careful listening?
   a. heart rate quickens
   b. respiration increases
   c. body temperature rises
   d. all of the above
   e. none of the above
   Answer: d   **Type: M**   **Pages: 256**   **Comprehension**

68. Which of the following is the best helpful paraphrase to "I'm really bummed out about my apartment situation."
    a. "So, you're bummed out, huh?"
    b. "Your apartment situation is bad?"
    c. "You're depressed because you haven't found a place to live yet?"
    d. "You should really get a new place; I agree."
    e. "It will all work out by next month."
    Answer: c   Type: M   Pages: 267   Analysis

69. Constructive criticism is a kind of listening response that falls into the category termed
    a. advising.
    b. judging.
    c. analyzing.
    d. supporting.
    e. questioning.
    Answer: b   Type: M   Page: 275   Comprehension

70. Before you meet with your professor, you think that she will talk "over your head." When you actually speak with her, you have a difficult time understanding what she is saying. Based on the information given above, the most likely cause of your listening problem is
    a. lack of effort.
    b. lack of advantages.
    c. faulty assumptions.
    d. rapid thought.
    e. preoccupation.
    Answer: c   Type: M   Page: 256   Application

71. Your roommate gives the appearance of listening to you, but you can tell from her responses that her mind is elsewhere. You could call her listening style in this instance
    a. stage hogging.
    b. insulated listening.
    c. pseudolistening.
    d. defensive listening.
    e. ambushing.
    Answer: c   Type: M   Page: 253   Application

72. Which of the following is the best helping paraphrase response for the statement: "I can't stand that class! The lectures are a waste of time, and the tests are full of nit-picking questions. I'm not learning anything."
    a. "Sounds like you're fed up with the class."
    b. "Sounds like you're thinking about dropping the class."
    c. "Sounds like the class has nit-picking tests and is a waste of time."
    d. "Sounds like you resent spending so much time on information you don't consider useful."
    e. "Sounds like you're fed up with school."
    Answer: d   Type: M   Page: 267   Application

73. Paraphrasing can be considered a form of
    a. perception checking.
    b. nonverbal communication.
    c. assertive communication.
    d. bypassing.
    e. emotional contagion.
    Answer: a   **Type: M**   **Pages: 115, 266–267 Synthesis**

74. The ability of a listener to think faster than a speaker can talk
    a. often contributes to poor listening.
    b. allows the listener to understand the speaker's ideas better.
    c. creates the potential for psychological noise in the listener.
    d. all of the above
    e. none of the above
    Answer: d   **Type: M**   **Page: 256**   **Comprehension**

75. The tentative nature of paraphrasing thoughts and feelings means that it is
    a. open-minded.
    b. longer.
    c. objective.
    d. brief.
    e. subjective
    Answer: a   **Type: M**   **Pages: 266–267**   **Synthesis**

76. "I think that the reason you're so confused is that you're trying to make everyone else happy and forgetting your own happiness." This statement is what type of listening response?
    a. supporting
    b. advising
    c. questioning
    d. paraphrasing
    e. analyzing
    Answer: e   **Type: M**   **Page: 273**   **Application**

77. "From what you've said, it sounds like you're mad at your boss for expecting you to drop your personal plans whenever he wants you to work. Is that right?" This statement is what type of response?
    a. supporting
    b. judging
    c. questioning
    d. paraphrasing
    e. analyzing
    Answer: d   **Type: M**   **Page: 265**   **Application**

78. "Sure it's unfair. But you shouldn't let that stop you. Life is unfair, so you're crazy to let it bother you." This statement is what type of response?
    a. supporting
    b. judging
    c. questioning
    d. paraphrasing
    e. parroting
    Answer: b　　　　**Type: M**　　　　**Page: 275**　　　　**Application**

79. Paraphrasing
    a. is a type of perception checking.
    b. helps to demonstrate empathy.
    c. encourages further self-disclosure.
    d. illustrates the transactional nature of communication.
    e. all of the above
    Answer: e　　　　**Type: M**　　　　**Pages:11, 115, 118, 265 Synthesis**

80. All of the following are described in the text as helping responses except
    a. analyzing.
    b. judging.
    c. repeating.
    d. supporting.
    e. paraphrasing.
    Answer: c　　　　**Type: M**　　　　**Pages: 263–275**　　　　**Comprehension**

81. "I just can't decide whether I can afford to move out on my own. Do you think I'll be able to handle it financially?" Which of the following is a prompting response to this statement?
    a. "I guess you're worried that you can't make it ."
    b. "I don't know, really. Do you think you will?"
    c. "You know best because it is your money."
    d. "I can't imagine why you'd spend all that money on rent when you can live at home for free."
    e. "If your parents could just help you out a little, then you could make it."
    Answer: b　　　　**Type: M**　　　　**Page: 263**　　　　**Application**

82. Which of the following is an informational paraphrase to the statement, "You've got to get those reports in on time or it looks bad for both of us."
    a. "Sounds like you're upset with me."
    b. "Could you help me out by reminding me when the deadlines are?"
    c. "Are you saying you're going to fire me if I don't?"
    d. "Because I didn't get the Murphy report done by last Friday, you and I are both in trouble?"
    e. "Those guys in upper management are too uptight about deadlines."
    Answer: d　　　　**Type: M**　　　　**Page: 288**　　　　**Application**

83. When choosing the best listening style, it is important to consider
    a. the situation.
    b. the other person.
    c. yourself.
    d. both a and b above.
    e. a, b, and c above.
    Answer: e   **Type: M**   **Pages: 278–279**   **Comprehension**

INSTRUCTIONS for questions 84–109: Match each statement with the helping listening style it characterizes.

    a. paraphrasing
    b. judging
    c. supporting
    d. advising
    e. analyzing

84. "That's a terrible idea!"
    Answer: b   **Type: Matching**   **Page: 275**   **Analysis**

85. "You ought to give it a try. You've got nothing to lose."
    Answer: d   **Type: Matching**   **Page: 274**   **Analysis**

86. "You're really afraid of failing, aren't you?"
    Answer: e   **Type: Matching**   **Page: 273**   **Analysis**

87. "Don't let it get you down. You're doing a great job."
    Answer: c   **Type: Matching**   **Page: 269**   **Analysis**

88. "Sure it's discouraging now, but it will be over soon."
    Answer: c   **Type: Matching**   **Page: 269**   **Analysis**

89. "So you're upset because Chris didn't pay you back?"
    Answer: a   **Type: Matching**   **Page: 265**   **Analysis**

90. "You'll never know what he thinks unless you ask."
    Answer: d   **Type: Matching**   **Page: 274**   **Analysis**

91. "Have you ever thought about just giving her what she wants?"
    Answer: d   **Type: Matching**   **Page: 274**   **Analysis**

92. "I can't believe it! He's really a jerk for saying that."
    Answer: b   **Type: Matching**   **Page: 275**   **Analysis**

93. "So you're hoping they'll call, but you're not sure what you'll say if they do?"
    Answer: a   **Type: Matching**   **Page: 265**   **Analysis**

94. "Of course you get pushed around. That's what happens when you don't tell people what you want."
    Answer: b   **Type: Matching**   **Page: 275**   **Analysis**

95. "If you can't be honest, you're not a real friend."
    Answer: b   **Type: Matching**   **Page: 275**   **Analysis**

96. "Sounds like you're mad at me for embarrassing you. Is that right?"
Answer: a   **Type: Matching**   **Page: 265**   **Analysis**

97. "You've always done fine in the past. Don't worry; you can do it this time, too."
Answer: c   **Type: Matching**   **Page: 269**   **Analysis**

98. "You'd be a lot happier if you stopped blaming everyone else for your problems."
Answer: b   **Type: Matching**   **Page: 275**   **Analysis**

99. "It seems to me you're only doing that to get back at him for cheating on you."
Answer: e   **Type: Matching**   **Page: 273**   **Analysis**

100. "Don't try so hard and you'll probably do better."
Answer: d   **Type: Matching**   **Page: 274**   **Analysis**

101. "Your problem isn't being too mean; you're afraid of being too nice!"
Answer: e   **Type: Matching**   **Page: 273**   **Analysis**

102. "The reason you're insecure is that money means a lot to you."
Answer: e   **Type: Matching**   **Page: 273**   **Analysis**

103. "Don't give up. You'll get it this next time."
Answer: c   **Type: Matching**   **Page: 269**   **Analysis**

104. "Your sister has a strong hold on you, and that's why you're afraid to face your parents."
Answer: e   **Type: Matching**   **Page: 274**   **Analysis**

105. "Are you saying that you're hesitant to take a math class for fear of failing?"
Answer: a   **Type: Matching**   **Page: 265**   **Analysis**

106. "Have you tried just talking to her about it?"
Answer: d   **Type: Matching**   **Page: 274**   **Analysis**

107. "I think you're still unsure of yourself because of all the moving you did as a child."
Answer: e   **Type: Matching**   **Page: 273**   **Analysis**

108. "I think it's a good idea and you're a good person."
Answer: b   **Type: Matching**   **Page: 275**   **Analysis**

109. "Hey, he didn't leave you the last time this happened; he won't this time."
Answer: c   **Type: Matching**   **Page: 269**   **Analysis**

110. We have all been selective, insulated, defensive, insensitive, and ambushing listeners. Give an example of each type of listening from your own personal experience. Illustrate any misunderstandings that developed as a result of your listening behavior.
Answer   **Type: E**   **Page: 253**   **Analysis**

111. Chapter Seven lists seven different types of listening responses. Imagine a speaker says the following remarks to you. Write seven responses to this situation—an example of prompting, questioning, paraphrase, support, analysis, advice and judgment. *"This woman at work never speaks to me. I mean, I come in and say something like, 'Hi, how are you?' and she just stares at me. Rude, right? How can a person just ignore someone?"*
Answer   **Type: E**   **Pages: 263–275 Application**

112. Describe an unsuccessful communication transaction in which you used a poor listening style to receive information. Discuss the advantages and disadvantages of using paraphrasing to improve the reception of the information.

Answer   **Type: E**   **Page: 269**   **Synthesis**

113. Describe the style(s) of listening you use most often when helping others. How successful are these styles? What makes them successful or unsuccessful? What might you do to increase your effectiveness as a helpful listener?

Answer   **Type: E**   **Pages: 263–276**   **Evaluation**

114. In your own words, describe what paraphrasing is and how it is used to help others solve their problems. Use real or hypothetical examples and concrete specific language to explain and illustrate your answer.

Answer   **Type: E**   **Pages: 265–267**   **Synthesis**

115. Read the following three hypothetical situations and discuss for each which of the seven listening responses described on pages 263–275 in your text might suit the situation and other person best. Explain why your choices are more likely to be helpful than the other types of listening responses.
- Your employer is giving complicated directions for a task you must do.
- A friend storms into the room clearly furious over something that happened to her while she was at school today.
- Your brother comes to you about a job offer that he's trying to decide about accepting.

Answer   **Type: E**   **Pages: 263–275**   **Application**
                                                               Evaluation

116. Recount an interpersonal situation in which you failed to listen effectively. Describe the factors which caused you to listen poorly. What could you have done to change those factors?

Answer   **Type: E**   **Pages: 256–258**   **Evaluation**

CHAPTER 8

COMMUNICATION AND
RELATIONAL DYNAMICS

1. Dialectical tensions arise when a relationship is new and tend to disappear after the first two years.
   Answer: F   **Type: T**   **Pages: 300–310**   **Knowledge**

2. Research reported in Chapter 8 indicates that long term relationships are most satisfying when the partners do everything together.
   Answer: F   **Type: T**   **Page: 301**   **Comprehension**

3. Of the three types of dialectical tensions, research indicates that young married couples report having the most difficulty with the openness versus privacy tension.
   Answer: F   **Type: T**   **Page: 302**   **Knowledge**

4. Your text suggests that while benevolent lies are common, the truth is always the best course of action.
   Answer: F   **Type: T**   **Pages: 323–324**   **Synthesis**

5. People with especially high or low self-esteem find "perfect" people more attractive than people who are competent but flawed.
   Answer: T   **Type: T**   **Page: 286**   **Knowledge**

6. Self-disclosure is more effective when it is used frequently by a communicator.
   Answer: F   **Type: T**   **Page: 310**   **Comprehension**

7. According to Chapter Eight, we are usually attracted to people who are similar to us.
   Answer: T   **Type: T**   **Page: 285**   **Comprehension**

8. To be good at self-disclosure you need to disclose frequently and steadily to keep up your skill.
   Answer: F   **Type: T**   **Page: 310**   **Comprehension**

9. Small talk typically occurs during the initiating stage of an interpersonal relationship.
   Answer: F   **Type: T**   **Page: 294**   **Knowledge**

10. The experimenting stage of interpersonal relationships is characterized by small talk.
    Answer: T   **Type: T**   **Page: 294**   **Knowledge**

11. Not only is the Internet increasingly being used to initiate relationships, but is being used to terminate them as well.
    Answer: T   **Type: T**   **Page: 299**   **Comprehension**

12. We can categorize interpersonal relationships as intimate or not by the place in which they occur.
    Answer: F   **Type: T**   **Page: 287**   **Synthesis**

13.   Self-disclosure must be frequent to be effective.
      Answer: F   **Type: T**   **Page: 310**   **Comprehension**

14.   According to Chapter Eight, we are more attracted to people who are good at what
      they do but admit their mistakes.
      Answer: T   **Type: T**   **Page: 286**   **Knowledge**

15.   The terminating stage of an interpersonal relationship can be quite short or drawn out
      over time.
      Answer: T   **Type: T**   **Page: 298**   **Knowledge**

16.   Any healthy relationship will go through all the ten stages of interpersonal
      relationships from initiating to terminating, as described in Chapter Eight of your
      text.
      Answer: F   **Type: T**   **Pages: 300**   **Knowledge**

17.   Cliches, the outer circle of the self-disclosure model in your text, are the most
      revealing type of communication.
      Answer: F   **Type: T**   **Page: 309**   **Knowledge**

18.   The most revealing level of self-disclosure usually involves talking about feelings.
      Answer: T   **Type: T**   **Page: 309**   **Knowledge**

19.   Bringing up feelings, like, "I feel uncomfortable when you drop by without calling,"
      is not appropriate to self-disclosure situations.
      Answer: F   **Type: T**   **Page: 313**   **Comprehension**

20.   After we get to know others, their liking for us becomes less of a factor in our
      attraction toward them.
      Answer: T   **Type: T**   **Page: 286**   **Synthesis**

21.   Reciprocal liking builds attractiveness.
      Answer: T   **Type: T**   **Page: 286**   **Knowledge**

22.   People are judged as attractive when they match the amount and content of their self-
      disclosure to the self-disclosure of others.
      Answer: T   **Type: T**   **Page: 316**   **Knowledge**

23.   A well-documented conclusion from research is that one act of self-disclosure usually
      begets another from the other party.
      Answer: T   **Type: T**   **Page: 311**   **Knowledge**

24.   When we self-disclose to strangers, it is usually for reciprocity or identity formation.
      Answer: T   **Type: T**   **Page: 311**   **Comprehension**

25.   It is quite possible to have a wide range of satisfying relationships without having
      much intimacy at all.
      Answer: T   **Type: T**   **Page: 287**   **Knowledge**

26.   Social circles merge and the relational partners take on a new relational identity in
      the intensifying stage of relationships.
      Answer: F   **Type: T**   **Page: 296**   **Comprehension**

27.   The strongest influence on why people disclose seems to be how well they know the
      other person.
      Answer: T   **Type: T**   **Page: 307**   **Knowledge**

28. Intimacy can come from intellectual sharing alone.
    Answer: T   **Type: T**   **Page: 287**   **Comprehension**

29. In interpersonal relationships, the rule is: The more self-disclosure the better.
    Answer: F   **Type: T**   **Page: 310**   **Comprehension**

30. The Johari Window model suggests that the amount of intimacy in a relationship is determined by the most open person.
    Answer: F   **Type: T**   **Page: 287, 310**   **Synthesis**

31. In most instances, the relational stage of bonding generates social support for the relationship.
    Answer: T   **Type: T**   **Page: 296**   **Knowledge**

32. Differentiation in relationships is always negative, since it is part of the "coming apart" process.
    Answer: F   **Type: T**   **Page: 297**   **Comprehension**

33. The circumscribing stage of interpersonal relationships involves total avoidance of the other.
    Answer: F   **Type: T**   **Page: 297**   **Comprehension**

34. Since they are honest and true, comments to another, like "I've always thought you were a bit flaky," have constructive effects in self-disclosure.
    Answer: F   **Type: T**   **Page: 314**   **Comprehension**

35. Many long-term relationships aren't characterized by a constant exchange of intimate details.
    Answer: T   **Type: T**   **Page: 304–305**   **Comprehension**

36. The deepest and most effective self-disclosure will include much detail about your past life.
    Answer: F   **Type: T**   **Page: 309**   **Comprehension**

37. Lies may help us avoid embarrassment.
    Answer: T   **Type: T**   **Page: 322**   **Comprehension**

38. The initiating stage of interpersonal relationships is usually brief.
    Answer: T   **Type: T**   **Page: 294**   **Comprehension**

39. Communication, during the initiating stage of interpersonal relationships, is usually characterized by lengthy investigations into the personality of the parties involved.
    Answer: F   **Type: T**   **Page: 294**   **Comprehension**

40. Self-disclosure on both sides is usually necessary for the development of a satisfying interpersonal relationship.
    Answer: T   **Type: T**   **Page: 316**   **Comprehension**

41. According to your text, the ease of self-disclosure is increased by including a third party in your discussion.
    Answer: F   **Type: T**   **Page: 307**   **Comprehension**

42. Hints are more direct than equivocal statements.
    Answer: T   **Type: T**   **Page: 323**   **Comprehension**

43. Most lies are told for the benefit of the recipient.

Answer: F   **Type: T**   **Page: 318**   **Comprehension**

44. All self-disclosure leads to liking or attractiveness.
    Answer: F   **Type: T**   **Page: 314**   **Comprehension**

45. Research shows that people are judged as attractive in proportion to the amount to which they disclose themselves to others, no matter what the situation.
    Answer: F   **Type: T**   **Page: 314**   **Comprehension**

46. Your text makes the case that hints, benign lies, and equivocations are sometimes ethical alternatives to telling the truth.
    Answer: T   **Type: T**   **Page: 323**   **Synthesis**

47. Self-disclosure is more effective when it is used in the context of a positive relationship.
    Answer: T   **Type: T**   **Page: 314**   **Knowledge**

48. Self-disclosure of personal thoughts and feelings may be inappropriate and risky in the work setting.
    Answer: T   **Type: T**   **Page: 314**   **Application**

49. Good listening skills are necessary aspects of your self-disclosure skills because you have to listen well to others in order to match the content and amount of your self-disclosure to theirs.
    Answer: T   **Type: T**   **Pages: 316**   **Synthesis**

50. Most self-disclosure is reciprocal.
    Answer: T   **Type: T**   **Page: 316**   **Comprehension**

51. You should avoid making disclosing statements that contain negative messages.
    Answer: F   **Type: T**   **Page: 313**   **Comprehension**

52. Self-disclosure can have the effect of an attack on the other person.
    Answer: T   **Type: T**   **Page: 314**   **Comprehension**

53. The best way to develop a positive interpersonal relationship is usually to begin that relationship by revealing a great amount of highly personal information about yourself.
    Answer: F   **Type: T**   **Page: 309**   **Knowledge**

54. People sometimes self-disclose to create a good impression.
    Answer: T   **Type: T**   **Page: 312**   **Knowledge**

55. According to the text, real self-disclosure does not involve attempts at control of the other.
    Answer: F   **Type: T**   **Page: 312**   **Comprehension**

56. If research in the text is accurate, your relationship will be likely to end if you discover your partner has told you a serious lie.
    Answer: T   **Type: T**   **Page: 321**   **Synthesis**

57. Physical intimacy is obviously the best type of relational intimacy.
    Answer: F   **Type: T**   **Page: 287**   **Evaluation**

58. The "Blind" window of the Johari model represents things about yourself that another may know about you, but you do not.
    Answer: T   **Type: T**   **Page: 310**   **Knowledge**

59. The "Unknown" window of the Johari model represents things about yourself that another knows, but you do not.
    Answer: F   **Type: T**   **Page: 310**   **Comprehension**

60. The social penetration model represents both the breadth and the depth of your self-disclosure with another person.
    Answer: T   **Type: T**   **Page: 307**   **Knowledge**

61. Just because we have revealed many different kinds of facts to another doesn't mean that we have an intimate relationship.
    Answer: T   **Type: T**   **Page: 309**   **Comprehension**

62. We form many relationships with others because they are like us in some ways and different from us in others.
    Answer: T   **Type: T**   **Page: 285**   **Comprehension**

63. Attraction to others is greatest when we perceive we are similar to them in a high percentage of important areas, like goals and beliefs.
    Answer: T   **Type: T**   **Page: 285**   **Comprehension**

64. Differences strengthen a relationship when they are complementary.
    Answer: T   **Type: T**   **Pages: 285**   **Knowledge**

65. Social exchange theory suggests that self-disclosure is an outdated semi-economic model of relationships.
    Answer: F   **Type: T**   **Page: 292**   **Comprehension**

66. The fact that we are attracted to competent people means that we need to appear flawless to others.
    Answer: F   **Type: T**   **Page: 286**   **Analysis**

67. Self-disclosure tends to draw people closer as long as the messages are perceived to be appropriate.
    Answer: T   **Type: T**   **Page: 286**   **Knowledge**

68. Constant self-disclosure is a useful goal for those of us trying to improve a relationship.
    Answer: F   **Type: T**   **Page: 313**   **Comprehension**

69. Not all self-disclosure draws people closer.
    Answer: T   **Type: T**   **Page: 314**   **Synthesis**

70. Research shows that deception threatens relationships.
    Answer: T   **Type: T**   **Page: 321**   **Knowledge**

71. Some lies are designed to make the relationship grow.
    Answer: T   **Type: T**   **Page: 318**   **Knowledge**

72. Circumscribing is the stage in the relationship process during which partners become emotionally closer.
    Answer: F   **Type: T**   **Page: 297**   **Knowledge**

73. Dialectical tensions exist in relationships when two incompatible forces or pressures exist at the same time.
Answer: T   Type: T   Page: 301   Comprehension

74. If a communicator is truly competent, he/she will be able to resolve the conflicting needs involved in dialectical tensions competently.
Answer: F   Type: T   Page: 301   Analysis

75. If faced with a choice to tell a face-saving lie or deliver an equivocal message, most people will tell the lie.
Answer: F   Type: T   Page: 321   Knowledge

76. In Chapter Eight's "Looking At Diversity" reading, Matt DeLanoy talks about how communicating on the Internet makes it easier to meet people since he
   a.   is very shy.
   b.   is overweight.
   c.   stutters.
   d.   is physically disabled.
   e.   none of the above
Answer: c   Type: M   Page: 293   Knowledge

77. In the "Is Misleading Your Spouse Fraud or Tact?" reading in Chapter Eight, Ronald Askew's wife
   a.   had an affair and lied about it.
   b.   concealed her lack of sexual attraction for him.
   c.   lied to him about a previous marriage.
   d.   Pretended she thought his jokes were funny.
   e.   None of the above.
Answer: b   Type: M   Page: 320   Knowledge

78. In the Chapter Eight Communication Transcript, Ramon discloses to his boss, Julie. Which of the following guidelines for self-disclosure did Ramon seem to ignore as he talked with Julie?
   a.   Ask yourself if the risk of disclosure is reasonable.
   b.   Determine if the self-disclosure is relevant to the situation at hand.
   c.   Decide if the other person is important to you.
   d.   Select the appropriate amount and type of self-disclosure.
   e.   Ramon ignored all of the guidelines.
Answer: d   Type: M   Page: 313–315   Analysis

79. According to your text, there are three alternatives to self-disclosure:
   a.   white lies, equivocation, and hinting.
   b.   empathy, evasion, and evaluation.
   c.   strategy, straightforwardness, and spontaneity.
   d.   lying, circling, and confessing.
   e.   stroking, withholding, and sandbagging.
Answer: a   Type: M   Page: 317–323   Knowledge

80. According to your text, all of the following are reasons to be somewhat deceitful in relationships except
    a. to guide social interaction.
    b. to empower others.
    c. to save face.
    d. to avoid conflict.
    e. to expand or reduce relationships.
    Answer: b   **Type: M**   **Pages: 317–319**   **Synthesis**

81. You've just delivered a speech to your classmates. None of them liked your speech very much. According to your text, which of the following is the response you are most likely to hear from them when you ask how you did?
    a. "You did a great job."
    b. "I'm nervous about my speech tomorrow."
    c. "I don't think it was a very good speech."
    d. "You made some interesting points."
    Answer: d   **Type: M**   **Page: 321**   **Application**

82. The Johari Window is an important device to help explore the role
    a. coding plays in communication.
    b. interpretation plays in clarifying understanding.
    c. feedback plays in negative relationships.
    d. self-disclosure plays in communication.
    e. affection needs play in strong relationships.
    Answer: d   **Type: M**   **Page: 310**   **Knowledge**

83. According to the text, which of the following is good advice about self-disclosure?
    a. Wait for the other person to open up before you do.
    b. The more self-disclosure, the better.
    c. Self-disclosure is "safest" in twosomes, and not around others.
    d. Most relationships are characterized by almost constant amounts of self-disclosure.
    e. It's best to accompany each piece of negative self-disclosure with a compliment to soften any hurt.
    Answer: c   **Type: M**   **Pages: 313–314**   **Synthesis**

84. The social penetration model by Altman and Taylor
    a. shows ways in which a relationship can be more or less intimate.
    b. suggests how relationships can operate on superficial or more personal levels.
    c. defines a relationship in terms of its breadth and depth.
    d. helps identify why certain relationships are strong or weak.
    e. all of the above
    Answer: e   **Type: M**   **Page: 307**   **Analysis**

85. According to the text, we are usually attracted to people who
    a. like us.
    b. are high self-disclosers.
    c. are perfect.
    d. approve of us even in ways we know are inaccurate.
    Answer: a   **Type: M**   **Pages: 286**   **Comprehension**

86. To qualify as self-disclosure, a statement must
    a. involve feelings.
    b. be intentional, significant, and not otherwise known.
    c. be reciprocated by the same type of statement from a partner.
    d. involve intimate information.
    e. be shared privately.
    Answer: b   **Type: M**   **Pages: 305, 307**   **Comprehension**

87. "I've never been out of this state" is an example of self-disclosure at which of the following levels?
    a. cliche
    b. fact
    c. opinion
    d. feeling
    e. interpretation
    Answer: b   **Type: M**   **Page: 309**   **Application**

88. "It's nice to meet you" is an example of self-disclosure at which of the following levels?
    a. cliche
    b. fact
    c. opinion
    d. feeling
    e. interpretation
    Answer: a   **Type: M**   **Page: 309**   **Application**

89. "I'm worried that you won't follow through on your commitment" is an example of self-disclosure at which of the following levels?
    a. cliche
    b. fact
    c. opinion
    d. feeling
    e. interpretation
    Answer: d   **Type: M**   **Page: 309**   **Application**

90. "I don't think you're telling the truth" is an example of self-disclosure at which of the following levels?
    a. cliche
    b. fact
    c. opinion
    d. feeling
    e. interpretation
    Answer: c   **Type: M**   **Page: 309**   **Application**

91. Quadrants of the Johari Window are
    a. open, narrow, blind, unknown.
    b. open, hidden, blind, unknown.
    c. broad, narrow, blind, unknown.
    d. open, hidden, neutral, unknown.
    e. open, closed, neutral, unknown.
    Answer: b   **Type: M**   **Page: 310**   **Knowledge**

92. Which of the following best fits the definition of self-disclosure given in this class?
    a. telling your romantic partner about your feelings toward him/her
    b. telling your college teacher about past grades
    c. telling your mother your weight
    d. telling your family physician about your health
    e. telling anyone anything about you
    Answer: a   **Type: M**   **Pages: 305, 307**   **Application**

93. According to Knapp's model of interaction stages, symbolic public gestures that show the world that a relationship exists usually occur in which stage in interpersonal relationships?
    a. experimenting
    b. intensifying
    c. bonding
    d. integrating
    e. circumscribing
    Answer: c   **Type: M**   **Page: 296**   **Knowledge**

94. When the target of self-disclosure is a friend, the most frequent reason people give for volunteering personal information is
    a. to get to know the other better.
    b. relationship maintenance and enhancement.
    c. defensiveness reduction.
    d. self-validation.
    e. manipulation.
    Answer: b   **Type: M**   **Page: 312**   **Knowledge**

95. With strangers as the target of self-disclosure, the most common reason people give for disclosing is
    a. defensiveness reduction.
    b. manipulation.
    c. reciprocity.
    d. relationship maintenance.
    e. relationship enhancement.
    Answer: c   **Type: M**   **Page: 311**   **Knowledge**

96. Which of the following changes does not typically occur in the intensifying stage of interpersonal relationships?
    a. Forms of address become more informal.
    b. The parties begin to take on an identity as a social unit.
    c. Feelings of commitment are directly expressed.
    d. Increased familiarity leads to verbal shortcuts.
    e. The parties begin to refer to themselves as " we."
    Answer: b   **Type: M**   **Page: 295**   **Synthesis**

97. Social exchange theory suggests that we often seek out people who can give us
    a. rewards greater than or equal to the costs we encounter in dealing with them.
    b. more self-esteem.
    c. relational rewards rather than physical ones.
    d. something in exchange for what we give them.
    e. both relational and physical things without demanding anything of us.
    Answer: a   **Type: M**   **Page: 292**   **Knowledge**

98. "This was a rotten idea" is an example of self-disclosure at which of the following levels?
    a. cliche
    b. fact
    c. opinion
    d. feeling
    e. interpretation
    Answer: c   **Type: M**   **Page: 309**   **Application**

99. "Why don't you go ahead and visit your friends without me this weekend. I'll stick around and catch up on my studies." This statement typifies which relational stage?
    a. integrating
    b. differentiating
    c. bonding
    d. terminating
    e. intensifying
    Answer: b   **Type: M**   **Page: 297**   **Application**

100. When two opposing or incompatible forces exist simultaneously in an interpersonal relationship, the struggle to achieve these opposing goals creates what is called a
    a. collectivistic tension.
    b. differentiating end state.
    c. counterfeit goal state.
    d. dialectical tension.
    e. proximity problem.
    Answer: d   **Type: M**   **Page: 301**   **Knowledge**

101. Conflicting desires for connection and independence in an interpersonal relationship lead to the
    a. connection-autonomy dialectic.
    b. cohesion-revolt dialectic.
    c. predictability-novelty dialectic.
    d. openness-privacy dialectic.
    Answer: a   **Type: M**   **Page: 301**   **Knowledge**

102. Conflicting desires for both intimacy and the lack of it in an interpersonal relationship lead to the
    a. connection-autonomy dialectic.
    b. cohesion-revolt dialectic.
    c. predictability-novelty dialectic.
    d. openness-privacy dialectic.
    Answer: d   **Type: M**   **Page: 301**   **Knowledge**

103. Of all the strategies for managing dialectical tensions, _____ is the least functional.
    a. denial
    b. disorientation
    c. alternation
    d. segmentation
    Answer: a   **Type: M**   **Page: 301**   **Knowledge**

104. Judith and Natalie work for the same employer and both women often talk at lunch together about their current romances, problems with family, and apartment headaches. Most Saturday afternoons they play tennis together. Which relationship stage do they seem to be in?
    a. initiating
    b. differentiating
    c. bonding
    d. intensifying
    e. circumscribing
    Answer: d   **Type: M**   **Page: 295**   **Application**

105. Molly makes an excuse not to attend a party she knows Jack is invited to. She's most
     likely in which stage with Jack?
     a. initiating
     b. avoiding
     c. circumscribing
     d. experimenting
     e. bonding
     Answer: b   **Type: M**   **Page: 298**   **Application**

INSTRUCTIONS for questions 106–110: Match the statement below with the term it best describes.

     a.   self-disclosure
     b.   Knapp's staircase model
     c.   Johari Window
     d.   social penetration
     e.   exchange

106. Model to explore the role of self-disclosure in relationships
     Answer: c   **Type: Matching**   **Page: 310**   **Knowledge**

107. Model to examine breadth and depth of relationships
     Answer: d   **Type: Matching**   **Page: 307**   **Knowledge**

108. Explains stages in relationships
     Answer: b   **Type: Matching**   **Page: 294**   **Knowledge**

109. Voluntarily revealing personal information
     Answer: a   **Type: Matching**   **Page: 305**   **Knowledge**

110. Theory explaining costs and rewards in relationships
     Answer: e   **Type: Matching**   **Page: 292**   **Knowledge**

INSTRUCTIONS for questions 111–115: Match the statement below with the relational stage it best
describes.

     a. avoiding
     b. circumscribing
     c. experimenting
     d. integrating
     e. differentiating

111. Relational partners attempt to reduce uncertainty and to decide if the relationship is
     worth pursuing.
     Answer: c   **Type: Matching**   **Page: 294**   **Knowledge**

112. Relational partners begin to share identities and their social circles merge.
     Answer: d   **Type: Matching**   **Page: 296**   **Knowledge**

113. Relational partners begin to withdraw from one another to avoid disagreement,
     interest in one another is shrinking.
     Answer: b   **Type: Matching**   **Page: 297**   **Knowledge**

114. Relational partners create physical distance between one another, make excuses to reduce contact.

Answer: a   **Type: Matching**   **Page: 298**   **Knowledge**

115. Relational partners often experience the first signs of the connection—autonomy dialectical tension.

Answer: e   **Type: Matching**   **Page: 297**   **Knowledge**

116. Discuss the relationship between risk and trust. Evaluate how these two are related to self-disclosure. Apply this discussion to a relationship in which you are involved.

Answer   **Type: E**   **Pages: 313–314**   **Evaluation**

117. Referring to the reasons for deceit outlined in your chapter, analyze a current relationship you are in according to the degrees of truthfulness and deceit. Are you satisfied with the level of honesty? Explain your answer.

Answer   **Type: E**   **Pages: 317–321**   **Analysis**

118. Using the social penetration model in your text, describe the breadth and depth of one important interpersonal relationship you have. Explain why you are satisfied/unsatisfied with this relationship.

Answer   **Type: E**   **Page: 307**   **Synthesis**

119. Describe one important relationship in which you are involved in terms of the stages of interpersonal relationships found in your text. Give specific behavioral examples that illustrate your relationship is in a particular stage. Give a history of your relationship as it relates to the stages of relationships found in your text and speculate as to the next stage you will move to or the stage at which you have stabilized.

Answer   **Type: E**   **Pages: 294–298**   **Evaluation**

120. Draw a Johari Window describing your relationship with an important person in your life. Comment on which parts of yourself you keep in the "hidden" area, and explain your reasons for doing so. Describe the benefits and costs of not disclosing these parts of your personality. Next, look at the size of the "blind" area model. Is the blind area large or small because of the amount of feedback you get from the other person, or because of the way you react to the feedback you do get? How would a window describing your partner's relationship with a mutual friend look similar to yours? Different? Explain. Are you satisfied with the kind of relationship your windows describe? If not, what could you do to change it?

Answer   **Type: E**   **Pages: 310–311**   **Evaluation**

121. Pick two people you know--one with whom you want to strengthen your relationship and one to whom you are not particularly attracted. Using the interpersonal attraction variables in the text, analyze the reasons why you want/don't want to form a relationship with each person.

Answer   **Type: E**   **Pages: 284–286**   **Analysis**

122. Discuss three types of intimacy in a relationship that is important to you. Explain your satisfaction with the intimacy or distance in each area. Relate any other factors (change, independence, culture, gender, etc.) that affect your intimacy in this relationship.

Answer   **Type: E**   **Pages: 287**   **Evaluation**

123. Relate the four levels of self-disclosure—clichés, facts, opinion, and feelings—to the following four stages of relationships—experimenting, integrating, differentiating and stagnating. What level of self-disclosure is most and least likely at each of these four stages.

Answer   **Type: E**   **Pages: 287**   **Synthesis**

124. Chapter Eight described five reasons people tell lies. Describe examples of lies you have told or have been told to you that illustrate three of the different reasons for lying identified in your text. Describe whether or not each of these lies was a "benevolent lie" or not and why.

Answer   **Type: E**   **Pages: 317–319**   **Synthesis**

CHAPTER 9

IMPROVING COMMUNICATION CLIMATES

1. Defensiveness is often a self-perpetuating cycle.
    Answer: T   **Type: T**   **Page: 339**   **Synthesis**

2. When your partner criticizes you, the best thing you can do is ignore the criticism so you won't get defensive.
    Answer: F   **Type: T**   **Pages: 342**   **Comprehension**

3. Remarks about a specific subject (i.e., appearance, intelligence, honesty) that make one person defensive might arouse little or no defensiveness in another.
    Answer: T   **Type: T**   **Page: 339**   **Analysis**

4. Once a progressive spiral has been established in a relationship, it is likely to continue indefinitely.
    Answer: F   **Type: T**   **Page: 337**   **Knowledge**

5. Your text recommends agreeing with criticisms that are untrue about you, since doing so will help you recognize ways you can improve.
    Answer: F   **Type: T**   **Page: 364**   **Comprehension**

6. It is possible to disagree with another person in a confirming way.
    Answer: T   **Type: T**   **Page: 334**   **Comprehension**

7. When you respond non-defensively to criticism, you can agree with the truth of what the critic is saying.
    Answer: T   **Type: T**   **Page: 363**   **Knowledge**

8. In order to deal effectively with criticism, it is necessary to acknowledge and accept the other's criticism.
    Answer: F   **Type: T**   **Pages: 334**   **Comprehension**

9. The most damaging kind of disconfirming response is disagreeing with the other person.
    Answer: F   **Type: T**   **Page: 334**   **Knowledge**

10. The clear message format should always be used in the order given in your text for best results.
    Answer: F   **Type: T**   **Page: 356**   **Analysis**

11. It's OK to reword the clear message format to suit your own particular style of speaking.
    Answer: T   **Type: T**   **Page: 356**   **Analysis**

12. You shouldn't have to repeat the clear message format if you express yourself clearly in the first place.
    Answer: F   **Type: T**   **Page: 356**   **Analysis**

13. Communication climates are a function of the tasks people perform rather than the way the people feel about one another.
    Answer: F   **Type: T**   **Page: 333**   **Comprehension**

14. Messages shaping the communication climate of a relationship can be both verbal and nonverbal.
    Answer: T   **Type: T**   **Page: 333**   **Comprehension**

15. Defensiveness in human communication is usually reciprocal.
    Answer: T   **Type: T**   **Page: 337**   **Synthesis**

16. Endorsement is the strongest type of confirming message.
    Answer: T   **Type: T**   **Page: 334**   **Knowledge**

17. The Gibb categories define behaviors that improve or hurt the communication climate.
    Answer: T   **Type: T**   **Pages: 345**   **Comprehension**

18. According to Chapter Nine, stating your intentions is an important element of a clear message.
    Answer: T   **Type: T**   **Page: 355**   **Knowledge**

19. Tangential responses are one type of disconfirming message.
    Answer: T   **Type: T**   **Page: 336**   **Knowledge**

20. Just recognizing the other person isn't enough to be considered confirming.
    Answer: F   **Type: T**   **Page: 333**   **Evaluation**

21. An acknowledgment statement is more confirming than a recognition statement.
    Answer: T   **Type: T**   **Page: 333**   **Evaluation**

22. Incongruent responses contain two messages that seem to deny or contradict each other.
    Answer: T   **Type: T**   **Page: 336**   **Knowledge**

23. Since ambiguous responses leave your partner unsure of your position, they would likely be interpreted as disconfirming.
    Answer: T   **Type: T**   **Page: 336**   **Comprehension**

24. An impervious response sends a disconfirming message because the other person is not responded to.
    Answer: T   **Type: T**   **Page: 336**   **Knowledge**

25. Whereas acknowledging others means you are interested in their ideas, endorsement means that you agree with them.
    Answer: T   **Type: T**   **Page: 334**   **Knowledge**

26. Even if you don't intend to ignore others, they might perceive you as avoiding them and get defensive.
    Answer: T   **Type: T**   **Page: 333**   **Knowledge**

27. We often reduce cognitive dissonance by using defense mechanisms.
    Answer: T   **Type: T**   **Page: 340**   **Comprehension**

28. When coping with criticism, it isn't a good idea to ask what else is wrong because it just brings up too much material to handle at one time.
    Answer: F   **Type: T**   **Page: 362**   **Comprehension**

29. Asking if anything else is bothering your critic won't help you cope with criticism because it encourages more defensiveness.
    Answer: F   **Type: T**   **Page: 362**   **Comprehension**

30. A controlling message can be verbal or nonverbal.
    Answer: T   **Type: T**   **Page: 345**   **Comprehension**

31. Behavior that fits into Gibb's category of "strategy" attempts to manipulate the other into doing what you want.
    Answer: T   **Type: T**   **Page: 345**   **Knowledge**

32. What Gibb describes as "spontaneity" means saying the first thing that comes into your mind.
    Answer: F   **Type: T**   **Page: 345**   **Comprehension**

33. A supportive climate usually results from the expression of empathy.
    Answer: T   **Type: T**   **Page: 346**   **Comprehension**

34. You have to use the Gibb category of "superiority" now and then because not all of us have the same talents.
    Answer: F   **Type: T**   **Page: 347**   **Knowledge**

35. Provisional statements often include words like "perhaps" and "from my perspective."
    Answer: T   **Type: T**   **Page: 347**   **Application**

36. Your text contains a humorous list of advice from Dave Barry designed to teach a person how to act according to which of Gibb's categories?
    a. empathy
    b. superiority
    c. displacement
    d. spontaneity
    e. problem orientation
    Answer: b   **Type: M**   **Page: 348**   **Analysis**

37. Intention statements can communicate
    a. where you stand on an issue.
    b. requests of others.
    c. descriptions of how you plan to act in the future.
    d. a, b, and c above.
    e. only interpretations of behavior.
    Answer: d   **Type: M**   **Page: 355**   **Comprehension**

38. Which of the following is the best example of a specific intention clearly stated to a partner?
    a. "I want you to be honest with me."
    b. "I want more understanding from you."
    c. "I need to talk about our relationship."
    e. "I want two hours to myself to read."
    Answer: e   **Type: M**   **Page: 355**   **Application**

39. Which of the following is an accurate feeling statement?
    a. "I feel like you're angry at me."
    b. "I feel like going home now."
    c. "I feel embarrassed when I do poorly on tests."
    d. "I feel you ought to be more careful."
    e. All of the above are feeling statements.
    Answer: c   **Type: M**   **Page: 353**   **Evaluation**

40. All of the following are disconfirming messages except
    a. interrupting the other person.
    b. giving ambiguous responses.
    c. ignoring the other person.
    d. using a problem-oriented approach.
    e. responding with cliches.
    Answer: d   **Type: M**   **Page: 336**   **Synthesis**

41. All of the following are behavioral descriptions except
    a. "I notice you're frowning."
    b. "I saw you walk out of the party."
    c. "Your behavior shows me you're angry."
    d. "You've shouted the last three times we've discussed money."
    e. "You haven't said 'I love you' in over a week."
    Answer: c   **Type: M**   **Page: 336**   **Application**

42. Which of the following is an interpretation?
    a. "I got an 'A' on my history paper."
    b. "My boyfriend is jealous."
    c. "I sure appreciate your help."
    d. "Would you tell me what you mean by that?"
    e. All of the above are interpretations.
    Answer: b   **Type: M**   **Page: 351**   **Application**

43. A consequence statement can describe
    a. what happens to you, the speaker.
    b. what happens to the person you're addressing or to others.
    c. why you're bothered or pleased by another's behavior.
    d. what happens without moralizing about it.
    e. all of the above.
    Answer: e   **Type: M**   **Page: 354**   **Synthesis**

44. All of the following are defense mechanisms except
    a. verbal aggression.
    b. compensation.
    c. displacement.
    d. apathy.
    e. endorsement.
    Answer: e   **Type: M**   **Pages: 340–341**   **Comprehension**

45. The most visible way disconfirming messages reinforce one another, as when one attack leads to another and another, is termed a(n)
    a. escalatory conflict spiral.
    b. de-escalatory conflict spiral.
    c. cognitive dissonance reaction.
    d. impervious dyad.
    e. pillow-talk incident.
    Answer: a   **Type: M**   **Page: 337**   **Knowledge**

46. The text suggested that you may react non-defensively to criticism by
    a. asking for a "time-out."
    b. guessing about the specifics of a critic's remarks.
    c. criticizing yourself.
    d. giving the reasons for your behavior.
    e. telling the critic to stop.
    Answer: b   **Type: M**   **Pages: 358**   **Comprehension**

47. Your instructor tells you how poor your writing ability is and how wrong it is for you not to work harder on it. That instructor used the Gibb category of
    a. description.
    b. evaluation.
    c. problem orientation.
    d. equality.
    e. provisionalism.
    Answer: b   **Type: M**   **Page: 344**   **Application**

48. According to research findings about defensiveness, when one person in a dyad acts in a defensive manner
    a. a counterattack is appropriate.
    b. the partner will be supportive.
    c. a defensive spiral usually results.
    d. perceptions are not realistic.
    e. self-disclosure usually takes place.
    Answer: c   **Type: M**   **Page: 337**   **Knowledge**

49. According to your text, the elements of a clear message are
    a. feeling, interpretation, assertion, and consequence.
    b. behavior, interpretation, feeling, assertion, and intention.
    c. behavior, assertion, aggression, and interpretation.
    d. behavior, interpretation, feeling, consequence, and intention.
    e. assertion, aggression, negotiation, interpretation, and intention.
    Answer: d   Type: M   Pages: 350–355   Synthesis

50. Another term which describes the Gibb defensive category of neutrality would be
    a. understanding.
    b. aggressive perception.
    c. positive/negative balance.
    d. displaced loyalty.
    e. indifference.
    Answer: e   Type: M   Page: 346   Knowledge

51. Use of "you" language as described in the text usually indicates that the speaker is
    a. making a sincere effort to describe the other person's point of view.
    b. being spontaneous.
    c. being evaluative.
    d. acting in a descriptive manner.
    e. acting in an empathetic manner.
    Answer: c   Type: M   Page: 344   Comprehension

52. Defensiveness is
    a. an emotion.
    b. accompanied by physiological symptoms.
    c. usually reciprocal.
    d. often unconscious.
    e. all of the above.
    Answer: e   Type: M   Pages: 339   Analysis

53. None of Gibb's categories of defensive behaviors arouse defensiveness unless
    a. the receiver of the message perceives them as threatening.
    b. the sender of the message intends to start a defensive spiral.
    c. both partners in the communication get defensive.
    d. the matching supportive behavior is ignored by the sender of the message.
    e. the self-concepts of both partners are threatened.
    Answer: a   Type: M   Pages: 344   Comprehension

54. Evaluative language is also described as
    a. "me" language.
    b. "it" language.
    c. "you" language.
    d. "neutral" language.
    e. "supportive" language.
    Answer: c   Type: M   Page: 344   Knowledge

55. The term that describes the quality of a personal relationship is
    a. mood.
    b. tone.
    c. climate.
    d. environment.
    e. foundation.
    Answer: c   **Type: M**   **Page: 333**   **Knowledge**

56. This chapter states that a defensive communicator protects his/her
    a. interpretations.
    b. sense data.
    c. perceived self.
    d. presenting self.
    e. none of the above
    Answer: d   **Type: M**   **Page: 339**   **Knowledge**

57. Gibb's categories provide a useful way for us to examine our
    a. self-concept.
    b. patterns of self-disclosure.
    c. defensive and supportive behaviors.
    d. manipulative behaviors.
    e. perceptual differences.
    Answer: c   **Type: M**   **Page: 339**   **Comprehension**

58. The communication climate in a relationship is determined by the
    a. roles each person has in the relationship.
    b. similarities of the parties.
    c. degree to which each person feels valued.
    d. amount of self-disclosure that occurs.
    e. listening and perceptual skills that each individual brings to the relationship.
    Answer: c   **Type: M**   **Page: 333**   **Knowledge**

59. A confirming response typically
    a. criticizes the other.
    b. agrees with or acknowledges the other.
    c. reveals deception.
    d. recognizes manipulation.
    e. controls the other.
    Answer: b   **Type: M**   **Pages: 333–334**   **Comprehension**

60. People who act in accordance with Gibb's category of equality communicate that
    a. everyone is equal in every way.
    b. while they may have greater talent in some areas, all have just as much worth as human beings.
    c. all human beings are created with the capacity to be equal in all areas.
    d. all of the above
    e. none of the above
    Answer: b   **Type: M**   **Page: 347**   **Comprehension**

61. "I've done all the research I need to about my business; I don't need to know anything else" is an example of the Gibb defensive category of
    a. evaluation.
    b. control.
    c. superiority.
    d. certainty.
    e. strategy.
    Answer: d   **Type: M**   **Page: 347**   **Application**

62. Communicators can resolve cognitive dissonance by
    a. revising the self-concept in the face of criticism.
    b. ignoring the dissonant information.
    c. distorting the dissonant information.
    d. attacking the source of dissonant information.
    e. all of the above.
    Answer: e   **Type: M**   **Page: 340**   **Comprehension**

63. Jenny says, "Beth, I'm really upset about how we divide the cooking chores." Beth retorts, "Speaking of cooking, my secretary brought in great cookies today." Beth's response is an example of a(n)
    a. impervious response.
    b. interrupting response.
    c. irrelevant response.
    d. impersonal response.
    e. tangential response.
    Answer: e   **Type: M**   **Page: 336**   **Application**

64. Robin asks her boss if she can take Friday afternoon off to clear up some legal problems. Her boss replies, "Seems like everybody has problems these days." The boss's reply is an example of a(n)
    a. impervious response.
    b. interrupting response.
    c. irrelevant response.
    d. tangential response.
    e. impersonal response.
    Answer: e   **Type: M**   **Page: 336**   **Application**

65. Molly asks her mother if she'll help her go through her wardrobe to see what needs to be thrown out. Mother replies, "Throwing out things is a great idea; help me with cleaning out this refrigerator, won't you?". Mother's reply is an example of a(n)
    a. impervious response.
    b. interrupting response.
    c. irrelevant response.
    d. tangential response.
    e. impersonal response.
    Answer: d   **Type: M**   **Page: 336**   **Application**

66. Carmen receives an E-mail message that is a question from Jack, but she doesn't respond to Jack's E-mail. Jack might interpret this as
    a. impervious.
    b. interrupting.
    c. irrelevant.
    d. tangential.
    e. impersonal.
    Answer: a   **Type: M**   **Page: 336**   **Application**

67. "You drink too much" is an example of the Gibb defensive category of
    a. evaluation.
    b. control.
    c. strategy.
    d. neutrality.
    e. superiority.
    Answer: a   **Type: M**   **Page: 344**   **Application**

68. Which of the following statements is the best supportive alternative to the accusation, "You just don't try hard enough."
    a. "You should try harder."
    b. "You give up too easily."
    c. "I'm worried you'll fail with two D's."
    d. "You should study two hours every night."
    e. "It's time we had a talk about trying."
    Answer: c   **Type: M**   **Page: 344**   **Analysis**

69. Ambiguous responses
    a. are conversational "take aways."
    b. are unrelated to what the other person has just said.
    c. ignore the other person's attempt to communicate.
    d. contain messages with more than one meaning.
    e. interrupt the other person.
    Answer: d   **Type: M**   **Page: 336**   **Knowledge**

70. Disconfirming responses loaded with cliches and other statements that never truly respond to the speaker are called
    a. impervious.
    b. interrupting.
    c. irrelevant.
    d. tangential.
    e. impersonal.
    Answer: e   **Type: M**   **Page: 336**   **Knowledge**

71. An old friend flashes you a smile across the room. You turn away. You have just given a disconfirming response categorized as
    a. impervious.
    b. interrupting.
    c. irrelevant.
    d. tangential.
    e. impersonal.
    Answer: a   **Type: M**   **Page: 336**   **Application**

72. Agreeing with a critic's perception of your behavior involves
    a. telling the critic she/he's right.
    b. saying you think she/he might interpret it that way.
    c. agreeing with the specifics of the criticism.
    d. all of the above.
    e. none of the above.
    Answer: b   **Type: M**   **Page: 364**   **Application**

73. Which of the following is a non-defensive response to the criticism, "You've really messed up that account now"?
    a. "Tell me what, in your mind, I did that upset you."
    b. "Not taking Mr. Kimble to dinner endangers the account?"
    c. "So you're upset that the account may be lost?"
    d. "Losing that account might really hurt our department?"
    e. All of the above respond non-defensively to that criticism.
    Answer: e   **Type: M**   **Pages: 358–364**   **Analysis**

74. An inconsistency between two conflicting pieces of information about one's self, attitudes, or behavior has been termed
    a. a defensive spiral.
    b. a supportive spiral.
    c. cognitive dissonance.
    d. an ambiguous response.
    e. intrapersonal conflict.
    Answer: c   **Type: M**   **Page: 340**   **Knowledge**

75. Psychological devices that resolve dissonance by maintaining a positive presenting image at the risk of distorting reality are called
    a. reaction formations.
    b. confirming responses.
    c. defense mechanisms.
    d. self-fulfilling prophecies.
    e. climate adjusters.
    Answer: c   **Type: M**   **Page: 340**   **Comprehension**

76. If others start criticizing you, one productive way to respond is to
   a. tell them to stop the criticism.
   b. point out that criticism is not productive.
   c. criticize them to show them how it feels.
   d. ask them for more details about what the criticism involves.
   e. just back off; there's no effective way to deal with this kind of "no-win" situation.
   Answer: d   **Type: M**   **Page: 358**   **Comprehension**

77. You can often respond non-defensively to criticism by agreeing
   a. with the critic's truthful statements.
   b. with the critic's judgment.
   c. with the critic's perception of the situation.
   d. both a and b above
   e. both a and c above
   Answer: e   **Type: M**   **Pages: 363–364**   **Comprehension**

78. All of the following are non-defensive responses to criticism recommended by your text except
   a. asking for more details about the criticism.
   b. paraphrasing the speaker's comments.
   c. asking about the consequences of your behavior.
   d. accepting the speaker's comments, even if you disagree.
   e. guessing about the details of the criticism.
   Answer: d   **Type: M**   **Pages: 387–391**   **Knowledge**

79. Defensive counterattacks take the form of
   a. verbal aggression and sarcasm.
   b. description and neutrality.
   c. facilitation and compromise.
   d. assertion and aggression.
   e. all of the above.
   Answer: a   **Type: M**   **Pages: 340–341**   **Knowledge**

80. If you emphasize how good you are in sports when someone criticizes your academic performance, you've used the defensive reaction called
   a. displacement.
   b. rationalization.
   c. repression.
   d. regression.
   e. compensation.
   Answer: e   **Type: M**   **Page: 341**   **Application**

81. Becoming defensive can be
     a. a way to prepare for self-disclosure.
     b. a way to avoid change.
     c. easy to change in ourselves and others once we recognize it.
     d. unavoidable in most instances.
     e. always undesirable.
     Answer: b   **Type: M**   **Page: 339**   **Comprehension**

82. Communication climates are a function of
     a. the way people feel about one another.
     b. the tasks people perform.
     c. individual personality characteristics.
     d. Gibb's functional theories.
     e. time, place, and context.
     Answer: a   **Type: M**   **Page: 333**   **Comprehension**

83. Jim's boss at the bank criticizes the way Jim handled a new account. Jim says
     nothing to his boss, but he's very short-tempered with his roommate that evening.
     Which defense mechanism is Jim most likely using?
     a. apathy
     b. displacement
     c. verbal aggression
     d. regression
     e. repression
     Answer: b   **Type: M**   **Page: 342**   **Application**

84. A defense mechanism that is characterized by a pretense of not caring is called
     a. repression.
     b. displacement.
     c. compensation.
     d. apathy.
     e. none of the above.
     Answer: d   **Type: M**   **Page: 342**   **Knowledge**

85. Just for fun, you flirted with an attractive person at a party last night. You know your
     partner is hurt, so you arrange a dinner at a favorite restaurant. You are most likely
     using the defense mechanism of
     a. verbal aggression.
     b. compensation.
     c. rationalization.
     d. apathy.
     e. displacement.
     Answer: b   **Type: M**   **Page: 334**   **Application**

86. Defensiveness is most likely to occur when
    a. an individual's presenting image is attacked.
    b. an individual's Johari Window is attacked.
    c. another person is problem-oriented.
    d. sender and receiver are experiencing identical environments.
    e. facilitative emotions are being exchanged.
    Answer: a   **Type: M**   **Page: 333**   **Comprehension**

87. Chapter Nine's Ethical Challenge, "Nonviolence: A Legacy of Principled Effectiveness," essentially explains how
    a. pacifism has been effectively used to achieve political goals since the 1800's.
    b. pacifism originated from Mahatma Gandhi.
    c. nonviolence, although deeply principled, has rarely been a practical strategy.
    d. pacifism has changed societies, but is rarely effective interpersonally.
    e. none of the above
    Answer: a   **Type: M**   **Page: 361**   **Comprehension**

88. In Chapter Nine's Communication Transcript when his boss criticizes him, his employee
    a. first becomes defensive, then uses several non-defensive strategies.
    b. responds very defensively, growing more and more hostile.
    c. quits the job because he perceives the criticisms as unreasonable.
    d. quickly agrees with his boss in order to diffuse his anger.
    e. contributes to a negative escalatory spiral by using sarcasm.
    Answer: a   **Type: M**   **Page: 365**   **Comprehension**

INSTRUCTIONS for questions 89–93: Match each description below with the appropriate defense mechanism.

    a. verbal aggression
    b. compensation
    c. rationalization
    d. repression
    e. regression

89. Stressing a strength in one area to cover up a perceived shortcoming in another area
    Answer: b   **Type: Matching**   **Page: 341**   **Knowledge**

90. Denying the existence of an unpleasant fact
    Answer: d   **Type: Matching**   **Page: 342**   **Knowledge**

91. Accusing a critic of the same fault another person claims you are guilty of
    Answer: a   **Type: Matching**   **Page: 340**   **Knowledge**

92. Offering a logical but untrue explanation of your behavior
    Answer: c   **Type: Matching**   **Page: 341**   **Knowledge**

93. Playing helpless to avoid facing attack
    Answer: e   **Type: Matching**   **Page: 341**   **Knowledge**

INSTRUCTIONS for questions 94–98: Match each defense mechanism with its description.

    a.   rationalization
    b.   sarcasm
    c.   apathy
    d.   physical avoidance
    e.   displacement

94. Disguising an attack with a barbed, humorous message
    Answer: b   **Type: Matching**   **Page: 341**   **Application**

95. Laughing off a close friend's criticism even though it bothers you
    Answer: c   **Type: Matching**   **Page: 342**   **Application**

96. Snapping at your roommate after being criticized by your boss
    Answer: e   **Type: Matching**   **Page: 342**   **Application**

97. Blaming your lack of exercise on a desire to conserve your energy
    Answer: a   **Type: Matching**   **Page: 341**   **Application**

98. Steering clear of someone who points out your flaws
    Answer: d   **Type: Matching**   **Page: 342**   **Application**

INSTRUCTIONS for questions 99–103: Match the type of disconfirming response with its behavioral description.

    a.   impervious
    b.   tangential
    c.   interrupting
    d.   impersonal
    e.   irrelevant

99. Shelley says, "Let's decide what we're doing this weekend after I get paid tomorrow," and you reply, " I'm really excited about getting an 'A' on my test."
    Answer: e   **Type: Matching**   **Page: 336**   **Analysis**

100. Vince says, "I'm so tired," and you reply, "Boy, everybody's got problems today."
    Answer: d   **Type: Matching**   **Page: 336**   **Analysis**

101. You see Denise smile at you, but you turn away.
    Answer: a   **Type: Matching**   **Page: 336**   **Analysis**

102. You begin talking before Lana is finished.
    Answer: c   **Type: Matching**   **Page: 336**   **Analysis**

103. Gail asks how your roommate is feeling; you tell her about your own health.
    Answer: b   **Type: Matching**   **Page: 336**   **Analysis**

INSTRUCTIONS for questions 103–111: Identify each of the following statements within quotation marks as according to the clear message format.

    a. feeling
    b. behavior
    c. interpretation
    d. consequence
    e. intention

103. "Whenever we fight, both of us wind up regretting it."
     Answer: d   **Type: Matching**   **Page: 354**   **Application**

104. "You've never used language like that before."
     Answer: b   **Type: Matching**   **Page: 351**   **Application**

105. "You're certainly touchy today."
     Answer: c   **Type: Matching**   **Page: 351**   **Application**

106. "I sure am grateful for your help."
     Answer: a   **Type: Matching**   **Page: 353**   **Application**

107. "I just want you to know how I feel."
     Answer: e   **Type: Matching**   **Page: 355**   **Application**

108. "I want that twenty dollars you owe me."
     Answer: e   **Type: Matching**   **Page: 355**   **Application**

109. "You're smoking again after you said you were quitting."
     Answer: b   **Type: Matching**   **Page: 351**   **Application**

110. "I guess you just don't like me."
     Answer: c   **Type: Matching**   **Page: 351**   **Application**

111. "I'm going to eat out tonight."
     Answer: e   **Type: Matching**   **Page: 355**   **Application**

112. "Because we were five minutes late, we couldn't be seated until intermission."
     Answer: d   **Type: Matching**   **Page: 354**   **Application**

113. "You seem pretty sure of yourself."
     Answer: c   **Type: Matching**   **Page: 351**   **Application**

114. "I'm uncomfortable about that."
     Answer: a   **Type: Matching**   **Page: 353**   **Application**

115. "You must not realize how silly you looked."
     Answer: c   **Type: Matching**   **Page: 351**   **Application**

116. "I want to study tonight."
     Answer: e   **Type: Matching**   **Page: 355**   **Application**

117. "It seems to me that you're just trying to set me against her."
     Answer: c   **Type: Matching**   **Page: 351**   **Application**

118. "I'm glad you're coming."
    Answer: a   **Type: Matching**   **Page: 353**   **Application**

119. "Quit teasing me!"
    Answer: e   **Type: Matching**   **Page: 355**   **Application**

120. "I can tell you're upset."
    Answer: c   **Type: Matching**   **Page: 351**   **Application**

121. "You're wearing that shirt I like."
    Answer: b   **Type: Matching**   **Page: 351**   **Application**

122. "You haven't popped your gum all evening."
    Answer: b   **Type: Matching**   **Page: 351**   **Application**

123. "I hope you'll visit again soon."
    Answer: e   **Type: Matching**   **Page: 355**   **Application**

124. "Since you're here, I've decided to relax."
    Answer: d   **Type: Matching**   **Page: 355**   **Application**

125. "Give me that book."
    Answer: e   **Type: Matching**   **Page: 355**   **Application**

126. "I know you wore that outfit to please me."
    Answer: c   **Type: Matching**   **Page: 351**   **Application**

127. "I'm really burned up about that bill."
    Answer: a   **Type: Matching**   **Page: 355**   **Application**

128. "You think this studying is easy for me."
    Answer: c   **Type: Matching**   **Page: 354**   **Application**

129. "I feel you should pay half."
    Answer: e   **Type: Matching**   **Page: 355**   **Application**

130. "Because you helped me and I felt relieved, I had time to cook for you."
    Answer: d   **Type: Matching**   **Page: 354**   **Application**

131. "Let's go to the movies."
    Answer: e   **Type: Matching**   **Page: 355**   **Application**

132. "I don't think you really mean that."
    Answer: c   **Type: Matching**   **Page: 351**   **Application**

133. "Ever since you said that I was wrong, I've been afraid to ask your opinion."
    Answer: d   **Type: Matching**   **Page: 354**   **Application**

134. "Tell me the truth."
    Answer: e   **Type: Matching**   **Page: 355**   **Application**

135. "I wish you'd call more often."
    Answer: e   **Type: Matching**   **Page: 421**   **Application**

136. Describe two of your important relationships in terms of communication climate. What factors contribute to the overall climate in each relationship? Describe

confirming and disconfirming behaviors for each relationship that lead you to your overall assessment.

Answer   **Type: E**   **Pages: 333–338**   **Analysis**

137. How do defensive behaviors work in the sphere of work relationships? Given your knowledge of Gibb's categories, what advice would you give to a manager?

Answer   **Type: E**   **Pages: 345–349**   **Application**

138. Pretend you have explained the Gibb categories of defensive and supportive behaviors to someone who knows you well. Ask this person which of the Gibb categories you use. Record the responses, giving a specific example for each category.

Answer   **Type: E**   **Pages: 345–349**   **Synthesis**

139. Pick the two defense mechanisms you most commonly use. For each, describe (a) a recent incident when you used it, (b) the part of your self-concept you were protecting, and (c) the consequences of your defensiveness. If you haven't used defense mechanisms recently, answer this question with defense mechanisms you have used in the past. Be specific.

Answer   **Type: E**   **Pages: 340–342**   **Synthesis**

140. Describe an important relationship in which you are involved in terms of a positive or negative "spiral" of behavior. Indicate how behaviors over the past six months (or any defined segment of time) have tended to "beget" similar behaviors in your relationship. Comment on the future direction of your spiral.

Answer   **Type: E**   **Page: 337**   **Evaluation**

141. Imagine the following scene: Your instructor (we'll call him Dr. Roberts) angrily thrusts your research paper back at you saying, *"This paper is not only late, it is full of errors."* Write a response to Dr. Roberts that demonstrates three different ways to respond using Chapter Nine's strategies for handling criticism non-defensively.

Answer   **Type: E**   **Pages: 358–364**   **Application**

142. Define cognitive dissonance. Give five examples from your life that illustrate this concept in action. Label any defensive behaviors you use to cope with cognitive dissonance.

Answer   **Type: E**   **Pages: 340**   **Synthesis**

143. Using the Clear Message Format (behavior, interpretation, feeling, consequence, and intention), write one gripe, request, appreciation, or some other message that you could share with a person who is important to you at this time in your life. (Don't use the message you already composed when we discussed this method in class.)

Answer   **Type: E**   **Pages: 350–356**   **Synthesis**

144. Use the Clear Message Format to write a message to one of two situations described below, identifying each of the five parts of the message.
A friend of yours is in the habit of borrowing your belongings and doesn't return them to you without you having to ask for them back several times. Now your friend is returning a sweater of yours and there's a stain on it. One of your friends has been especially supportive lately, has called often, spent time getting you out socially and even prepared dinner for you to help you get through a difficult time.

Answer   **Type: E**   **Pages: 350–356**   **Application**

CHAPTER 10

MANAGING INTERPERSONAL CONFLICTS

1. According to your text, direct aggression is never justified.
   Answer: F   **Type: T**   **Pages: 379**   **Knowledge**

2. Research cited in the text states that strong marriages are characterized by productive expressions of conflict, among other things.
   Answer: T   **Type: T**   **Page: 375**   **Knowledge**

3. Destructive fights often start because the initiator confronts a partner who isn't ready for a confrontation.
   Answer: T   **Type: T**   **Page: 398**   **Knowledge**

4. Handling conflict assertively guarantees that you'll get what you want.
   Answer: F   **Type: T**   **Page: 383**   **Comprehension**

5. Interdependence must exist between two parties in order for a conflict to exist.
   Answer: T   **Type: T**   **Page: 374**   **Knowledge**

6. A conflict can exist only when both parties are aware of a disagreement.
   Answer: T   **Type: T**   **Page: 373**   **Knowledge**

7. Chapter Ten admits that there are situations when direct aggression is the only realistic option.
   Answer: T   **Type: T**   **Page: 379**   **Knowledge**

8. Avoidance and accommodation are both forms of nonassertive behavior.
   Answer: T   **Type: T**   **Pages: 376**   **Comprehension**

9. One key to the win-win approach to conflict resolution is to look for the single best solution at the beginning of your conversation.
   Answer: F   **Type: T**   **Page: 400**   **Comprehension**

10. Win-lose or win-win outcomes to conflicts can often be products of self-fulfilling prophecies.
    Answer: T   **Type: T**   **Page: 405**   **Analysis**

11. The text says that "counting to ten" applies to win-win problem solving.
    Answer: T   **Type: T**   **Page: 405**   **Analysis**

12. As long as one person in the relationship is aware of the disagreement, a conflict exists.
    Answer: F   **Type: T**   **Page: 373**   **Knowledge**

13. The win-win approach to conflict resolution requires parties to reach a solution through compromise.
    Answer: F   **Type: T**   **Page: 395**   **Knowledge**

14. "You can live happily ever after" is the ultimate theme of *Looking Out/Looking In*.
    Answer: F   **Type: T**   **Page: 405**   **Comprehension**

15. With enough skill you should be able to use win-win problem solving successfully in almost any conflict.
    Answer: F   **Type: T**   **Page: 396**   **Knowledge**

16. When people express hostility in obscure ways, "passive aggression" occurs.
    Answer: T   **Type: T**   **Page: 379**   **Knowledge**

17. The win-win approach to conflict resolution requires each party to compromise by giving up something he or she wants.
    Answer: F   **Type: T**   **Page: 395**   **Knowledge**

18. In win-win problem solving, it's important to request specific change from your partner as early as possible in the "fight."
    Answer: F   **Type: T**   **Page: 395**   **Comprehension**

The most common way people make requests is by being direct and honest.
    Answer: F   **Type: T**   **Page: 381**   **Knowledge**

The metaphorical ways we have to describe conflict often create self-fulfilling prophecies in terms of how we approach conflict.
    Answer: T   **Type: T**   **Pages: 67, 372**   **Synthesis**

21. The most positive metaphor for conflict, proposed in Chapter Ten, is to compare conflict to a sporting event.
    Answer: F   **Type: T**   **Page: 372**   **Comprehension**

22. A full-fledged conflict will not occur unless the individuals involved try to prevent one another from achieving their goals.
    Answer: T   **Type: T**   **Page: 374**   **Comprehension**

23. Research indicates that nonassertion is the least common way couples deal with their conflicts.
    Answer: F   **Type: T**   **Page: 376**   **Knowledge**

24 Direct aggression is described as physical attacks and swearing, but does not include teasing or nonverbal gestures.
    Answer: F   **Type: T**   **Page: 378**   **Knowledge**

25. Gender is the most important variable in determining conflict style.
    Answer: F   **Type: T**   **Page: 389**   **Knowledge**

26. The situation at hand and the behavior of the other person in the conflict are more powerful determinants of a person's conflict style than gender.
    Answer: T   **Type: T**   **Page: 389**   **Knowledge**

27. Some scholars assert that conflict style is often determined simply by a person's biological makeup.
    Answer: T   **Type: T**   **Page: 392**   **Knowledge**

28. In a survey of conflict views of college men and women, women were described as being
   a. more concerned with maintaining the relationship during a conflict.
   b. more concerned with power in the conflict.
   c. more interested in the content of the conflict.
   d. more ego-involved in the conflict than men.
   e. all of the above.
   Answer: a   **Type: M**   **Page: 389**   **Comprehension**

29. Complementary and symmetrical conflict styles have been shown to produce
   a. marriages that got back together after conflict.
   b. couples who find other mates while getting divorced.
   c. a greater percentage of divorces that are settled amicably.
   d. both "good" results as well as "bad" ones.
   e. divorces that only have the facade of politeness.
   Answer: d   **Type: M**   **Page: 385**   **Comprehension**

30. Individuals in low-context cultures typically resolve conflict by
   a. avoidance.
   b. indirect communication.
   c. nonassertion.
   d. all of the above
   e. none of the above
   Answer: d   **Type: M**   **Pages: 376, 390**   **Synthesis**

31. An uncontrolled, spontaneous "explosion," a "Vesuvius," is
   a. encouraged by your text as a first step to solving conflict.
   b. therapeutic when you feel it's impossible to be relational and your partner understands what you're doing.
   c. a great way of eliminating defensive behaviors by "clearing the air."
   d. one way to make sure your partner will listen to you.
   e. all of the above.
   Answer: b   **Type: M**   **Page: 405**   **Comprehension**

32. Win-win problem solving is seldom used because
   a. there is a lack of awareness of it.
   b. emotional reflexes prevent constructive solutions.
   c. it requires both persons' cooperation.
   d. win-win problem solving is actually the most used problem-solving style of all.
   e. a, b, and c above
   Answer: e   **Type: M**   **Page: 397**   **Comprehension**

33. A person who buys a piece of new furniture, finds it damaged, and says nothing because he doesn't want to confront the retailer, is engaging in the personal conflict style of
   a. nonassertion.
   b. direct aggression.
   c. indirect communication.
   d. assertion.
   e. none of the above

   Answer: a   Type: M   Page: 376   Application

34. You're angry that your neighbor's cat uses your child's sandbox as a litter box, so you deposit a collection of sand and droppings on your neighbor's front porch. You've engaged in the personal conflict style described as
   a. nonassertion.
   b. direct aggression.
   c. indirect communication.
   d. assertion.
   e. passive aggression.

   Answer: b   Type: M   Page: 377   Application

35. In order for a conflict to exist, two interdependent parties must perceive
   a. incompatible goals.
   b. scarce rewards.
   c. interference from the other party in achieving their goals.
   d. a, b, and c above.
   e. both a and c above.

   Answer: d   Type: M   Pages: 373–374   Knowledge

36. You are upset with your friend Laura because she's borrowed some clothes and not returned them. You badmouth Laura to some mutual friends, telling them Laura is "undependable." You've engaged in the personal conflict style described as
   a. nonassertion.
   b. direct aggression.
   c. passive aggression.
   d. assertion.

   Answer: c   Type: M   Page: 379   Application

37. When people deliver subtle aggressive messages (involving feelings of resentment, anger, or rage that they aren't able or willing to express directly), and they still maintain the front of kindness, they are engaging in what psychologist George Bach calls
   a. defense arousal.
   b. nonverbal conflict.
   c. pseudo-messages.
   d. crazymaking.
   e. one-up conflict resolution.

   Answer: d   Type: M   Page: 380   Knowledge

38. A possible pitfall of using passive aggression is that
   a. the object of your indirect aggression may just miss the point.
   b. a short-range "win" may lose in the long run.
   c. you deny yourself and the other party a chance of building any kind of honest relationship.
   d. All of the above are possible pitfalls involved with the use of passive aggression.
   e. Passive aggression really has no pitfalls.
   Answer: d   **Type: M**   **Page: 380**   **Comprehension**

39. Conflict rituals are
   a. inherently wrong.
   b. the best way to solve the variety of conflicts that are part of any relationship.
   c. almost always positive.
   d. unacknowledged but repeating patterns of dealing with conflict.
   e. all of the above.
   Answer: d   **Type: M**   **Page: 387**   **Comprehension**

40. The "ownership" of a problem almost always belongs to
   a. the person who brings it up.
   b. the person to whom the complaint is directed.
   c. the person with the lowest amount of self-disclosure.
   d. the person with the greatest amount of passive aggressive behavior.
   e. the most assertive person.
   Answer: a   **Type: M**   **Page: 397**   **Comprehension**

41. You and your partner's pattern of managing disagreements that repeats itself over time is called your
   a. relational conflict style.
   b. cognitive dissonance pattern.
   c. harmony/disharmony pattern.
   d. "Vesuvius."
   e. clear message format.
   Answer: a   **Type: M**   **Page: 384**   **Knowledge**

42. In the Communication Transcript in Chapter Ten, Chris tries to resolve a conflict with her roommate Terry over cleaning their apartment by
   a. relying on authority as a source of power.
   b. using the "Vesuvius" method to get Terry's attention.
   c. appealing to their mutual self-interests.
   d. employing "crazymaking" strategies.
   e. none of the above
   Answer: c   **Type: M**   **Pages: 402–403**   **Comprehension**

43. "Crazymakers" are
    a. undiagnosed schizophrenics who use aggressive behaviors.
    b. disguised forms of aggression.
    c. people who have been driven to distraction by noncommunicative partners.
    d. humorous greeting cards that express aggression.
    e. none of the above.
    Answer: b   **Type: M**   **Page: 380**   **Comprehension**

44. All of the following are true about conflict, except
    a. conflict is natural.
    b. every relationship of any depth at all has conflict.
    c. conflict can be beneficial.
    d. people typically have similar conflict styles.
    Answer: d   **Type: M**   **Pages: 373–376**   **Synthesis**

45. Which suggestion does your text offer if you don't meet with success when following
    the six steps in win-win problem solving?
    a. Go back and repeat the previous step.
    b. Start again at step one.
    c. Skip the difficult step and move on.
    d. Step away and begin the process again another time.
    e. all of the above are advised.
    Answer: a   **Type: M**   **Page: 401**   **Comprehension**

46. Studies of different cultures and conflict reveal that
    a. assertiveness is valued worldwide.
    b. North Americans avoid confrontation more than other cultures studied.
    c. individualistic cultures are less assertive than collective ones.
    d. the assertiveness appropriate in North America would be rude and insensitive in
       collectivist cultures.
    e. all of the above are true.
    Answer: d   **Type: M**   **Pages: 390–392**   **Comprehension**

47. One of the best methods to use to describe your problem and needs to a partner
    during conflict resolution is
    a. paraphrasing.
    b. perception checking.
    c. the clear message format
    d. high-level abstractions.
    e. emotional description.
    Answer: c   **Type: M**   **Page: 397**   **Knowledge**

48. Rhonda complains to Collin that she's tired of their weekend routine. Irritated, Collin
    snaps back that he's tired of her complaining. Their conflict pattern reflects which of
    the following conflict styles?
    a. complementary
    b. symmetrical
    c. tangential
    d. conditional

e.   none of the above

Answer: b   **Type: M**   **Pages: 384–385**   **Analysis**

49.   Studies of intimate and aggressive relational conflict styles find that
   a.   the pattern partners choose may reveal a great deal about the kind of relationship they have chosen.
   b.   the intimate-nonaggressive style fails to handle problems.
   c.   intimate-aggressive partners avoid conflicts.
   d.   intimacy and aggression are opposites and thus not productive topics for study.
   e.   intimacy and aggression work best in symmetrical relationships.

Answer: a   **Type: M**   **Page: 386**   **Comprehension**

50.   A win-win "fight" is recommended as a positive way of handling conflict because it
   a.   allows for clear expression of differences and wants.
   b.   guarantees that your demands will be met.
   c.   lets dyads express conflict by physical aggression which is not harmful.
   d.   allows for spontaneous expression of feelings.
   e.   forces one partner to come to see the other's needs.

Answer: a   **Type: M**   **Pages: 404–405**   **Synthesis**

51.   You hint to your partner that you've been feeling neglected lately by mentioning how many nice things your friend's partner has done. You've used the personal conflict style called
   a.   indirect communication.
   b.   nonassertive behavior.
   c.   direct aggression.
   d.   passive aggression.
   e.   assertion.

Answer: a   **Type: M**   **Page: 381**   **Application**

52.   In order to decide which conflict style you should use, you should consider
   a.   the situation.
   b.   the receiver.
   c.   your goals.
   d.   a, b, and c above.
   e.   the other person's conflict style most of all.

Answer: d   **Type: M**   **Page: 383**   **Comprehension**

53.   The best way to boost the odds of a partner's cooperation toward a win-win solution to a conflict is to
   a.   alternate conflict styles between accommodation and aggression.
   b.   demonstrate your own willingness to compromise some of your goals.
   c.   utilize indirect communication to preserve your partner's presenting self.
   d.   explain the ways the partner will benefit.
   e.   all of the above

Answer: d   **Type: M**   **Page: 405**   **Analysis**

54.   Conflict rituals
   a.   are always damaging.

    b.   should be replaced with compromise.

    c.   most often involve avoidance by both of the participants in the conflict.

    d.   become problems when they are seen as the only way to resolve problems.

    e.   are defined as ways partners use guilt and intimidation to fight dirty.

Answer: d   **Type: M**   **Page: 388**   **Knowledge**

55.   Norman and Fredrick seem to argue all the time. Coworkers describe the two as hot-heads, but recognize that the two men seem to like sparring and are very close friends. Their conflict style is best described as

    a.   Nonintimate-Aggressive.

    b.   Nonintimate-Nonaggressive.

    c.   Intimate-Aggressive.

    d.   Intimate-Nonaggressive.

Answer: c   **Type: M**   **Page: 386**   **Analysis**

56.   Leah and Rachel have never gotten along. Rachel says that the best way for them to continue to work in the same office is to do their best to avoid one another. Their conflict style is best described as

    a.   Nonintimate-Aggressive.

    b.   Nonintimate-Nonaggressive.

    c.   Intimate-Aggressive.

    d.   Intimate-Nonaggressive.

Answer: b   **Type: M**   **Page: 386**   **Analysis**

57.   Despite their very different personalities, Sandra and Maureen have been able to share an office together by agreeing to disagree when a conflict comes up that might threaten their friendship. Their conflict style is best described as

    a.   Nonintimate-Aggressive.

    b.   Nonintimate-Nonaggressive.

    c.   Intimate-Aggressive.

    d.   Intimate-Nonaggressive.

Answer: d   **Type: M**   **Page: 386**   **Analysis**

58.   At which step in the Win-Win negotiation process would you utilize the clear message format described in Chapter Nine?

    a.   Identify the problem

    b.   Negotiate a solution

    c.   Make a date

    d.   Describe your problem and needs

    e.   Consider your partner's point of view

Answer: d   **Type: M**   **Page: 398–399**   **Knowledge**

59.   At which step in the Win-Win negotiation process would brainstorming appropriate?

    a.   Identify the problem

    b.   Negotiate a solution

    c.   Make a date

    d.   Describe your problem and needs

    e.   Consider your partner's point of view

Answer: b   **Type: M**   **Page: 398–399**   **Knowledge**

60. Of the following statements, which most accurately describes the part gender plays in conflict style?
   a. Gender is less important in determining conflict style than the behavior of the other person in the conflict.
   b. Research indicates that the stereotype of women as passive is nearly 90% accurate.
   c. There are virtually no discernible differences between the conflict styles of men and women
   d. When actual behaviors are observed, women are more likely to withdraw from discussion issues than men are.

   Answer: a   **Type: M**   **Page: 389**   **Knowledge**

INSTRUCTIONS for questions 61–65: Match each of the following crazymakers with its description.

   a. mind reader
   b. crisis tickler
   c. guilt maker
   d. pseudoaccommodator
   e. avoider

61. When this person's partner brings up a problem, she pretends to be busy with the laundry.

   Answer: e   **Type: Matching**   **Page: 380**   **Comprehension**

62. This person pretends that there's nothing wrong when his partner brings up a conflict.

   Answer: d   **Type: Matching**   **Page: 380**   **Comprehension**

63. This person handles conflict by trying to make her partner feel responsible for causing her discomfort.

   Answer: c   **Type: Matching**   **Page: 380**   **Comprehension**

64. This person almost brings what's bothering him to the surface, but never quite comes out and expresses himself.

   Answer: b   **Type: Matching**   **Page: 380**   **Comprehension**

65. Instead of expressing her feelings honestly, this person explains what her partner "really" means or what's "really wrong."

   Answer: a   **Type: Matching**   **Page: 380**   **Comprehension**

INSTRUCTIONS for questions 66–70: Match each of the following crazymakers with its description.

   a. joker
   b. withholder
   c. gunnysacker
   d. trivial tyrannizer
   e. trapper

66. James tells Sarah he wants her advice, and when she offers it, he becomes very angry and accuses her of trying to tell him what to do.

   Answer: e   **Type: Matching**   **Page: 380**   **Analysis**

67. Elaine deliberately cranks up the volume on her music, knowing that it irritates her mother.

    Answer: d   **Type: Matching**   **Page: 380**   **Analysis**

68. Jeffrey kept all his frustrations to himself and then when his sister asked him to run an errand for him he erupted, telling her all the ways he felt she had imposed upon him in the past two weeks.

    Answer: c   **Type: Matching**   **Page: 380**   **Analysis**

69. Renee refused to speak to Henry for two days.

    Answer: b   **Type: Matching**   **Page: 380**   **Analys**

70. Thomas laughed off his business partner's comments that he was shirking some of his work responsibilities by saying, "And who got out of the wrong side of the bed today?"

    Answer: a   **Type: Matching**   **Page: 380**   **Analysis**

71. Explain a current conflict you are having with a friend or loved one. Apply the win-win method to arrive at a solution using all six steps as though you were speaking to your partner.

    Answer   **Type: E**   **Pages: 397**   **Synthesis**

72. Chapter Ten states that compromise hardly deserves the positive image it seems to carry. Describe a time when you compromised to settle a conflict. Did your experience present a more negative or more positive outcome? What is your view of compromise as a conflict resolution outcome?

    Answer   **Type: E**   **Page: 394**   **Evaluation**

73. In a short essay, defend or refute the following statement: "Conflict is a destructive behavior."

    Answer   **Type: E**   **Pages: 375**   **Evaluation**

74. Describe a time that you were in a conflict and the other person was not cooperating in resolving that conflict. According to Chapter Ten, what are the various alternatives you have in handling this situation?

    Answer   **Type: E**   **Pages: 392–405**   **Analysis**

75. Do you think it is a good idea to "give in" or "give up" in a conflict? If you answered "yes," describe the circumstances that would warrant giving in. If you answered "no," explain why not.

    Answer   **Type: E**   **Pages: 394**   **Evaluation**

76. Imagine a conflict which cannot be solved. What have you learned about interpersonal communication that might enable you to cope with a conflict that can not be resolved?

    Answer   **Type: E**   **Pages: 1-405**   **Evaluation**

77. Pick the two crazymakers you use most often. For each, describe the circumstances in which the crazymaker is used, the function which the crazymaker serves, the consequences of using the crazymaker, and any alternative behavior which would be more constructive.

    Answer   **Type: E**   **Pages: 380**   **Evaluation**

78. "In order for there to be winners, there have to be losers." Discuss this statement by examining an interpersonal conflict in which you have been involved.

    Answer   **Type: E**   **Page: 397**   **Synthesis**